Shirley Jackson, Influences and Confluences

The popularity of such widely known works as "The Lottery" and *The Haunting of Hill House* has tended to obscure the extent of Shirley Jackson's literary output, which includes six novels, a prodigious number of short stories, and two volumes of domestic sketches. Organized around the themes of influence and intertextuality, this collection places Jackson firmly within the literary cohort of the 1950s. The contributors investigate the work that informed her own fiction and discuss how Jackson inspired writers of literature and film. The collection begins with essays that tease out what Jackson's writing owes to the weird tale, detective fiction, the supernatural tradition, and folklore, among other influences. The focus then shifts to Jackson's place in American literature and the impact of her work on women's writing, campus literature, and the graphic novelist Alison Bechdel. The final two essays examine adaptations of *The Haunting of Hill House* and Jackson's influence on contemporary American horror cinema. Taken together, the essays offer convincing evidence that half a century following her death, readers and writers alike are still finding value in Jackson's words.

Melanie R. Anderson is Instructional Assistant Professor of American Literature at the University of Mississippi, USA.

Lisa Kröger is an independent scholar in the USA.

Shirley Jackson, Influences and Confluences

Edited by
Melanie R. Anderson and Lisa Kröger

LONDON AND NEW YORK

First published 2016
by Routledge

2 Park Square, Milton Park, Abingdon, Oxfordshire OX14 4RN
52 Vanderbilt Avenue, New York, NY 10017

Routledge is an imprint of the Taylor & Francis Group, an informa business

First issued in paperback 2019

Copyright © 2016 selection and editorial matter, Melanie R. Anderson and Lisa Kröger; individual chapters, the contributors

The right of Melanie R. Anderson and Lisa Kröger to be identified as the authors of the editorial material, and of the authors for their individual chapters, has been asserted in accordance with sections 77 and 78 of the Copyright, Designs and Patents Act 1988.

All rights reserved. No part of this book may be reprinted or reproduced or utilised in any form or by any electronic, mechanical, or other means, now known or hereafter invented, including photocopying and recording, or in any information storage or retrieval system, without permission in writing from the publishers.

Notice:
Product or corporate names may be trademarks or registered trademarks, and are used only for identification and explanation without intent to infringe.

British Library Cataloguing in Publication Data
A catalogue record for this book is available from the British Library

Library of Congress Cataloging-in-Publication Data
Names: Anderson, Melanie, editor. | Kröger, Lisa, editor.
Title: Shirley Jackson, influences and confluences / edited by
  Melanie R. Anderson and Lisa Kröger.
Description: Burlington, VT : Ashgate, 2016. | Includes bibliographical
  references and index.
Identifiers: LCCN 2015045577 (print) | LCCN 2016006396 (ebook) |
  ISBN 9781472481894 (hardcover : alk. paper) |
Subjects: LCSH: Jackson, Shirley, 1916–1965—Criticism and interpretation. |
  Women and literature—United States—History—20th century.
Classification: LCC PS3519.A392 Z89 2016 (print) |
  LCC PS3519.A392 (ebook) | DDC 818/.5409—dc23
LC record available at http://lccn.loc.gov/2015045577

ISBN: 978-1-4724-8189-4 (hbk)
ISBN: 978-0-367-88194-8 (pbk)

Typeset in Times New Roman
by Apex CoVantage, LLC

Contents

List of figures vii
Editors and contributors viii
Acknowledgments xi

Introduction 1
MELANIE R. ANDERSON AND LISA KRÖGER

1 **"We know only names, so far": Samuel Richardson, Shirley Jackson, and exploration of the precarious self** 7
JENNIFER PRESTON WILSON AND MICHAEL T. WILSON

2 **A failed experiment: Family and humanity in *The Sundial*** 25
S. T. JOSHI

3 **Perception, supernatural detection, and gender in *The Haunting of Hill House*** 35
MELANIE R. ANDERSON

4 **Speaking of magic: Folk narrative in *Hangsaman* and *We Have Always Lived in the Castle*** 54
SHELLEY INGRAM

5 ***The Road Through the Wall* and Shirley Jackson's America** 76
RICHARD PASCAL

6 **"Laughing through the words": Recovering housewife humor in Shirley Jackson's *We Have Always Lived in the Castle*** 97
ANDREA KRAFFT

7 **"Listening to what she had almost said": Containment and duality in Shirley Jackson's *We Have Always Lived in the Castle*** 111
ASHLEIGH HARDIN

8 Knowing and narration: Shirley Jackson and the campus novel   123
   JAMES E. DOBSON

9 The haunting of *Fun Home*: Shirley Jackson and Alison Bechdel's
   queer Gothic neodomesticity   142
   JILL E. ANDERSON

10 The tower or the nursery? Paternal and maternal re-visions
   of Hill House on film   160
   SHARI HODGES HOLT

11 Girl anachronism: *We Have Always Lived in the Castle* and
   the depiction of adolescent psychosis in *Excision* (2012)
   and *Stoker* (2013)   183
   BERNICE M. MURPHY

   Index   201

Figures

10.1	The low-angle perspective of exterior shots of Hill House emphasizes the structure's power over its occupants	162
10.2	Robert Wise typically photographs the inhabitants of Hill House from a high angle. Dr. Markway, Luke, Theo, and Eleanor (from left to right) climb the main staircase, one of the house's many phallic structures	163
10.3	A striking dissolve transition foreshadows Eleanor's eventual spectralization and assimilation by the haunted house	163
10.4	The phallic tower of Hill House attracts Eleanor's gaze just prior to a ghostly sexual assault	163
10.5	The *mise-en-scène* of interior scenes frequently parallels Eleanor with images of female immobility and imprisonment	164
10.6	In Jan De Bont's adaptation, an empowered Eleanor prepares for her confrontation with Hugh Crain atop the phallic staircase	175
10.7	Christian iconography transforms Eleanor into a female messiah who sacrifices herself to defeat the patriarch	175
10.8	As psychic detective, Eleanor relies on technologies such as photography to communicate with the dead. The flipping pages of a photo album bring still photographs to life, allowing Eleanor's great-great-grandmother to reveal stories of patriarchal abuse	178

Editors and contributors

Jill E. Anderson is an assistant professor of English and women's studies at Tennessee State University. She is currently at work on a book manuscript on queer ecocriticism and Cold War culture, which examines how Cold War novels, film, and comics challenge the dominant iterations of nature at the intersection of sexuality and environmentalism. Her work has appeared in *Ecozon@*, *Margaret Atwood Studies*, *The Journal of Ecocriticism*, and various essay collections, including the forthcoming *This Book Is an Action: Feminist Print Culture and Activist Aesthetics*.

Melanie R. Anderson is an instructional assistant professor of English at the University of Mississippi, where she teaches courses in American literature. Her research interests are in supernatural literature and American Gothic. She is the author of *Spectrality in the Novels of Toni Morrison* (2013), and she coedited (with Lisa Kröger) *The Ghostly and the Ghosted in Literature and Film: Spectral Identities* (2013). *Spectrality in the Novels of Toni Morrison* was a finalist for a 2014 Ohioana Library Association Award and won the 2014 South Central MLA Book Prize.

James E. Dobson is a lecturer of English at Dartmouth College. He has published critical essays on major figures, including Mark Twain, Lucy Larcom, and Ambrose Bierce, and on the digital humanities and computational methods.

Ashleigh Hardin is a doctoral candidate at the University of Kentucky. Her dissertation, "The Age of Intervention: Addiction, Culture, and Narrative During the War on Drugs," focuses on narratives of addiction and recovery in late twentieth- and early twenty-first-century fiction, television, and film. She has presented her research at meetings of the American Literature Association, the International Society for the Study of Narrative, and the Cultural Studies Association.

Shari Hodges Holt is an instructional assistant professor of English at the University of Mississippi, where she teaches courses in literature and film studies. She has authored articles on Charles Dickens, Gothic fiction, and film adaptations of literature, and she is the coauthor of *Ouida the Phenomenon* (University of Delaware Press, 2008).

Editors and contributors ix

Shelley Ingram is an assistant professor of English at the University of Louisiana at Lafayette. Her major research interests include folklore and cultural theory, twentieth-century American literature, Southern literature, and critical race theory.

S. T. Joshi is the author of *The Weird Tale* (1990), *The Modern Weird Tale* (2001), and *Unutterable Horror: A History of Supernatural Fiction* (2012). His award-winning biography, *H. P. Lovecraft: A Life* (1996), was later expanded as *I Am Providence: The Life and Times of H. P. Lovecraft* (2010). He is a two-time winner of the World Fantasy Award, and has also won the Bram Stoker Award, the British Fantasy Award, and the International Horror Guild Award.

Andrea Krafft is Marion L. Brittain Postdoctoral Fellow at the Georgia Institute of Technology's School of Literature, Media, and Communication. She completed her PhD in English at the University of Florida in August of 2015. Her research interests include twentieth-century American literature, speculative fiction, domesticity, humor writing, and advertising studies.

Lisa Kröger holds a doctorate in English literature and languages from the University of Mississippi. Her academic interests include Gothic and horror literature, specifically works by British women writers of the late eighteenth through the early nineteenth centuries. Along with Melanie R. Anderson, Kröger has edited the essay collection *The Ghostly and the Ghosted in Literature and Film: Spectral Identities* (2013), and her work has appeared in publications such as S. T. Joshi's *The Encyclopedia of the Vampire: The Living Dead in Myth, Legend, and Popular Culture* (2011) and the essay collection *EcoGothic*, edited by Andrew Smith and William Hughes (2013). She works as a freelance writer and editor, when she's not living life among the savages.

Bernice M. Murphy is a lecturer in popular literature at the School of English, Trinity College Dublin. She edited the 2005 collection *Shirley Jackson: Essays on the Literary Legacy* and has published several previous articles on her work. Her recent publications include *The Highway Horror Film* (2014) and *The Rural Gothic in American Popular Culture* (2013). She is currently writing a guide to *Key Concepts in Contemporary Popular Fiction* for Edinburgh University Press, and coediting (with Elizabeth McCarthy) the collection *Lost Souls: Essays on Gothic Horror's Forgotten Writers, Directors, Actors and Artists* for McFarland. She is cofounder and was coeditor (during 2006–12) of the online *Irish Journal of Gothic and Horror Studies* and has directed the Trinity College M.Phil. in Popular Literature since 2009.

Richard Pascal has published several articles on Shirley Jackson. He has held visiting fellowships at the University of Canterbury in New Zealand and at the University of New Mexico. Currently he holds the position of visiting fellow at the Australian National University's School of Literature, Languages and Linguistics.

Jennifer Preston Wilson, associate professor of English at Appalachian State University, is coeditor, with Elizabeth Kraft, of *Approaches to Teaching the*

Novels of Henry Fielding (2015). Her essays include "*Clarissa*: The Nation Misrul'd" (2003), "'One Has Got All the Goodness, and the Other All the Appearance of It': The Development of Darcy in *Pride and Prejudice*" (2004), and "On Honor and Consequences: The Duel in *The Small House at Allington*" (2012).

Michael T. Wilson is an associate professor of English at Appalachian State University. His most recent publications include "'You give a damn about so many things I don't': Hemingway's Gendered Sentimentalism in 'The Snows of Kilimanjaro' and 'The Short, Happy Life of Francis Macomber'" in *The Sentimental Mode: Essays in Literature, Film and Television* (2014) and "'Absolute Reality' and the Role of the Ineffable in Shirley Jackson's *The Haunting of Hill House*" in *The Journal of Popular Culture* (2015). He is currently exploring the depiction of violence in popular American mystery and crime novel series.

Acknowledgments

The editors wish to thank the brilliant contributors, who shared our vision and our love of Shirley Jackson, and without whom there would be no collection. A very sincere expression of gratitude is due for their hard work and intelligent ideas, which they so kindly shared with us. Thank you also to the anonymous readers, as well as to the publishing team, for making sure this manuscript was the best it could be. To Benjamin F. Fisher, thank you for your years of mentorship.

Melanie R. Anderson cannot name here all of the friends, mentors, and colleagues from Thomas More College and the University of Mississippi, who over the years have been an encouragement on this academic path. Many thanks must go to her coeditor, Lisa Kröger, with whom it is always a pleasure to pursue these projects. Additional thanks go to Joan Wylie Hall for the enjoyable and interesting conversations about the work of Shirley Jackson. Last but never least, she is grateful for the love, support, and patience of her parents, Paul and Deborah Anderson; her siblings, Justin and Stephanie; her grandparents, Earl and Aline Beil; and Bobbie, one of the best of man's best friends.

Lisa Kröger would like to thank her coeditor and friend, Melanie R. Anderson, with whom writing is always an enjoyable adventure. Here's to many more joint projects in the future. She would also like to thank her husband, Robbie, for being an unending source of encouragement and courage, and her sons, Leo and Eli, for being an unending source of joy and love, even when the term "raising demons" seems all too appropriate.

Introduction

On April 28, 2014, the *New Yorker* published "The Man in the Woods," at the time a previously unpublished short story by Shirley Jackson. The story appeared over sixty years after the *New Yorker* made Jackson famous when it published "The Lottery," a story that garnered a mass of letters from angry readers. In "Biography of a Story," Jackson remembered the calm before the sudden storm of communication: "June 28, 1948 . . . was the last time for months that I was to pick up the mail without an active feeling of panic" (211). She admitted of the story, "It was not my first published story, nor my last, but I have been assured over and over that if it had been the only story I ever wrote or published, there would be people who would not forget my name" (211). Indeed, nearly seventy years later, Shirley Jackson's name is still on the tongues of readers and literary critics alike. The timing of the appearance of "The Man in the Woods" anticipated forthcoming publications, about and by Jackson. Critic Ruth Franklin is completing a new biography, and two of Jackson's children, Laurence Jackson Hyman and Sarah Hyman DeWitt, have recently released a collection of their mother's previously unpublished work, including the aforementioned story "The Man in the Woods," titled *Let Me Tell You: New Stories, Essays, and Other Writings*. This renewed interest in Jackson's fiction is timely, as 2015 marked the fiftieth anniversary of her death. And, as the publication of "The Man in the Woods" suggests, Jackson's allure has only increased among readers in the past decades since "The Lottery" rocked the literary world and caused readers to cancel their subscriptions to the *New Yorker* and complain to Jackson of their anger, confusion, and, sometimes, gruesome curiosity through loads of mail.

A closer examination of "The Man in the Woods" reveals many of the themes that permeate Jackson's body of work. It is a familiar story to readers of her canon: the story adopts a fairy-tale tone as it follows an outsider who is confronted with a barbaric ritual in an environment that initially seems to be safe and innocuous. Christopher, the story's protagonist, is a lonely wanderer. He, like many of Jackson's main characters, has lost his way, walking simply "because he had nothing else to do." The wayward and marginalized outcast finding a place outside of society is common throughout Jackson's writings. From Natalie in *Hangsaman* to Eleanor in *The Haunting of Hill House* to Merricat in *We Have Always Lived in the Castle,* her protagonists often feel as if they are on the fringes of society, if not completely isolated, and much of their separate journeys involves creating their own safe place, their own society outside of the mainstream world. Christopher wanders into the woods, a setting that is at once familiar, in its winding paths, and at the same time uncanny, as evidenced by the cat who joins him, whose presence the narrator describes as simultaneously surprising and "oddly" comforting to the wanderer. As the two push deeper into the woods, the story develops an almost mythical structure. Their destination lands them in a timeless setting, among women who have existed "for a long time," perhaps for eternity, who exude warmth and a feeling of home that is, at once, comfortable but possibly magical.

As would be expected of any good fairy tale, Christopher and his cat stumble upon a quaint cottage in the woods. The house is described as "a comfortable-looking, settled old house, made of stone," but like any setting in a fairy tale, this one has a sinister mood underneath its cozy veneer. Once inside, Christopher finds a scene of domestic tranquility, as two women are cooking a meal and the home is filled with "the unbelievable beauty of warmth, light, and the smell of onions." Upon the introduction of Mr. Oakes, the man of the house, Christopher begins to realize that the hospitality he has received might come with a price. Like the ritual at the heart of Jackson's short story "The Lottery," another inexplicably obligatory and violent ritual seems preordained for Mr. Oakes and Christopher to ensure that this quaint cottage in the woods has a capable and strong caretaker. As with many of Jackson's stories, tradition often comes with a steep price. Perhaps this is at the heart of why her writings remain applicable today: her stories often question the traditions that society takes for granted and highlight the mindless conformity and prejudices that exist in the shadows. Her work encourages us to discover the unfair, and sometimes even barbaric, origins of customs that society has insisted keep civilization afloat and question whether those very customs are doing more harm than good, hopefully leading to a repudiation of our darker impulses. As Judy Oppenheimer suggests, "It was Shirley's genius to be able to paint homey, familiar scenes . . . and then imbue them with evil – or, more correctly, allow a reader to see the evil that had been obvious to her all along" (101). For Oppenheimer, Jackson strived to create moments in her stories where "the comforting limits of the real world . . . dissolved, and the reader was left standing at a misty crossroads, gazing into an abyss – other worlds, other possibilities, unnamed terrors" (102).

From the late 1940s until her death in 1965, Jackson produced six novels, one unfinished novel, two collections of domestic sketches, scores of short stories, collected and uncollected, and a few children's books. During her writing career, she was one of the most well-known and well-connected authors of the American literary scene. Because of her work for literary magazines and the academic and critical connections of her husband, Stanley Edgar Hyman, Jackson's social and professional circles included such luminaries as Malcolm Cowley, Kenneth Burke, Ralph Ellison, J.D. Salinger, and numerous figures in the publishing sphere. She churned out reams of short stories that were published in the *New Yorker*, *Good Housekeeping*, and *Woman's Home Companion*, among other magazines. Jackson's work transcended popularity to critical acclaim as well. Darryl Hattenhauer attests to her many accolades in his study *Shirley Jackson's American Gothic*, noting that she was often anthologized among the best writers of her day and new writers were often compared to her, in addition to canonical writers, such as William Faulkner and Katherine Anne Porter (2). Angela Hague also cites Jackson's achievements:

> During her lifetime Jackson's work frequently appeared on the *New York Times Book Review*'s list of the "Best Fiction" of the year. . . . *The Haunting of Hill House* was nominated for the National Book Award in 1960, "Louisa, Please Come Home" won the Edgar Allan Poe Award in 1961, and in 1965 Syracuse University presented Jackson with the Arents Pioneer Medal for Outstanding Achievement. "The Possibility of Evil," published in the *Saturday Evening Post* three months after Jackson's death in August, 1965, won a posthumous Edgar Allan Poe Award the following year.
>
> (91 note 2)

Despite a successful career, her literary legacy since her death has rested on "The Lottery" and her supernatural masterpiece *The Haunting of Hill House*. Her work has been relegated to the edges of popular culture and a small niche of literary studies. Alexis Shotwell White observes, "It is notable that almost all existing scholarship bemoans the lack of sufficient scholarship on Jackson" (138 note 2). With the exception of two movie adaptations of her 1959 novel *The Haunting of Hill House* and a small cadre of scholarly devotees, the public and academic critical realms have largely ignored Jackson's vast influence on the literature of her contemporary moment and the late twentieth and early twenty-first centuries. Illustrating the lasting legacy of *The Haunting of Hill House* in the American horror genre, Stephen King has cited Jackson as an important influence, and she often is considered the godmother of the modern American Gothic haunted house. Incarnations of Hill House can be seen everywhere, from Richard Matheson's *Hell House* (1971), to Ann Rivers Siddons's *The House Next Door* (1978), to Peter Straub's *Ghost Story* (1979), to Mark Z. Danielewski's *House of Leaves* (2000). Without forgetting this aspect of Jackson's impact on later writers, this collection of essays will build on previous work and continue to amplify Jackson's presence in American literature beyond her influence on the horror genre. To that purpose, these essays are organized around three categories of influence. The essays in the pages to come address influence on Jackson's work and her place as a successor to her literary forebears; they place Jackson more firmly within her cohort and the literary scene of the 1950s and 1960s; and finally, they address her legacy that is apparent in more recent literature and films.

The first section of the collection, which intends to look at the authors and works that influenced Jackson's writings, includes essays by Jennifer and Michael Wilson, S. T. Joshi, Melanie R. Anderson, and Shelley Ingram. In their essay "'We know only names, so far': Samuel Richardson, Shirley Jackson, and Exploration of the Precarious Self," Jennifer and Michael Wilson explore Jackson's interest in eighteenth-century fiction, particularly that of Samuel Richardson. They argue that Richardson's psychologically fraught narratives of incremental seduction, abduction, rape, and madness are essential influences on Jackson's fiction, and they emphasize the conflicts between each writer's heroines and societal expectations and oppressions. Joshi, adding to the scant critical attention paid to *The Sundial*, examines Jackson's focus on misanthropy in the novel and traces this theme back to satirists like Jonathan Swift and Ambrose Bierce in his essay "A Failed Experiment: Family and Humanity in *The Sundial*." Continuing this work of placing Jackson's fiction within a larger literary tradition, in "Perception, Supernatural Detection, and Gender in *The Haunting of Hill House*," Melanie R. Anderson explores Jackson's interests in supernatural and mystery fiction and suggests that she uses tropes of paranormal investigations and occult detective fiction of the late nineteenth and early twentieth centuries to interrogate the place of women and women's experience in 1950s America. In "Speaking of Magic: Folk Narrative in *Hangsaman* and *We Have Always Lived in the Castle*," Shelley Ingram examines the ways in which Jackson undercuts authenticity and belief through conscious and playful manipulation of myth, ritual, fairy tale, and legend, focusing on *We Have Always Lived in the Castle* and *Hangsaman*.

For Jackson's place in her literary cohort and the concerns of 1950s and 1960s America, there are pieces by Richard Pascal, Andrea Krafft, Ashleigh Hardin, and James E. Dobson. In his "*The Road Through the Wall* and Shirley Jackson's America," Pascal posits that Jackson's later novels all deploy elements of the Gothic in social criticism in order to steal into the domain of suburban realists, such as John O'Hara, James Gould Cozzens, and John Cheever. He finds this suburban realist social commentary in her earlier works as well, focusing on her first novel and her most famous story to illustrate how social cohesiveness comes at the expense of punishing difference. Krafft's "'Laughing Through the Words': Recovering Housewife Humor in Shirley Jackson's *We Have Always Lived in the Castle*" aims to show how Jackson's humor works in tandem with her use of the Gothic to subvert the dominant containment narrative of the 1950s. Moreover, this humor connects her to other women writers of the time who were using domestic comedy to subvert the status quo. In her essay, "'Listening to what she had almost said': Containment and Duality in Shirley Jackson's *We Have Always Lived in the Castle*," Hardin, looking also at the feminist viewpoint addressed in Jackson's works, views her final novel as an indictment of the limited opportunities women had for writing themselves out of midcentury authoritative narratives of domestic constraint. Dobson's piece, "Knowing and Narration: Shirley Jackson and the Campus Novel," serves as a transition point by placing Jackson's novel *Hangsaman* in the long tradition of the American campus novel from the turn of the century up to Donna Tartt.

After Jackson has been examined in various literary traditions and among her peer groups, the collection turns to a more current examination of her influence on later fiction and film through essays by Jill E. Anderson, Shari Hodges Holt, and Bernice M. Murphy. In her essay "The Haunting of *Fun Home*: Shirley

Jackson and Alison Bechdel's Queer Gothic Neodomesticity," Jill E. Anderson traces the ways in which Jackson in *The Haunting of Hill House* and Alison Bechdel in her graphic memoir *Fun Home* use hauntings to disrupt narratives of domestic normativity, and she suggests that *Fun Home* revisits aspects of Jackson's earlier novel in order to create a contemporary neodomestic memoir. The pivot to film adaptation and influence comes in the final two essays. In "The Tower or the Nursery? Paternal and Maternal Re-visions of Hill House on Film" Hodges Holt examines how the two film adaptations of *The Haunting of Hill House* demonstrate the novel's relevance to feminist and postfeminist discourse and show Jackson's anticipation of coming feminist movements and redefinitions of female subjectivity. Lastly, Murphy's "Girl Anachronism: *We Have Always Lived in the Castle* and the Depiction of Adolescent Psychosis in *Excision* (2012) and *Stoker* (2013)" addresses the influence of Merricat Blackwood's madness for later incarnations of the "bad child" and dangerous adolescent females in horror cinema. Through their confused existence in the spaces between reality and fantasy, these young women challenge repressive male figures in their lives and often use violence to achieve freedom from familial and social control. Murphy traces a creative link from Jackson's final complete novel to the films *Excision* (2012) and *Stoker* (2013).

Read as a whole, this collection of essays introduces readers to Shirley Jackson's work beyond "The Lottery," *The Haunting of Hill House*, and even *We Have Always Lived in the Castle*. It demonstrates Jackson's place in the greater canon of English and American literature, as well as shows her influence upon her peers and the literature that would follow her brief but productive writing career. After half a century following her death, readers and writers alike are still finding value in her words. For a writer as engaged in the American literary landscape of the late 1940s through the early 1960s as Shirley Jackson, scholarship on her work has not fully explored the diversity of her oeuvre, the historical connections and theoretical implications of her fiction, nor the lasting impact of her art. The following essays are offered as a beginning to, and as a critical appeal for, what we hope will be a resurgence and expansion in Jackson scholarship.

Melanie R. Anderson and Lisa Kröger, editors
September 2015

Works cited

Friedman, Lenemaja. *Shirley Jackson*. Boston: Twayne, 1975. Print.
Hague, Angela. "'A Faithful Anatomy of Our Times': Reassessing Shirley Jackson." *Frontiers: A Journal of Women Studies* 26.2 (2005): 73–96. Print.
Hall, Joan Wylie. *Shirley Jackson: A Study in Short Fiction*. New York: Twayne, 1993. Print.
Hattenhauer, Darryl. *Shirley Jackson's American Gothic*. Albany: SUNY P, 2003. Print.
Jackson, Shirley. "Biography of a Story." *Come Along with Me: Part of a Novel, Sixteen Stories, and Three Lectures*. 1968. Ed. Stanley Edgar Hyman. New York: Penguin, 1995. 211–24. Print.

———. "The Man in the Woods." *Newyorker.com*. Condé Nast, 1 Apr. 2014. Web. 6 Apr. 2015.

King, Stephen. *Danse Macabre*. Updated Ed. New York: Gallery Books, 2010. Print.

Murphy, Bernice M., ed. *Shirley Jackson: Essays on the Literary Legacy*. Jefferson, NC: McFarland and Company, 2005. Print.

Oppenheimer, Judy. *Private Demons: The Life of Shirley Jackson*. New York: Putnam, 1988. Print.

Shotwell, Alexis. "'No Proper Feeling for Her House': The Relational Formation of White Womanliness in Shirley Jackson's Fiction." *Tulsa Studies in Women's Literature* 32.1 (Spring 2013): 119–41. Print.

1 "We know only names, so far"

Samuel Richardson, Shirley Jackson, and exploration of the precarious self

Jennifer Preston Wilson and Michael T. Wilson

Shirley Jackson scholars have occasionally noted her interest in eighteenth-century English fiction, but they have done so only in passing. Critic Lenemaja Friedman observes that in *The Haunting of Hill House*, Dr. Montague, "like Miss Jackson, is fond of the eighteenth-century novel, for he reads Richardson's novels for relaxation before retiring: *Pamela*, then *Clarissa*, and later *Sir Charles Grandison*" (123). Darryl Hattenhauer adds that "Samuel Richardson was a particular favorite for Jackson, who saw him as 'an emblem of fairness and love'" (24), while Dara Downey and Darryl Jones delve a bit deeper to argue that "Dr. Montague reads *Pamela* and attempts to read *Sir Charles Grandison* as a corrective to the supernatural chaos of the haunted house" (221). Downey and Jones further contend that "Jackson herself looked back to the eighteenth century for a vision of social harmony now vanished, for, in her own words 'an insistence on a pattern imposed precariously on the chaos of human development'" (221), a quotation which Judy Oppenheimer repeats in her biography of the writer (125). All of these critics, however, move on quickly from the idea of a Richardsonian influence and gloss over the elements of Jackson's words which we find most interesting: "a pattern imposed *precariously* on the *chaos* of human development" (emphasis ours). Nor do their readings note the extent to which the deeply psychological individual and familial conflicts inherent in those eighteenth-century novels, rather than their "vision of social harmony," are mirrored in Jackson's fiction.[1]

In fact, Samuel Richardson's and Shirley Jackson's novels deploy psychologically complex plots of family conflict that are remarkably similar, when stripped of their extraneous historical effects. Their fictions ask questions about the integration of the self within Gothically drawn domestic environments and share a striking repetition of motifs: the use of female character foils to expose fears about the individual's ability to assert herself against social conventions, a focus on fraught child-parent relationships that shape the heroine's allegiances in conscious and unconscious ways, and the deliberate staging of conflict within evocative formal settings, such as the summerhouse, to frame significant trials and transformations. This essay will study Richardson's and Jackson's heroines who struggle with questions of identity at the most basic psychological levels, including moments of surreal contemplation of one's own name and awareness of the power of words and human reliance on word formulae – mottoes, adages, proverbs, folksongs, charms, lists, letters – to define and protect the self. The cumulative effect of Jackson's sustained incorporation of Richardsonian tropes suggests that Richardson's influence on Jackson operated at even deeper levels than those of style and character development. In the end, Jackson, like Richardson, uses these insights into language to approximate the experience of the traumatized mind.

Jackson followed Richardson at perhaps the broadest level by isolating and examining the individual as a unique formation of specific familial contexts. In Richardson's novels, which tell the stories of young women in social, physical, and spiritual peril through the letters those women write and receive, the epistolary form provides readers a constant reminder of themes of identity and family through the repetition of the signature line. This refrain reinforces the idea that the exploration of the heroine's character is the essence of the plot. When Pamela Andrews signs off to her parents in her early letters with such phrases as "*Your dutiful and honest daughter*" (24), "*Your afflicted* PAMELA" (27), and "*Your distressed daughter*" (64), we already see the endurance under suffering that will define her character for generations of readers to come.[2] Likewise, the signature of "Your once highly favoured, but now most unhappy, kinswoman, CL. HARLOWE" (252) expresses the plot of Richardson's second novel in a nutshell – Clarissa's tragedy occurs because the spiritual idealism that distinguishes her ultimately sets her against the greed and tyranny of her *nouveau riche* family. In *Sir Charles Grandison*, Harriet Byron is a paragon of honesty and frankness. Her most frequent signature, "*Your Harriet Byron*" (1.15), conveys her fidelity to those people and principles she has embraced as her own. Each of these Richardsonian protagonists faces a family problem that is emblematized in her name, and thus restated with each letter's close. For Pamela, the Andrews' laboring class status prompts Mr. B to pursue her as a potential mistress rather than court her as a wife; Clarissa's family disallows her a choice of marriage partner; meanwhile, Harriet attains symbolic membership as an honorary "sister" in the Grandison family, but that closeness only furthers love with her already bespoken "brother." The emphasis on these women's names acts as a constant reminder of these domestic conflicts.

Familial dilemmas and mysteries entwined with issues of naming and identity also erode the psyches of characters in Jackson's fiction. *The Sundial* foregrounds the formative powers of names from the moment one passes the giant ironwork "H" on the front gates of the Halloran estate, which proclaims the family's fading prominence over the nearby village it once dominated. When the daughter of the original owner, Aunt Fanny, receives an apparent prophecy, she does so within a context of repeated family conflict that leaves her vulnerable to uncanny events. She has been triply traumatized by the recent death of her nephew, an ultimatum issued by her sister-in-law, and an eerie sense that reality is coming unrooted in the garden of the Halloran house, a site featuring a hedge maze shaped in the letters of her mother's name. From this psychologically fraught setting, she hears a voice calling "FRANCES HALLORAN," a summons that terrifies her:

> This was fear so complete that Aunt Fanny, once Frances Halloran, stood with nothing but ice to clothe her; *was* there something there? Something?

Then she thought with what seemed shocking clarity: it is worse if it is not there; somehow it must be real because if it is not real it is in my own head; unable to move, Aunt Fanny thought: It is real.

(25–26)

Aunt Fanny is positioned precariously between her current identity and her most essential identity as a child, as young Frances. Ironically, she chooses to believe in the call to the child with very self-protective, adult logic. The mature "Aunt Fanny" reasons that in order to be "not mad" what she senses must have substance – the voice must be "real"; the reverberating words "Frances Halloran" can make sense only as a message from someone who knew her in her long-ago past, her father. This process of an adult mind explaining away a nonrational experience occurs again when Aunt Fanny ushers her grandniece, Fancy, up to the rooms housing the furniture of Fanny's childhood home, an unsettling simulacra of a house-within-a-house. The elderly aunt explains the rules of how the staged house functions, but Fancy, her name itself signifying imaginative power, runs off in boredom (163–64). The closeness apparent in the names of Fanny/Fancy belies this separation, however, and Jackson shows how the child still lurks under the surface of the adult façade. We sense the threatening and imminent mental collapse of a mad Aunt Fanny abandoning herself to a perpetual indulgence in her girlhood space.

In Jackson's *The Bird's Nest*, the name-invoking summons issues in the other direction, from child to parent, but with the same tone of world-shattering urgency. Betsy, one of the multiple personalities that manifest in the heroine, Miss Richmond, seeks her mother in New York, quietly chanting her name in a desperate attempt to stay focused and complete her quest: "'My mother's name is Elizabeth Richmond, and my name is Betsy and my mother always called me Betsy and I was named after my mother. Betsy Richmond'" (89). The shared name between mother and daughter is a memento of the affection Betsy remembers from her past, but it also suggests that until she resolves her relationship with her mother, she will not be able to supersede the three other personalities within Miss Richmond and develop on her own as an adult. Marta Caminero-Santangelo analyzes Betsy's crisis as an attempt to move past the Lacanian mirror stage: "Betsy now views the whole world or at least everyone she meets in New York, as extensions of herself, and the dramatic triangle involving Robin [her mother's love interest], her mother, and Betsy is replayed again and again" (75). Everything and everyone Betsy turns to – the dictionary in her suitcase, the phonebook consulted on the street, commuters on the bus – are all connected with the mother; her mission is one of memory and language as she confusedly replays the same script, holding on to her mother's name as a thread to lead her through the maze.

Betsy's clutching at names represents a cognitive process that is practiced by Jackson's other characters. Her identification with her same-sex parent, "Elizabeth Richmond," most immediately resembles the psychology of Aunt Fanny in *The Sundial*, who negotiates the garden maze by imagining the curves of her mother's name, Anna, outlined in relief by the hedgerows (95). As a child, Fanny worked relentlessly to lose herself in the maze in spite of the fact that she never could willfully forget its secrets. The primacy of naming rituals and cultivated memories also figures in *The Haunting of Hill House*, where names and identities are understood by difference, highlighting the arbitrary nature of signs. Luke Sanderson initiates this conversation by reasoning from what he thinks he already knows. He suggests,

> "shouldn't we get acquainted? We know only names, so far. I know that it is Eleanor, here, who is wearing a red sweater, and consequently it must be Theodora who wears yellow – "
> "Doctor Montague has a beard," Theodora said, "so you must be Luke."
> "And you are Theodora," Eleanor said, "because *I* am Eleanor."
>
> (43)

This playful sorting of selves later becomes more sinister as the house repeatedly calls on Eleanor by name. She experiences this appropriation as an assault on the property of her being and cannot understand why she should be singled out from the rest of the company.

Jackson's insistent use of the name as a key to the mysteries of the self repeats techniques developed centuries earlier by Richardson. In *Clarissa*, the child is isolated in resistance to the family's demands that she marry the rich, yet toad-like, Mr. Solmes. As she muses over her predicament, she fears that she will never live up to what she once promised to be, as delineated in her grandfather's will: "my dearest and beloved grand-daughter Clarissa Harlowe . . . from infancy a matchless young creature in her duty to me, and admired by all who knew her as a very extraordinary child" (53). These reverberating words of praise defining "Clarissa Harlowe" clash with her immediate disobedience to her family. As Margaret Anne Doody argues, in Clarissa's resistance to her parents' choice of Solmes, "[she] is already bricked up in a family tomb. Her mind runs upon burial alive" (*Natural Passion* 191). Moreover, she cannot remain "beloved" and "matchless" when engaged in secret correspondence with Sir Robert Lovelace, the libertine nobleman who has fallen out of favor with her relations. Richardson's Clarissa, like Jackson's Aunt Fanny, finds herself in conflict with the very reality surrounding her. The Harlowe family's utter neglect of Lovelace and his suit panics Clarissa into fearing his potential retaliation. Her anxiety takes over so entirely that she believes she must accommodate his desire to maintain their communications to prevent bloodshed.

Feeling manipulated into wrongdoing, Clarissa asks her friend Anna Howe, "can I give a sanction immediately to [Lovelace's] deluding arts? – can I *avoid* being angry with him for tricking me thus, as I may say (and as I have called it to him), out of myself?" (382). Clarissa is caught in a trap. She implicitly knows that it is her duty as daughter to decline forbidden correspondence, just as Aunt Fanny knows that the likeliest explanation of the voice she hears is her own madness. They both, however, engage in situational thinking to bring about a desired outcome. Clarissa imagines Lovelace's threats of violence as reality and reasons that she has no option but to write to him. In this way, she is tricked out of her full self. Fanny imagines a voice calling to her and reasons she has no option but to heed it. For Clarissa, the split has tragic consequences. Immediately after her rape, she loses her sense of reason, constantly writing and tearing up her letters. In one paper addressed to her "dear honored papa," she says that "I don't presume to think you should receive me – no, indeed – my name is – I don't know what my name is! – I never dare to wish to come into your family again!" (890). This sense of disintegration continues later when she attributes her declining health to "inward decay" (1276).

Clarissa's undoing down to the loss of her own name even more strongly presages *The Haunting of Hill House*, when Eleanor reads the large chalk lettering that materializes on the wall, spelling out "HELP ELEANOR COME HOME" (107). She feels immediately violated by this appropriation of her identity in a way she cannot fully explain:

> Those letters spelled out *my* name, and none of you know what that feels like – it's so *familiar* . . . Look. There's only one of me, and it's all I've got. I hate seeing myself dissolve and slip and separate so that I'm living in one half, my mind, and I see the other half of me helpless and frantic and driven and I can't stop it.
>
> (118)

Eleanor struggles to describe how the wall's possession of the visible form of her name splits her in two, with the material half of her being sliding away and leaving her mind stranded alone. She accuses Hill House of a "divide and conquer" strategy reminiscent of Lovelace's plan to destroy Clarissa's "pride of being corporally inviolate" before gaining full possession of his captive (879). These thefts of names thus mark a halfway point to complete loss of self, and the fractured protests of both Clarissa and Eleanor reflect the damage already inflicted.

In the sense that each emphasizes the female struggle to attain and maintain self-possession, *Clarissa* and *Hill House* stage an identical contest on one fundamental level: will a woman be brought to consent to her own spiritual destruction, to sign her name to her own ruin? Lovelace reasons that his attempts on Clarissa's virtue will do harm only if she allows her own seduction, while if she happens to prevail, her virtuous defense will only add to her reputation and glory. This rationale allows him postpone justice to the wronged lady, while he works to bring about his ulterior purpose of gaining a mistress who "will be mine upon my own terms" (886). Eleanor likewise realizes the "game" that Hill House is playing with her in order to dominate and destroy her, but she is unable to resist its seduction:

> in the churning darkness where [Eleanor] fell endlessly nothing was real except her own hands white around the bedpost . . . It is too much, she thought, I will relinquish my possession of this self of mine . . . "I'll come," she said aloud.
>
> (150)

The high-contrast image of Eleanor's white-knuckled hands desperately clinging amid an infinite fall into darkness signifies her finite capacity for self-possession capitulating to the House's seemingly unlimited assault. Hill House quiets instantly upon Eleanor's promise, much as Lovelace does when Clarissa writes to him with a seeming surrender of her earlier unequivocal denial. Clarissa has learned of the depth of Lovelace's deception and the certainty of his pursuit. By calculating on his worldly interpretation of her words, she commits a slant-lie:

> Sir, I have good news to tell you. I am setting out with all diligence for my father's house. I am bid to hope that he will receive this poor penitent with a goodness peculiar to himself... So, pray, sir, don't disturb or interrupt me – I beseech you don't – You may in time, possibly, see me at my father's, at least, if it be not your own fault.
>
> (1233)

By speaking allegorically of her heavenly father, Clarissa feigns consent and signs her name to a document that suggests an eventual reconciliation with Lovelace. This small, strategic shift in her usual prose wards off Lovelace's pursuit and thereby allows her time to accept another suitor: Death. Eleanor, trapped in an even more hostile universe than Clarissa, where death and Hill House are ultimately the same, finds that her own forced consent to the House seals her mortal and perhaps immortal fates.

Richardson and Jackson often situate this battle between the individual's freedom and consent within a polyphonic narrative structure that moves through mystery, tension, expectation, and release. In *The Bird's Nest*, a seemingly simple allusion to a nursery rhyme about names, "Elizabeth, Elspeth, Betsy, and Bess," hides a complex plot based on psychoanalytic research into multiple personality disorder and the Romance trope of reunion with one's mother. The reader's gradual discoveries parallel those of the therapist, Dr. Wright, as he treats Miss Richmond and the four identifiable aspects of her self – Lizzie, Beth, Betsy, and Bess. This multivocal technique parallels the quartet of letter writers in *Clarissa* – the eponymous heroine, her friend Anna Howe, the rake Robert Lovelace, and his friend John Belford. Just as we participate in *Clarissa*'s epistolary unfolding, we become acquainted with each of Miss Richmond's four voices by its distinctive tone or worldview as it plays out over time, eventually coming to know all of them so well as to predict their responses. The clamor of these voices simultaneously serves to emphasize and obscure the fact that the silent center of *The Bird's Nest* is Miss Richmond's mother, who died mysteriously six years earlier; her daughter's conflicted reaction to this loss pushes her differing personalities into complex oppositions and alliances.

In this sense, Jackson internalizes Richardson's use of voice-as-conflict by placing even stronger emphasis on the disintegration of the female protagonist. At one session with Dr. Wright, "Betsy" schemes with him by answering a few questions about her mother while another personality, "Lizzie," is asleep. Betsy whispers,

> I know whose mother you mean, old man. The one she – (here she shut her lips, and grinned mysteriously, and put her finger to her mouth in a childlike gesture of secrecy) – Talking about Lizzie when her back is turned, my dear! For shame!
>
> (67)

In this conspiratorial aside, Betsy, initially the most sinister and malicious of the personalities, hints that the more externalized Lizzie has some hidden involvement with her mother that she will not release. Jackson pits Lizzie's repression against the raucous Betsy, a trickster driven to escape the controlled containment of the other personalities.

Throughout Jackson's novels, such maternal loss and trauma unloose the child into a divisive world of conflicting social edicts, strongly reflecting Richardson's own use of this theme in *Pamela*. Eleanor Vance first approaches Hill House in a vulnerable state precisely because of her long years caring as an unpaid, frequently criticized nurse for her own domineering mother:

> the only person in the world that she genuinely hated, now that her mother was dead, was her sister . . . her years with her mother had been built up devotedly around small guilts and small reproaches, constant weariness, and unending despair.
>
> (3)

In this passage, the stuff of which Eleanor's life has been "built" includes daily sniping against a background of infinite service. Her sacrifice makes her at once a hateful and a devoted daughter. Roberta Rubenstein argues for the centrality of the mother image in *The Sundial* as well, observing a "split between the 'good mother' [Anna] for whom the daughter longs – protective and idealized, but absent – and the 'bad mother' – the predatory and tyrannical Mrs. Halloran" (134). In Richardson's *Pamela*, the heroine also loses her mother figure, the noblewoman to whom she is maid and companion, and the narrative of Pamela's "great Trouble" originates from this point. As her predatory new Master pursues her, Pamela finds herself protected – for good or evil – by the housekeepers at his two estates. The "civil" Mrs. Jervis and the "wicked" Mrs. Jewkes bifurcate the maternal role into nurturing protection and bawdy corruption (15, 107). As such, they can be interpreted as externalized components of Pamela's reaction to mother-loss.

Pamela's crisis of female roles manifests in her clothing as she casts off the fine silk dresses that her Lady had bestowed upon her and takes up a country garb, mirroring Eleanor's mental crisis in Hill House and her willful destruction of the seductive Theodora's clothes as a means of identity-reformation. Pamela is conscious of clothing as signifier and yearns for unity between her dress and her worldly fortune. As she writes to her parents, "I now long to get my Business done, and come to my New-Old Lot, again, as I may call it" (38). The awkward wording in this quotation represents the jarring psychological transition that Pamela faces in erasing her intellectual and fashionable development over the past few years and returning to the impoverished "Lot" that had been hers in childhood. These abrupt shifts in identity are even more jarring because they are largely out of Pamela's control, reactive to Mr. B's advances and requiring constant vigilance. Richardson's method of "writing to the moment" captures the terror of not knowing how to respond or why things are happening, much as Jackson's techniques unveil Eleanor's conflicted feelings at Hill House. Jackson mimics Richardson's "to the moment" prose when Eleanor feels both envy and hatred for Theodora and destroys her clothing: "'I suppose she'll have to wear my clothes' [Eleanor said] . . . she had never felt such uncontrollable loathing for a person before" (115–16). In this passage, Eleanor attempts to erase the differences between herself and the despised Theodora by forcing a crisis where they will look alike. She acts in a passive-aggressive fashion, setting up a situation where she will be forced to succumb to Theodora's needs. This pattern later repeats in her surrender to Hill House's demands and echoes her earlier servitude to her mother: "It is too much, [Eleanor] thought, I will relinquish my possession of this self of mine, abdicate, give over willingly what I never wanted at all; whatever [the house] wants of me it can have" (150).

The entanglement of multiple selves, naming, and identity is likewise presented as a precarious ordeal in Richardson's *Sir Charles Grandison* and Jackson's *Hangsaman*, where a susceptible heroine finds herself divided amid competition with more favored peers. The histories of Harriet Byron and Natalie Waite both begin with an obliquely portrayed scene of rape or violation hurtling them forward into a new environment, where they must function without guardians or much-needed worldly experience. In this "test" they find themselves shaken down to the very foundations of identity in their sense of their own names. Richardson's novel portrays a violent abduction from a masquerade, after which Harriet reels in shock, worrying that "I am afraid that I never shall be what I was" (1.159). Her rescuer, Sir Charles Grandison, encourages her to accept the fate that threatened her and allow him to intervene; he urges her to "let us turn this evil appearance into real good. I have two sisters: The world produces not more worthy women. Let me henceforth boast that I have three" (1.144). His flourish of familial acceptance, meant to lighten Harriet's sense of obligation, actually confuses her further with its offer of a new identity and reality. Her grateful love for the hero who saved her must now be shunted aside into sisterly acceptance of a "brother" who did no more than his duty in saving her honor. Mark Kinkead-Weekes observes this irony, noting that "The more she loves, the more unsatisfactory will she find the brothering and sistering she ought to welcome" (301). Harriet's watchfulness over her new siblings and speculations about Sir Charles's personal secrets compromise her usual candor. Eventually, though, her new identity as Charles's third sister allows Harriet access to his history and opens up her awareness of her double and rival, Clementina della Porretta, "the Miss Byron of Italy" (3.53). Lady Clementina comes from a venerable aristocratic family, has a prior attachment to Sir Charles, and is so simultaneously devoted and devout that she goes mad in conflict between her love for him and her native religion. When Clementina exalts herself by choosing Catholicism over a worldly path, Harriet must decide if she will follow her double's example and idealistically discard her love for Sir Charles because he can offer her only the half-heart of a "rejected man." As Kinkead-Weekes argues, "It is this insecurity, not only psychologically but morally, that lies behind her resistance to the pressure of Sir Charles for a quick marriage" (385). What is a contest of piety for Clementina is one of "delicacy" for Harriet (3.16), where her pride of self calls on her to be appropriately scrupulous, but not descend into petty "punctiliousness" (3.78).

Just as Harriet Byron's fears eventually manifest as Clementina, a more ethereal, alluring, and dramatic version of herself, Jackson's Natalie Waite enters college filled with a self-doubt that brings her to imagine the companionship of a more confident friend. When Natalie initially introduces herself to her housemates, she lacks a firm sense of self, even wondering,

> *Is* it my name? . . . afraid for a minute that she had appropriated the name of the next girl, or of someone she had met slightly once and remembered only in the recesses of her mind which seemed called upon unreasonably to function now, socially, and without experience.
>
> (55)

Freshman Natalie's existential unease only increases the longer she is on campus. The more she questions herself and imagines alternate realities (maybe she is not real, but only a figment of someone else's mind), the more she gains interest in a girl named "Tony," who may or may not be "real," and who seems to fit as poorly as Natalie into the conventional female student world, but remains defiant rather than cowed by her isolation. Lenemaja Friedman touts Jackson's precision in imbuing Tony with just enough material being to make her seem like a legitimate new friend who is actually present in the "real" world of Natalie's life on campus (87–89). Because of this convincing portrayal, in the penultimate scene in the woods, readers find themselves as confused and lost as Natalie becomes. As Tony becomes more elusive and moves through the trees, "seeming not to put her feet down," we are forced to reassess her apparent reality (212). From this new, unsettled vantage, it seems more likely that Natalie's self-questioning has led to an externalization of Tony from within her own psyche; after all, "Natalie" and "Tony" are both variants on the name Antonia. In summoning up this new "strange character," as she calls her, Natalie satisfies her need for someone to befriend and legitimize her identity, only to find that Tony ultimately turns against her (138).

Natalie's story, like that of Harriet Byron, is one where a woman is taken over by the identity-story of the other; Richardson's and Jackson's heroines waste away and become specter-like followers of their active doubles, who determine the moves of the game (either through Clementina's turns of conscience or Tony's dealing of the tarot deck). Just as they seem most vulnerable, though, Harriet and

Natalie surprise themselves by mustering an inner limit that preserves them from the influences that have been dominating their minds (*Hill House*'s Eleanor arguably also does so, but too late, immediately before her death). As these women assert independence, we see how difficult it is to step aside from the reinforcement provided by their doubles. Harriet "*justly* fears . . . she never shall be able to make that figure to HERSELF, which is necessary for her own tranquility" (3.77), Natalie laments that "*One is one and all alone and evermore will be so*" (214), and both are cognizant of the lasting effects of their decisions across time. With this awareness, they finally reject self-abnegation and servitude to an Other, and move toward uncertain but self-possessed outcomes.

A key component of Harriet's and Natalie's self-possession is their capacity for narrative. Indeed, a major resemblance between all of Richardson's and Jackson's female protagonists is their tendency to rehearse, reinforce, and question their identities by retelling stories about their lives, past, present, and future. Pamela's identity as a "scribbl[er]" is integral to her upward mobility (100). She works out her thoughts and plans as she writes the account of her struggles against the incursions of Mr. B. At the same time, she reconciles her conduct with her family's rigorous Protestantism and her reading of secular texts, such as *Hamlet* and *The Rape of Lucrece*. Jackson's early novels also feature female writers who are attempting to come of age and into their own. In *Hangsaman*, Natalie Waite's writing, closely directed and sharply critiqued, is intended by her overbearing father to be her key to development. Her 10:00 a.m. conferences with her father are given priority in the family schedule, but when she is shipped off to a college whose brochure proclaims, "Theory is nothing, experience all" (49), she is unprepared for the vicious competition between her peers. Pamela and Natalie try to write themselves into a more stable, self-possessed state of being as their family beliefs and systems are strained to collapse and their social "betters" do not adhere to expected roles. Just as Pamela's parents use correspondence to exhort their daughter ("resolve to lose your Life sooner than your Virtue" . . . *Your loving Father and Mother*), Mr. Waite pressures Natalie with letters from home, counseling her to "scrutinize carefully anyone aspiring to be your friend," yet then proffering his own "friendly" advice (20, 118).

The critique of Richardson's and Jackson's young women writers extends to more severe methods of silencing. The censorship imposed upon Clarissa Harlowe resembles that meted out to Harriet Merriam in Jackson's *The Road Through the Wall* for correspondence considered dangerous by her family. In each novel, the tyrannical control of parents includes the violent confiscation of writing materials and attempted silencing of young women's independent voices. Clarissa faces down psychological warfare within her family as she is imprisoned in her room, deprived of her "standish and all its furniture" (324), and informed that all of her relations have bound themselves in league against her by signing a document. These early scenes of censorship establish a grim tone that builds to eventual tragedy, leading Margaret Anne Doody to declare that "Freedom is very much at the centre of Richardson's novels" (*Natural Passion* 11). Clarissa ultimately dies a martyr of her family's stony-hearted oppression, and yet exonerates their actions by acknowledging her own original fault of disobedience. Similar issues of freedom and familial disorder provide the starting point for Jackson's first novel. When Harriet Merriam arrives home from school, she finds herself confronted by a steely-faced mother:

> The word "letters" carried Harriet hastily up the stairs and into her room; if there had been a lock on the door she might have been able to lock herself in, but she slammed the door violently, and then walked miserably over to her desk, although she knew, had seen from the doorway, that it was open. The slant-top, which should have been securely locked, was dropped down to make the table surface, and Harriet's small papers and notebooks lay as she kept them, mercilessly neat, put back in the pigeonholes, perhaps even put back more carefully than Harriet, who loved them, ever did.
> (11)[3]

The multiple levels of violation – of her ownership of the room, of her prized writing desk (a gift from her father), and of her very private writing – bring the girl to tears in this scene. Harriet grows increasingly distraught as she imagines her mother, positioned in her daughter's space, reading what is not hers to read. The traumatic afternoon worsens with a "scene" at dinner (with Harriet once again remanded to her room), the burning of all of Harriet's notebooks by her mother, and a "reconciliation" where Harriet is told that she will be allowed to learn some recipes to cook under the supervision of her mother. Over time, she accepts and internalizes this punishment and learns to parrot her mother's prejudices, a frightening conformity that shows how easily children are bullied into becoming younger versions of their parents.

In their shared focus on writerly protagonists, Richardson and Jackson also explore the ways that their characters circumvent censorship and gain power for themselves. Pamela and Clarissa often hide their writings next to their bodies, and at one point Pamela worries that her expanding shape may betray her secret: ". . . I begin to be afraid my Writings may be discover'd; for they grow large! I stitch them hitherto in my Under-coat next my linen" (130–31). She hides her writing because it is personal and judgmental of her earthly "Master's" behavior on the higher authority of her religious faith. As she repeatedly stitches packets of paper to her undercoat, Pamela's prolific writing swells around her, evoking the fullness of pregnancy; this fruitfulness of her wit circumvents Mr. B's literal impregnation of her body – as he crudely hints, "I wish I had thee as quick another Way, as thou art in thy Repartees" (70). In *The Bird's Nest*, writing is also a matter of survival. Miss Richmond's writing surges with hateful profanity composed by one of her subsumed personalities who is attempting to come forward. These missives critique the dominant personality, Lizzie, yet are valued by her as well as a sign of her importance: "Someone had written her lots of letters, she thought fondly, lots of letters; here were five. She kept them all in a red valentine box" (18). Like Pamela, Miss Richmond seeks to preserve her correspondence in an intimate fashion, away from the censoring eyes of the reigning authority, in this case her Aunt Morgen. The valentine box chosen as a hiding place symbolizes the deeply intertwined relationship between the different facets of herself, where even a hostile message can be interpreted as a sign of love.

Another sort of concealment is cultivated as Richardson and Jackson employ what might be termed a palimpsestic or encrypted sort of writing to represent the identity crises of their characters. Richardson's final heroine, Harriet Byron, has no option but to share the ostensibly private letters that everyone knows she is constructing and thus requests to hear. She absents herself from company so frequently to write that Charlotte Grandison blames her for her diligence: "Your nasty scribbling! Eternally at your pen" (1.396). Despite the privacy that goes into the creation of her correspondence, Harriet faces overt scrutiny once her letters are publically read, discussed, and analyzed by all her acquaintances; as such, the public nature of her private letters forms an ongoing test of her character. Harriet's primary trait of "'Frankness' means acknowledging to the group (as best one can) one's feelings, hopes, wishes, real desires – and that cannot be done without acknowledging the group's right to speak on the matter, to arrange, to judge, to reshape the individual's emotions and wishes into some socially acceptable form" (Doody, "Identity" 113). Harriet does, however, find a way to get around the problem of public performance. In Volume Two, Letter Six, she arranges a code with her cousin Lucy, the usual reader of the mail, so that in articulating the contents for all to hear Lucy can skip over private passages from Harriet that are marked with an image of a pointing hand and meant for Lucy's eyes alone (1.290). This scheme highlights one of the key questions of *Grandison*: where should generous openness end and proper pride of self begin? Only a reader with access to the entirety of Harriet's letters, public and coded, can judge Harriet's response to this dilemma. In Jackson's *The Bird's Nest*, writing becomes a similar instrument of subversion rife with character revelation when the determined Betsy personality infiltrates the professional work of Miss Richmond through willed control of her writing hand. Betsy is not yet strong enough to manifest completely, yet her ascendancy over Miss Richmond's hand symbolizes significant agency, power, and expression. With protagonists who are intelligent enough to both perform and subvert the conventions of discourse, Richardson and Jackson pursue similar methods of letting repressed voices of dissent criticize the *status quo*.

The strongly parallel, multivocal forms of these authors' novels likewise expand outward to the way in which fragments of folksongs, adages, psalms, mottoes, rhymes, and literary allusions serve to reflect the characters' belief in the great power of words to shape reality. In Richardson's works, the heroines weave the events of their confined lives into artistic media, such as poems and psalm-settings that parallel biblical and contemporary events. Pamela's letters, in particular, display the influence of her Protestant upbringing as she filters her own story through Christian exegesis. For example, Mrs. Jewkes is a "Jezebel" (126), and Mr. B an "Amnon" (53), among a stream of steady references and reflections. Pamela's religious allusions always remain grounded in her immediate observations and thus remain psychologically realistic for the fifteen-year-old servant that she is. Besides following biblical typology, Pamela's imagery fits within the basic story format of the fable, a form that Richardson knew well after adapting L'Estrange's *Fables of Aesop and Other Eminent Mytholo*gists just two years before composing his first novel.

Jackson's works are similarly full of allusions and folk references, especially those associated with childhood. Her characters engage in age-old games, such as Tin-Tin, repeat lies from Shakespeare, contemplate mottoes engraved within their homes, sing carols, remember nursery rhymes, and fend off singsong chants. When Jackson incorporates these invasive words, the characters typically are feeling threatened; what might be pleasurable or comforting instead takes on a darker tone. Jackson is fully alive to the sinister side of childhood and the way its rituals victimize children and predict their destruction. Her recurring use of such devices constructs a Richardsonian atmosphere of uncertainty and fear that is more subtle than the Gothic variety of fiction that would emerge at the end of the eighteenth century and dominate thereafter. The imagery she resorts to is at once nostalgically juvenile and uncannily tainted. Such use of multistability and the ambiguity it creates can be found, for instance, in *The Haunting of Hill House*, when Eleanor Vance reiterates Feste's song from *Twelfth Night*. In Shakespeare's comedy, this piece occurs during a night of carousing and thus it expresses the unity and happiness of the servants' after-hours party. Its lines, "In delay there lies no plenty . . . Present mirth hath present laughter . . . [and] Journeys end in lovers meeting," all stress action and fulfillment (19, 30). At first, this allusion seems to tell us that Eleanor is a romantic and perhaps a bit of a naive fool, but as these words keep infiltrating her thoughts, we wonder if Hill House has seized control of the contents of her memory, exerting its influence to push its relationship with her to "Journey[']s end" and the finality of death, or, worse, an eternity locked preternaturally within the house. Jackson never resolves the question, leaving the reader with a disturbing uncertainty. Unresolved ambiguity is a favorite technique of Samuel Richardson as well, who wanted to encourage the judgment of his audience and strove to make many components of his fiction debatable, even encouraging feedback from readers of his drafts so that he could adjust character portrayals toward the unresolvable (Keymer xvii–xviii). The most well-known example of this mixed portrayal is the characterization of Lovelace as *heroically* villainous, virtuous enough to attract Clarissa Harlowe's interest but flawed enough that readers would not valorize a morally unacceptable rake.

Amid all these allusions, underlying and destabilizing every other element, Richardson and Jackson stress the subjectivity of words themselves. Pamela argues with Mr. B:

> Would it not shew that I could bear anything from you, if I did not express all the Indignation I could express, at the first Approaches you make to what I dread? . . . And what is left me but Words? And can these Words be other than such strong ones, as shall shew the Detestation, which, from the Bottom of my Heart, I have for every Attempt upon my Virtue?
>
> (210)

Pamela is well aware of the half-life of words; she chooses the strongest ones she can summon up because, ultimately, words are all she has to define and defend herself. As a servant, she is regarded as a part of the household owned by Mr. B, yet here she speaks with force to set a guard around her body and her values.

Like Pamela, Jackson's characters repeatedly realize, utilize, and are victimized by the power and danger of words. In *The Road Through the Wall*, Marilyn Perlman loots Thackeray for words that will give her authority: "from *Vanity Fair* she had gleaned 'adorable' and 'fearsome' and 'horrid'" (16). Others wallow in their insufficiency at finding the right words. In the same novel,

> Harriet [Merriam] looked down at the "Dearest George" on the pink paper, and read on, in her own writing, "Let's run away and get married. I love you and I want to – " The letter ended there, because Harriet had not been able to think of what she wanted to do with George.
>
> (12)

In *Hangsaman*, Lizzie also laments her dearth of words:

> I wonder what I would say to a psychoanalyst. I wonder where people find words for all the funny things inside their heads. I keep turning around in circles and finding how well things fit together, but nothing is ever complete.
>
> (107)

In these passages, Jackson's characters trace words up to the brink of a chasm of collapsing identity and sanity they cannot traverse. In mapping where the words break off, the reader can follow the contours of that journey and sense the threat of that imminent collapse. We see human weaknesses, fears, and cruelties that are suggested but all the more powerful because unsaid.

Although the instability of language thus prefigures the dangers confronting a self-possessed, stable name and identity within the world, the forces of evil in Richardson's and Jackson's works attempt to solidify language into a set reality. In *The Sundial*'s apocalyptic twilight, domineering heiress Orianna Halloran literally publishes her list of "instructions" for the new, tiny society of relatives, servants, and houseguests that she intends to control in much the same narrative-driven fashion that Mr. B advances his "Articles" for cohabitation and "Rules" for marriage in *Pamela*. Soon thereafter Orianna is found dead at the bottom of the staircase with the inquiring motto "WHEN SHALL WE LIVE IF NOT NOW? . . . painted in black gothic letters touched with gold over the arched window at the landing," a question that she failed to answer in her attempts to force language to serve her own selfish ends (2). Later, her body is removed outside, next to the sundial with its own legend inquiring, "WHAT IS THIS WORLD?" (219). In this moment, Orianna, who "never liked the inscription," resembles Arcite, the character from Chaucer's "The Knight's Tale" who voiced the question too late (219). Both are shortsighted fighters for immediate dominance. Other tyrants who attempt to impose their own language on others include Mr. Harlowe, Clarissa's father, who issues a damning curse against her once she has left his house, and Mr. Hugh Crain, original inhabitant of Hill House whose book, "MEMORIES, *for* SOPHIA ANNE LESTER CRAIN," contains moral lessons replete with gruesome depictions of consequences should one fail to follow them (123). This tome is offensive in multiple ways – in warping the unknowing childhood of his daughter and in destroying other books to harvest their illustrations – making "MEMORIES" an Ur-book of sins that characterizes all of life as damnation and darkness.

By foregrounding names, multivocal effects, and the process of writing, Richardson and Jackson explore language's approach to nearly ineffable states of being. Both authors' fictions are particularly interested in what we can learn about the traumatized mind through language use. In the aftermath of rape, both Clarissa Harlowe and Natalie Waite experience a lag in their usually keen powers of expression. Clarissa does not seem herself after the violation; she is subject to intensive shifts of mood because of the drugs that were secretly administered to her, although the language of her writing hints at great lucidity behind a veneer of madness. Her writing is fragmentary, and as she creates, she tears up the papers that she writes. Lovelace gets his hands on several scraps and has them transcribed for Belford; they proceed circularly through half-assembled thoughts, riddles, exclamations, and comparisons to the natural world, not communicating sense in a linear fashion, but cumulatively giving a portrait of a mind trapped in time between her habitual self and this new state she has entered. In Paper X, Clarissa pens Otway's lines from *Venice Preserved* describing "my divided soul, / That wars within me, / And raises ev'ry sense to my confusion," a self-division also reflected in the typography that includes scattered quotations from her reading memory rendered sideways around the main column of type (893). This document of Clarissa's scattered mind portrays the flood of recriminations, the mental dissonance of her reason attempting to piece together what has happened. Similarly, after drinking too much at her parents' party, Natalie Waite wakes up the morning after her apparent rape and enjoys

> the clear uncomplicated moment vouchsafed occasionally before consciousness returned. Then, with the darkening of the sunlight, the sudden coldness of the day, she was awake and, before perceiving clearly why, she buried her head in the pillow and said, half-aloud, "No, please no" . . . If she got out of bed it would be true; if she stayed in bed she might just possibly be really sick, perhaps delirious. Perhaps dead. "I will not think about it," she said, and her mind went on endlessly, Will not think about it, will not think about it, will not think about it.
>
> (43)

Natalie's denial enables her to perform her previous self at the breakfast table. All through the family ritual, though, the undercurrent of Natalie's mind recurs, "Will not think about it." Like the shredding of paper by Clarissa, the shredding of Natalie's memory, over and over again, shows that for both traumatized young women, all of reality has been warped. The price of living is mental vigilance to repress or sublimate the most traumatic day of their lives.

Repressed fears also afflict the eponymous Pamela and Miss Richmond of *The Bird's Nest* as they inevitably encounter that which they wish to avoid. Richardson's heroine, terrified by trying to choose the right course of action, sinks down into no action at all. In her best chance for escape, she imagines threats where there are none:

> I looked, and saw the Bull, as I thought, between me and the Door; and another Bull coming towards me the other way: Well, thought I, here is double Witchcraft, to be sure! Here is the Spirit of my Master in one Bull; and Mrs. *Jewkes*'s in the other.
>
> (153)

Once she is returned to confinement, Pamela looks back and sees that what she imagined to be bulls were really only peacefully grazing cows. Her mental image of sexualized, threatening beasts overcomes her actual sense of vision, leaving her so shaken that she hobbles back into captivity rather than continue her attempted escape. In *The Bird's Nest*, Elizabeth Richmond breaks apart into separate personalities because some components of her being want to look back and understand her mother's death. Betsy, most motivated to "find" her mother, is alert to old threats that used to thwart her access to her parent. Her worries about her mother's boyfriend, Robin, cause her to anticipate him on the streets and in the hotels of New York, much as Pamela sees what she most fears as she tries to escape Mr. B's house:

> And [Betsy] could hear him after her, down the hall and down the stairs, praying not to stumble, not Robin again, it wasn't fair, not after all she'd done, not after all she'd tried, not Robin again, it wasn't fair, no one could do *that* again, praying to move quickly enough, to be safely out of it and away before he could touch her, to be safely out of it.
>
> (125–26)

The short, panicked lines of this passage convey Betsy's anxiety over "*that*" – the repressed secret of her youth, having dallied with her mother's boyfriend in order to break up their relationship. Her reiteration "it wasn't fair" and desire to be "safely out of it" suggest that her childish attempt to play at being her mother turned into sexual activity that she could not control. Now, all younger men evoke shades of "Robin" for her, a phobia that has forestalled her own development into adulthood.

Thus influenced by Richardson's intensely psychological studies of his heroines, and repeatedly incorporating his techniques and tropes into her own fiction, Jackson's novels investigate what happens when trauma obscures a coherent sense of self. Both authors destabilize traditional markers of identity, such as names and family structures, in order to suggest that human affective bonds pose little refuge against change. Their multivocal novels highlight the instability of language, particularly the fragmenting, slippery language which their protagonists use as an attempt to shore up their identities, forcing readers to interact actively with the range of possible interpretations of any given event and character. Mark Kinkead-Weekes calls this mode of narrative construction "dramatic form": "creating through the characters and allowing them to produce the changing situations" (425). Richardson and Jackson, although separated by two hundred years, thus argue that human identity, even in the confines of a fictive character, constantly shifts under the weight of questions about the nature of consciousness itself. The results are fascinating, character-driven plots that involve their readers in unresolved and unresolvable questions about instrumentality and freedom.

Notes

1 Jackson herself acknowledged an abiding interest in Richardson's portrayal of good and evil, asking, "Is a sinful man the less sinful because his crimes are against a standard more rarified than ours?" (217). See "Notes on an Unfashionable Novelist (Samuel Richardson, 1689–1761)" in *Let Me Tell You: New Stories, Essays, and Other Writings*, ed. Laurence Jackson Hyman and Sarah Hyman DeWitt, New York: Random House, 2015. 215–18.
2 Although *Pamela* was a popular sensation in the 1740s and beyond, readers interpreted the heroine's trials quite differently. "Pamelists" admired her adherence to a code of Christian virtue and "anti-Pamelists" critiqued her religiosity as a cover for her real code – self-interest. For more on this debate and its aftermath, see Thomas Keymer and Peter Sabor, *Pamela in the Marketplace: Literary Controversy and Print Culture in Eighteenth-Century Britain and Ireland*, Cambridge: Cambridge UP, 2009.
3 Biographer Judy Oppenheimer argues that Jackson worked through issues from her own childhood in many of her characterizations, the portrayal of Harriet Merriam being a notable example. Like Harriet, Jackson had a deep need for privacy and resented her mother and grandmother invading her desk and rifling through her writings (23–24, 124).

Works cited

Caminero-Santangelo, Marta. "Multiple Personality and the Postmodern Subject: Theorizing Agency." Murphy 52–80.
Doody, Margaret Anne. "Identity and Character in Sir Charles Grandison." *Samuel Richardson: Tercentenary Essays*. Eds Margaret Anne Doody and Peter Sabor. Cambridge: Cambridge UP, 1989. 110–45. Print.
———. *A Natural Passion: A Study of the Novels of Samuel Richardson*. Oxford: Clarendon, 1974. Print.
Downey, Dara and Darryl Jones. "King of the Castle: Shirley Jackson and Stephen King." Murphy 214–36.
Friedman, Lenemaja. *Shirley Jackson*. Boston: G.K. Hall, 1975. Print.
Hattenhauser, Darryl. *Shirley Jackson's American Gothic*. New York: State U of New York P, 2003. Print.
Jackson, Shirley. *The Bird's Nest*. New York: Penguin, 2014. Print.
———. *Hangsaman*. New York: Penguin, 2013. Print.
———. *The Haunting of Hill House*. New York: Penguin, 2006. Print.

———. *Let Me Tell You: New Stories, Essays, and Other Writings*. Eds. Laurence Jackson Hyman and Sarah Hyman Dewitt. New York: Random House, 2015. Print.

———. *The Road Through the Wall*. New York: Penguin, 2013. Print.

———. *The Sundial*. New York: Penguin, 2014. Print.

Keymer, Thomas and Peter Sabor. Pamela *in the Marketplace: Literary Controversy and Print Culture in Eighteenth-Century Britain and Ireland*. Cambridge: Cambridge UP, 2009. Print.

Keymer, Tom. *Richardson's Clarissa and the Eighteenth-Century Reader*. Cambridge: Cambridge UP, 1992. Print.

Kinkead-Weekes, Mark. *Samuel Richardson: Dramatic Novelist*. Ithaca: Cornell UP, 1973. Print.

Murphy, Bernice M. *Shirley Jackson: Essays on the Literary Legacy*. Jefferson, NC: McFarland and Company, 2005. Print.

Oppenheimer, Judy. *Private Demons: The Life of Shirley Jackson*. New York: G.P. Putman's Sons, 1988. Print.

Richardson, Samuel. *Clarissa; or, the History of a Young Lady*. Ed. Angus Ross. London: Penguin, 1985. Print.

———. *The History of Sir Charles Grandison*. Ed. Jocelyn Harris. 3 vols. London: Oxford UP, 1972. Print.

———. *Pamela; or, Virtue Rewarded*. Eds. Thomas Keymer and Alice Wakely. Oxford: Oxford UP, 2001. Print.

Rubenstein, Roberta. "House Mothers and Haunted Daughters: Shirley Jackson and the Female Gothic." Murphy 127–49.

2 A failed experiment

Family and humanity in
The Sundial

S. T. Joshi

Misanthropy as a philosophical doctrine has been espoused by a tiny proportion of the human race, even among those intellectuals who are well aware of the overall deficiencies – moral, intellectual, cultural, and physical – of the human race. This is understandable: given the seemingly instinctive urge to perpetuate the species, the espousal of misanthropy – and its practical corollary, the call for the destruction or elimination of the race – is inherently repulsive to the majority of humans, especially as a kind of selective misanthropy leads to such undoubted evils as racism, misogyny, and terrorism.

How, then, does one justify a misanthropic approach to life? There are any number of plausible scenarios whereby the extirpation of our species can be seen as right and fitting (see Joshi, *God's Defenders* 273–78), but most misanthropes relent to the extent of pointing to the general contemptibility of the race as a whole while singling out a few individuals for approval or beneficence. Ambrose Bierce, the great American journalist and fiction writer, engaged in this argument on one occasion when defending the harshness of his literary, moral, and political judgments in his newspaper columns against a critic accusing him of a broader-based misanthropy:

> John Bonner, does it really seem to you that contempt for the bad is incompatible with respect for the good? – that hatred of rogues and fools does not imply love of bright and honest folk? Can you really not understand that what is unworthy in life or letters can be known only by comparison with what is known to be worthy? He who bitterly hates the wrong is he who intensely loves the right; indifference to the one is indifference to the other thing. Those who like everything love nothing; a heart of indiscriminate hospitality becomes a boozing ken of tramps and thieves. Where the sentimentalist's love leaves off the cynic's may begin. You have lived and written to little purpose if you have yet to learn why the good do not make the bad behave themselves.
>
> (*Sole Survivor* 215–16)

All this sounds very noble and even morally upright, but in practice it appears that Bierce took great relish in lambasting the "boozing ken of tramps and thieves" and found relatively few individuals who corresponded to the "bright and honest folk" he is claiming to champion.

There is, moreover, a significant overlap between misanthropy (however that term is interpreted or applied) and satire – an overlap that begins at least as early as Juvenal and proceeds down through such figures as Jonathan Swift, Bierce, Evelyn Waugh, H.L. Mencken, Nathanael West, Gore Vidal, and many others. It is at this intersection that we may profitably study much of Shirley Jackson's work, in particular her inscrutable novel *The Sundial* (1958).

Jackson once wrote in her diary, "Nothing has the power to hurt which doesn't have the power to frighten" (quoted in Oppenheimer 42). This single statement may be all we need to gauge how Jackson's extensive contributions to nonsupernatural terror, or psychological suspense, fuse elements from misanthropy and satire to generate horror, very much in the manner of Ambrose Bierce. Bierce's landmark story collection, *Tales of Soldiers and Civilians* (1891; revised in 1910 as *In the Midst of Life: Tales of Soldiers and Civilians*), features a succession of tales that systematically emphasize how the protagonists' human frailties – cowardice, envy, irrational fear, jealousy – can backfire upon them, with horrific consequences. His most famous story, "An Occurrence at Owl Creek Bridge," is a tour de force in depicting the lengths to which a desperate man, about to be hanged as a spy during the Civil War, can fantasize escaping from his captors. In "The Man and the Snake" a man is frightened literally to death by a snake that proves to be a toy. "A Watcher by the Dead" and "A Tough Tussle" exhibit characters succumbing to the perceived terror of a dead body. Bierce became such a master at this kind of psychological torture (a torture that extends both to his protagonists and to his readers) that Maurice Lévy stated, "One is almost tempted to believe that one day he decided to instill fear into his contemporaries *by hatred*, to gain revenge on them" (14, emphasis in original).

I am not aware of any documentary evidence that Jackson read Bierce; but since Bierce's reputation as both a writer of horror fiction and a classic exponent of Civil War fiction had been established by the time she reached her maturity, it seems unlikely that Jackson could not have sampled him during her college or even her high-school years. Much of her short fiction has a distinctively Biercian flavor – derived no doubt from a roughly similar temperament rather than from any direct literary influence.

Her most famous story, "The Lottery" (1948), could, on one level, be interpreted as a condemnation of the kind of "mob mentality" that we also see, in more limited form, in *The Sundial*: a tradition of stoning selected individuals in order to ensure good crops has continued down to the present day, long after the folly of such sympathetic magic and ritual has been exposed by scientific advance. "One Ordinary Day, with Peanuts" (1955), a story that surprisingly remained uncollected during her lifetime, is another prototypical example. In this tale, a man leaves home in the morning and seems intent on accomplishing nothing but good; through a succession of actions he seems, both to himself and to others, to be benevolence itself. He comes home, meets his wife, and tells her how his day went. She tells him about hers. She tells of all the nasty and unpleasant things she has done. What will happen the next day?

> "Fine," said Mr. Johnson. "But you do look tired. Want to change over tomorrow?"
> "I *would* like to," she said. "I could do with a change."
> "Right," said Mr. Johnson.
>
> (*Just an Ordinary Day* 304)

That is virtually the end of the story. In other words, the qualities of benevolence and malevolence can be put on and taken off with the insouciance of changing one's hat or coat – it makes no moral difference in the end.

Misanthropy as terror probably reaches its height in Jackson's work in the late novel *We Have Always Lived in the Castle* (1962), a searing portrayal of the hatred that the Blackwood family feels for the townspeople who have ostracized them. Merricat Blackwood (who, it turns out, is a murderess) expresses the following sentiments to herself early in the narrative:

> I wish you were all dead, I thought, and longed to say it out loud. Constance said, "Never let them see that you care," and "If you pay any attention they'll only get worse," and probably it was true, but I wished they were dead. I would have liked to come into the grocery some morning and see them all, even the Elberts and the children, lying there crying with the pain and dying. I would then help myself to groceries, I thought, stepping over their bodies, taking whatever I fancied from the shelves, and go home, with perhaps a kick for Mrs. Donell while she lay there. I was never sorry when I had thoughts like this; I only wished they would come true.
>
> (15–16)

The course of the narrative – entirely told from the Blackwood family's point of view with the townspeople depicted as virtually faceless "trash" (17) whose hatred is spiteful and irrational – encourages the reader to agree with Merricat's sentiments here.

The Sundial presents misanthropy in a somewhat more restrained or indirect manner, but it can nonetheless be seen as a driving force in the text, as multiple characters exhibit a loathing for one another that fuels the twists and turns of the narrative. The novel tells the superficially absurd story of an aristocratic family, the Hallorans, who become convinced that the entire world will be consumed by fire and that their spacious home will be all that is left standing, and they will thereby become the source for a newer and presumably better human race. The novel ends inconclusively, and we never learn whether the impending cataclysm has occurred or will occur. In my judgment, the novel is a pungent exploration of a nearly universal misanthropy that is a central element in Jackson's philosophical and aesthetic outlook.

Jackson's biographer, Judy Oppenheimer, states that *The Sundial* grew directly out of an unpleasant incident in her adopted home of North Bennington, Vermont, where she led a campaign to oust an elderly schoolteacher who had been physically and emotionally abusive toward her daughter Sally. In the course of her campaign against the teacher, however, Jackson aroused the hostility of the town, which largely took the teacher's side and made Jackson feel even more isolated in the close-knit community than before (see Oppenheimer 213–15). While it is unlikely that this single incident was the catalyst for *The Sundial*, it is evident that Jackson's general sense of isolation from the community of North Bennington had much to do with the bitter and cynical tone of the novel.

From the point of view of genre, *The Sundial* occupies a kind of middle ground between such clearly supernatural works as *The Haunting of Hill House* (1959) and such tales of psychological aberration as *The Bird's Nest* (1954) and *We Have Always Lived in the Castle*. The matter of the "truth" or reality of the impending destruction of the world remains unresolved to the end; and, although there are a few incidents in the novel that might be interpreted supernaturally, I believe we are to see the prophecy – ludicrous on its face – as fundamentally false, and false in a way that augments the essential misanthropy underlying the entire work. Although Jackson (as Gore Vidal did in the novel *Kalki* [1978]) would no doubt take great relish in the extirpation of nearly the whole of humanity, the overwhelming likelihood that the world will remain intact, even as the Hallorans calmly await its destruction, augments the misanthropic element by refusing to single out the Hallorans as any better than the ignorant townsfolk they scorn.

Jackson may have given a subtle nod to the genre implications of the novel by a disquisition about Strawberry Hill, the eccentric neo-Gothic mansion built by Horace Walpole in the eighteenth century (see *Sundial* 168–69). Jackson was no doubt well aware that Walpole was also the originator of the Gothic novel with *The Castle of Otranto* (1764), and the rambling, multistory Halloran house is indeed a miniature "Gothic castle" in much the same sense as the Blackwood house in *We Have Always Lived in the Castle*. And, as in many works of Gothic fiction, the convoluted byways of these "castles" suggest the unstable mental and psychological states of their inhabitants.

It is of interest to note that some reviewers of the novel detected the misanthropy that underlies it – but they did so in a naively censorious manner that reflects the conventional view that such a philosophical stance is itself morally evil and unjustified. Harvey Swados, in tones of magisterial condemnation, wrote,

> Why is it then that the book finally leaves such a small impression? For one reader it is primarily because, while Miss Jackson is an intelligent and clever writer, there rises from her pages the cold fishy gleam of a calculated and carefully expressed contempt for the human race.
>
> Pleasure in the vileness that human beings can commit one upon the other soon palls, particularly [if] it is unaccompanied by any imaginary representation of the specific moral gravity of a good human being. The result is that the figures in this literary landscape become less and less human and more and

more simply the vehicles for an extended bitter joke that ends after several hundred pages by being merely tedious.

(20)

This is a moral criticism masquerading as an aesthetic judgment, and the fallacy of the latter paragraph is that it is entirely plausible to assume that there simply are no "good human beings" to form a counterweight to the bad ones. Somewhat less judgmentally, David L. Stevenson noted that the novel "is a macabre and comical morality of the human id, in which all the characters are articulate and capable of decision only at the level of their most primitive wishes for power, their subliminal feelings of hate, greed, lust" (58). William Peden wrote disapprovingly, "For all its wry humor, the novel seems to me to be primarily a bleak inquiry into what can only be called the idiocy of mankind" (16).

For a relatively short novel, *The Sundial* features a bewildering array of characters, not all of whom are depicted quite as fully and three-dimensionally as one could have wished. It would be helpful to keep in mind the various figures who strut throughout the novel:

Richard Halloran, son of the deceased builder of the house, now confined to a wheelchair and with a tenuous hold on reality.

Mrs. Orianna Halloran, Richard's wife and the dominant figure (in every sense of the term) in the work, always seeking to maintain her preeminence against all challengers.

Fanny Halloran, Richard's sister, an unmarried and aging woman (she is forty-eight but seems and acts older), snobbish and intolerant, striving as best she can to battle with Orianna for supremacy in the household, and the one who claims to have heard the prophecy of cataclysm from the ghost of her dead father.

Maryjane Halloran, widow of Richard and Orianna's son Lionel. She is a flighty ex-librarian who seeks only to gain whatever she can from the family she has married into.

Fancy Halloran, Maryjane's young daughter, seemingly a sweet, innocent child but also animated by cold self-interest.

Essex, a young man hired to catalogue the library and who aims to sidle up to whoever he believes can improve his own fortunes.

Miss Ogilvie, Fancy's governess, timid and put-upon.

At later stages of the novel, several other individuals appear on the scene and take up residence in the house:

Mrs. Willow, a friend of Orianna, plain-speaking and a bit coarse.

Arabella and Julia, her daughters; Arabella is the pretty one, and Julia the smart one.

Gloria Desmond, the seventeen-year-old daughter of Orianna's cousin, seemingly endowed with psychic powers.

Captain Scarabombardon, a stranger whom Fanny has brought to the house from the village, apparently for reproductive purposes when the new Eden dawns. His name is fictitious, having been arbitrarily assigned to him by Fanny.

There are any number of other minor characters – chiefly various denizens of the nearby village – but they play very small roles in the action.

The novel opens strikingly with the bland assertion by Maryjane (an assertion believed by her daughter, Fancy) that Orianna has killed her own son, Lionel, by pushing him down the stairs. Was this done in order to allow Orianna unfettered dominance in the household? It would certainly appear so. Her very name is no accident, for it clearly evokes Gloriana, the nickname given to Queen Elizabeth I. The name Oriana is a character (a British princess) in the medieval Spanish romance *Amadis de Gaula* (c. 1304) and was used in a musical work, *The Triumphes of Oriana* (1601), a collection of madrigals assembled by Thomas Morley and dedicated to Elizabeth I.

Orianna's heartlessness and dismissiveness toward the remaining members of the household are amply displayed by her appalling comment about her own son ("We could very well do without Lionel" [14]) and by her subsequent plans to dismiss Essex, put Miss Ogilvie in a cheap boardinghouse, banish Aunt Fanny to the tower room, send Maryjane back to the library where she worked before marrying Lionel, and keep Fancy for herself as the ultimate heir of the house.

It is shortly after this revelation that Fanny, in the garden near the eponymous sundial, has the vision (or fantasy) that her dead father is speaking to her, declaring that there is danger everywhere except in the house. Although Orianna scoffs at the vision, a snake suddenly emerging out of the fireplace convinces Maryjane that Fanny is speaking the truth. Soon thereafter, Fanny hears the prophecy that governs the subsequent action in the novel:

> Aunt Fanny was listening to her father, repeating to them what he told her. With a happy smile on her face and her eyes shut, she listened with a child's care, and spoke slowly, word for word. Aunt Fanny's father had come to tell these people that the world outside was ending. Neither Aunt Fanny nor her father expressed any apprehension, but the world which had seemed so unassailable to the rest of them, the usual, daily world of houses and cities and people and all the small fragments of living, was to be destroyed in one night of utter disaster. Aunt Fanny smiled, and nodded, and listened, and told them about the end of the world.
>
> (35)

Subsequently she concludes ruefully, "Humanity, as an experiment, has failed" (36).

Because of this revelation, Fanny seems to be gaining the upper hand in the household; indeed, it is stated that Orianna had "no choice" (41) but to believe Fanny. But Orianna quickly seizes the moment. To her it is of no consequence whether Fanny's prophecy is true or false; all she is concerned about is emerging on top when the new dispensation (if there is any) comes.

It is at this point that the Willow family and, soon thereafter, Gloria Desmond appear. Gloria occupies a critical function in the novel, seemingly confirming the prophecy by participating in a kind of spiritualist exercise whereby she looks deeply into a mirror taken from the wall and placed flat on a table. By this means she ascertains that the day of reckoning will be a few months from the time the novel opens – specifically, August 30. It is here that the supernatural appears to enter into the novel. One of Gloria's visions depicted the family sitting placidly at breakfast; some weeks later, that precise scenario, with numerous details from Gloria's vision, occurs (139). Still later, Gloria tells Fancy that she has never seen Orianna in any of her visions of the world after August 30 (171) – a point that will gain relevance later.

Although the novel focuses almost relentlessly on the multifarious struggles for power, influence, and supremacy within the Halloran household, including the rambling house and capacious grounds, the unnamed village nearby also comes in for some attention. A long and otherwise anomalous passage going into elaborate detail about a teenage girl, Harriet Stuart, who killed her family but was acquitted (70–71) is evidently meant to suggest that the moral, intellectual, and cultural level of the villagers is even lower than that of the aristocratic Hallorans.

Numerous other passages reinforce this impression. On a trip to the village, Miss Ogilvie – in spite of strict instructions to the contrary – speaks of the coming cataclysm with a drugstore clerk; and although she explicitly declares (in accordance with Jackson's own antireligious bent) that it would be nothing like the Last Judgment (84), the clerk tells his mother, who is a member of a small club called the True Believers, whose (admittedly unorthodox) Christian leanings are unmistakable. In a grotesque episode where some of the True Believers visit the Halloran house, it is revealed that they believe that spacemen from Saturn are coming to take them away. "We wish you a pleasant journey," Orianna says with bland sarcasm (93).

At a party thrown for the villagers on the day before the expected cataclysm, Essex takes great pleasure in teasing a number of the villagers. He soberly declares that Miss Ogilvie's taciturnity has an odd source: "Miss Ogilvie as a child was violated by a band of Comanche Indians in a lonely farmhouse on Little Wicked Bend River" (187). This, and other obviously fabricated tales, is credulously believed by the villagers.

But if the villagers are contemptible in numerous ways, the denizens of the Halloran household are scarcely less so. That, by general consensus, the thousands of books in the library are not only removed but also burned to make way for supplies that will presumably be needed after the cataclysm is a pungent symbol for the collapse of intellect that is overrunning all members of the household in the wake of Fanny's preposterous prophecy. Various characters from time to time do express a mild skepticism about the veracity of the prophecy, but the others summarily reject these doubts.

The character exhibiting the greatest skepticism is Julia Willow, who declares flatly at one point (in reference to herself and the Captain), "We don't believe that crap, any of it" (122). Orianna, now in total charge of the situation, declares that Julia is free to leave with the Captain; in fact, she cleverly gives the Captain a check for an unspecified but apparently enormous sum of money, blandly remarking, "We are not going to need it any more" (125). The very size of this check causes the Captain to have doubts of his own skepticism: If Orianna is so convinced of the coming cataclysm, perhaps it would be prudent to stay on at the house? He does so, leaving Julia in the lurch.

Julia is nevertheless determined to leave by herself, and Orianna provides her with a driver from the village to take her to a larger "city" some distance away. Is Jackson setting up a scenario whereby it becomes (supernaturally) impossible for anyone to leave the house? Let us examine precisely what happens to Julia. The Captain's desertion of her is a significant blow, but she tries to carry on in his absence. The driver of the car proves to be a surly individual who attempts to take advantage of the situation by demanding an increasingly higher fee for his services, to the point that Julia abruptly leaves the car and proceeds on foot. At this point a surreal atmosphere supervenes, but what has really happened is that she simply gets lost in the dark and falls down a steep hill toward the river. She awakens the next morning back at the Halloran house with Orianna delivering a snide and gloating taunt: "My dear . . . if you continue uncooperative I shall not let you go to the city again" (137). Nothing supernatural has actually occurred. It is nothing more than Julia's (and, by extension, any other potentially skeptical character's) physical and emotional weakness that prevents them from leaving the house in the face of the collective insanity overwhelming its denizens.

In a revealing passage, Essex recites the motto (from Chaucer) that adorns the sundial: "What is this world? What asketh man to have? / Now with his love, now in his colde grave, / Allone, with-outen any companye." Orianna makes a deliberately ambiguous comment. "'I do not care for it,' Mrs. Halloran said, caressing the W of WORLD" (149). This could mean either that she does not care for the quotation or that she does not care for the world (i.e., that she is herself a misanthrope, or at best a cynic and a pessimist). The latter interpretation is emphasized when Essex asks, in reference to the world following the cataclysm, "Do you think we will be happy there?" Orianna replies, "No . . . But then, we are not happy here" (149–50). The new world will be pretty much as wretched and miserable as the old.

It is young Gloria who, a little surprisingly, expresses the most pungent misanthropy in the novel. In a remarkable discussion with Fancy about the outside world, Gloria offers a blanket condemnation:

> "There's nothing there," Gloria said with finality. "It's a make-believe world, with nothing in it but cardboard and trouble." She thought for a minute, and then said, "If you were a liar, or a pervert, or a thief, or even just sick, there wouldn't be anything out there you couldn't have."
>
> Fancy bent over the doll house. "Anyway," she said, "I don't care how shabby it is. I'm not afraid of bad people, and of not being safe."
>
> "But there aren't any *good* people," Gloria said helplessly. "No one is *any*thing but tired and ugly and mean. I *know*."
>
> (167)

But if the outside world offers nothing of value, the Halloran house (and household) is little better. At the very outset we are told that, in the opinion of its builder, the house "should contain everything" (8). In other words, it is a microcosm of the world at large. And the motley array of denizens in the house, for all the aristocratic pretensions of some of them, is a fittingly vile amalgam of the varied human failings embodied by the villagers.

The climax of the novel only augments the general misanthropy underpinning it. By this time, all doubt as to the reality of the impending cataclysm has disappeared, and a kind of mob mentality has taken over the entire Halloran household. Even those who had previously expressed skepticism are doing nothing but planning for life after the destruction of the world.

In a stunning confirmation of Gloria's vision, which suggested that Orianna would not be around following the cataclysm, Orianna is found dead on the fateful day of August 30. She has been pushed down the stairs, exactly as she presumably pushed her own son some weeks earlier. Who is the culprit? Without saying so, Jackson strongly implies it is little Fancy. Perhaps taking hints from the image of corrupted innocence in Henry James's *The Turn of the Screw*, Jackson has throughout the novel portrayed Fancy as far from the sweet little girl she appears. At the very outset her ruthless megalomania is etched keenly: "Fancy ran her hand richly along the soft hearth rug. 'It's going to belong to me when my grandmother dies,' she said. 'When my grandmother dies, no one can stop the house and everything from being mine'" (17). And who else but Fancy could have been responsible for the existence of a doll, clearly representing Orianna, that is stuck full of pins and placed on the sundial (104–5)? Orianna may in fact have signed her own death warrant when she told Fancy that the crown (really just a gold band) she is wearing to symbolize her own supremacy in the household will go to Fancy only "When I am dead" (200). Sure enough, Fancy snatches up the crown from the dead Orianna's head without the slightest remorse or grief: "'My crown!' Fancy said suddenly, and bolted down the stairs" (216). If Fancy is the kind of ruler that the new dispensation offers, the new world will truly be no better than the old.

But is that cataclysm actually going to occur? Jackson deliberately keeps the reader in suspense to the end. She merely concludes the novel with a scene in which the remaining denizens of the Halloran household exchange utterly trivial and fatuous small talk while waiting stolidly for the destruction of the world. She enjoys teasing the reader with suggestions that that cataclysm may in fact be coming. In the days leading up to the climactic August 30, strange phenomena are noted throughout the nation:

> Toward the end of August the weather turned strange; various and unusual phenomena were reported from one end of the country to the other: freak snow storms, hurricanes, hail from a clear sky. . . . There were cases of death from heat and death from drowning and death from wind in each morning's newspaper, along with statements that the earth's surface was being lowered into the oceans at the rate of two inches a century; a volcano which had been dormant for five hundred years erupted, blasted its surrounding countryside, and fell asleep again forever.
>
> (179)

This may be an amusing anticipation of global warming, but Jackson knows (and expects her skeptical readers to know) that each one of these incidents can be plausibly be accounted for naturalistically. And in that final scene there is one more hint of the cataclysm: "'I thought I heard a crash,' Julia said, turning her hands nervously. 'Probably one of the trees going down,' Aunt Fanny said. 'The best thing for you, dear, is to try not to notice. Try to think of something else'" (221). The crash of a single tree is insufficient to establish the extraordinary notion that the entire world is somehow coming to an end, and Fanny's deadpan response is only a further indication of her utter failure to realize the truly apocalyptic nature of the calamity that she professes to believe.

The Sundial portrays humanity as a failed experiment in and out of the Halloran household, so that it scarcely makes a difference whether the cataclysm predicted by Fanny occurs. For all the elaborate preparations that the Hallorans engage in to ensure the renewal of the race, there is little indication that – if that apocalypse were actually to happen – the new crop of human beings would be much better than the old. Moreover, the high probability that the Hallorans are merely waiting around delusionally for a new dispensation that is only a product of their neurotic imaginations points to Jackson's refusal to single out any member of our species, however high-born or self-important, as much better than his or her fellows. It is a cheerless vision of humanity that Jackson portrays in *The Sundial*, but it is also a fitting vehicle for the mordant satire that she wielded with customary aplomb.

Works cited

Bierce, Ambrose. *A Sole Survivor: Bits of Autobiography.* Eds. S. T. Joshi and David E. Schultz. Knoxville: U of Tennessee P, 1998. Print.
Jackson, Shirley. *Just an Ordinary Day.* Eds. Laurence Jackson Hyman and Sarah Hyman Stewart. New York: Bantam, 1997. Print.
———. *The Sundial.* 1958. New York: Penguin, 2014. Print.
———. *We Have Always Lived in the Castle.* 1962. New York: Popular Library, n.d.
Joshi, S. T. *God's Defenders: What They Believe and Why They Are Wrong.* Amherst, NY: Prometheus Books, 2003. Print.
Lévy, Maurice. *Lovecraft: A Study in the Fantastic.* Trans. S. T. Joshi. Detroit: Wayne State UP, 1988. Print.
Oppenheimer, Judy. *Private Demons: The Life of Shirley Jackson.* New York: G. P. Putnam's Sons, 1988. Print.
Peden, William. "The 'Chosen Few.'" *Saturday Review of Literature* XLI (8 March 1958): 18. Print.
Stevenson, David L. "The Lost Audience." *Nation* (2 August 1958): 58. Print.
Swados, Harvey. "What Is This World?" *New Republic* (3 March 1958): 19–20. Print.

3 Perception, supernatural detection, and gender in *The Haunting of Hill House*

Melanie R. Anderson

Contrary to popular belief, which tends to label Shirley Jackson as a Gothic writer, she not only wrote horror or supernatural tales but also had a tendency to incorporate aspects of the supernatural into many of her works. Even though they are not ghost stories, her novels *Hangsaman* (1951), *The Bird's Nest* (1954), *The Sundial* (1958), and *We Have Always Lived in the Castle* (1962) and her final, unfinished novel, *Come Along with Me* (1968), do contain elements that could be construed as supernatural. These elements often develop characters typical of Jackson's fiction – marginalized women who use the supernatural either as a bid to gain power or, more likely, as a symbol of their ghostliness and lack of agency. For example, in the fragment *Come Along with Me*, Angela Motorman "dabble[s] in the supernatural" (10), and in *The Sundial*, on the day her conniving sister-in-law plans to kick her out of the Halloran ancestral home, spinster Fanny Halloran hears the disembodied voice of her deceased father, the patriarch of the Halloran family, announce the apocalypse and tell her that she is favored among the family members. Jackson's tendency to flavor her writing with the uncanny could have played a role in her eventual slide into relative obscurity in the American academy, a course that happily looks to be reversing.[1] As Bernice M. Murphy notes,

> Jackson has often been sidelined as too commercial, too generic or too popular. Yet . . . Jackson's work has a great deal to offer. . . . Her writing provides a fascinating portrait of American womanhood during a period of significant change. She excelled at dramatizing the anxiety and claustrophobia experienced by so many . . . American women during the postwar period.
>
> (19)

This lack of critical attention for reasons of genre and popularity did not include Jackson's famous (or infamous) short story "The Lottery" or her novel *The Haunting of Hill House* (1959), but even so these two narratives point to one of the central tenets of her canon: evil lurks in the most ordinary of circumstances and can surprise one at any moment. Another important aspect of her fiction is her masterful use of the supernatural as a metaphor for this lurking presence of evil, latent and overt in her writing, particularly in oppressions of a patriarchal society, and in the victims' sometimes doomed attempts to create possibilities for a life within these strictures.

To this end, with its setting of a ghost hunt at a haunted mansion, Jackson's supernatural masterpiece, *The Haunting of Hill House*, to a greater degree than her other works, becomes an excellent test case for her connections between women and the supernatural. In this novel she combines her interests in mystery and supernatural fiction, thus recycling such late nineteenth- and early twentieth-century materials as the reports of psychical societies and narratives of occult detection into her own version of a ghost-hunting expedition. Jackson manipulates the trappings of these narrative forms to subvert their patriarchal underpinnings and open a space for the investigation of the very real terrors of 1950s American culture for women. This failed search for spirits becomes an exploration of the conflict between authoritative and subjective narratives. Consequently the novel contains two levels: on the surface is Dr. Montague's paternal, rational, and supposedly scientific quest to explain the supernatural, whereas underneath that investigation and unnoticed by Montague is Eleanor's real struggle as she attempts to find a home in a society that does not value her as an unprotected and unattached woman. The inexplicable and dangerous supernatural atmosphere in Hugh Crain's Hill House is a microcosm of the damaging world Eleanor faced before she arrived, embodied in her own family relationships, or the lack thereof. These competing narratives and perceptions suggest Jackson's use of the plot of occult detection as a handy fictional translation point for the experience of women who, by circumstance or choice, do not fit the accepted scripts of behavior in a patriarchal society.

The paranormal that peppers Jackson's creative work, even those stories ostensibly received as humorous sketches of family life, stems from her own interest in the supernatural, an interest that was no secret in the literary world of the 1950s and early 1960s.[2] As a result of the marketing of her work, her intellectual and creative curiosity about witchcraft and magic became almost immediately intertwined with her literary persona. In order to achieve a broader, more popular audience, her husband, Stanley Hyman, wrote a biographical blurb for her first novel, *The Road Through the Wall* (1948), that included the line that Jackson was "perhaps the only contemporary writer who is a practicing amateur witch" (Oppenheimer 138), and Jackson continued this thread of publicity in her own biographical sketch for *The Lottery and Other Short Stories* (1949). Claiming that she was "tired of writing dainty little biographical things that pretend I am a trim little housewife in a mother hubbard stirring up appetizing messes over a wood stove," she wrote an autobiographical sketch that included a haunted house with a ghost in the attic, magic incantations, and voodoo dolls (139).[3] She uses these touches of the supernatural to undermine the traditional connotations of "housewife." As she repeatedly insists in her family stories, she can inhabit multiple roles – she can be Stanley Hyman's wife and Shirley Jackson the author. As a writer, she has the possibilities afforded by imagination, and she snatches at the power represented by creativity for her professional persona. For my purposes of showing how Jackson uses the supernatural to represent the horror of reality for women trapped in a patriarchal system, we can take note of a description of the "supernatural" by one of her four children. In an interview with Judy Oppenheimer, Barry described his mother's interest in the occult as curiosity about mysterious processes of human consciousness rather than a strict belief in spirits:

> Is the ... supernatural ... ghosts of dead people, or another way of verbalizing other sides of the mind, other sides of emotion? ... If you see a ghost walk across the room, have you seen a ghost or are you hallucinating? There's no way to tell. As with a lot of things where there's no way to tell, it makes absolutely no difference. It's equally real whether it exists in your head or in the room ... So there is no difference between unknown parts of the human mind and the supernatural.
>
> (223)

In essence, the supernatural becomes a question of perception – proving that something concrete exists is nearly impossible and not as important as exploring *why someone believes she saw it*. As Jackson wrote after her first novel was published,

> I've had for many years a consuming interest in magic and the supernatural. . . . I think this is because I find there so convenient a shorthand statement of the possibilities of human adjustment to what seems to be at best an inhuman world.
>
> (Oppenheimer 125)

One of the settings that Jackson consistently revisits in her explorations of the supernatural and inhuman is the structure of the house. In her essay "Experience and Fiction" (anthologized by Hyman in the posthumously published collection *Come Along with Me*), Jackson explains how she developed her ideas for the novel she just finished – *The Haunting of Hill House*. While humorously emphasizing that she "had not the remotest desire to see a ghost," she outlines careful research that included reading all of the supernatural fiction she could find and speaking with people who claimed to have experienced hauntings. From this research, she emphasizes a particular study of a haunted location and its influence upon her work. Critic Judie Newman describes the influence of the haunting of Borley Rectory on Hill House, but she notes that the report on Ballechin House is more likely the one that Jackson references here (182).[4] What is most interesting about Jackson's description of this haunting is her emphasis on perception:

> I happened ... to read a book about a group of people, nineteenth-century psychic researchers, who rented a haunted house and recorded their impressions of the things they saw and heard and felt in order to contribute a learned paper to the Society for Psychic Research. They thought that they were being terribly scientific and proving all kinds of things, and yet the story that kept coming through their dry reports was not at all the story of a haunted house,

it was the story of several earnest, I believe misguided, certainly determined people, with their differing motivations and backgrounds. I found it so exciting that I wanted more than anything else to set up my own haunted house, and put my own people in it, and see what *I* could make happen.

(*Come Along with Me* 200–1)

After this lengthy description, Jackson admits that she felt compelled to write her haunted classic, flippantly commenting, "By then it was abundantly clear to me that I had no choice; the ghosts were after me" (203). A reading of this report, *The Alleged Haunting of B – House*, shows its influence on *The Haunting of Hill House*, for similarities are numerous. The report is composed of notes and journals from the investigation – much like Dr. Montague wishes to construct his report of Hill House – and the hauntings have interesting echoes. The report of the investigation of Ballechin House, like that of Hugh Crain's estate, records mysterious banging sounds like cannonballs striking on doors, speculation about nuns, the involvement of spectral dogs, and ghosts experienced by sensitive investigators through telepathic visions. Additionally, there is a mistrust of the techniques of female mediums on the part of the investigators that finds resonance in Montague's dismissals of his wife's work with a planchette in Hill House as being unscientific. In spite of these parallels, Jackson emphasizes her focus on the story underneath the investigation. She notes, "I do not think that the Society for Psychic Research would accept me as a qualified observer; I think, in fact, that they would bounce me right out the door." This suggested rejection results from her interest not in proving the paranormal but in "learning how people feel when they encounter the supernatural" (202). At this point she is not so much interested in pursuing actual ghosts, per se, in her writing; rather she is intrigued by the possibilities that ghosts (and their accompanying narratives) offer for exploring the human mind, emotions, and identity.

These questions of subjectivity most likely influence the way Jackson handles the "haunting" in Hill House. Even though she promised her publisher ghosts galore in the novel, it is never clear exactly what is haunting the house – there are no apparitions within its walls.[5] This decision to avoid obvious specters follows her emphasis on perception and the highly subjective nature of "hauntings." But it also follows quite closely occult and psychical theories of ghosts and haunted homes that had been developing since the late 1800s in the British and American Societies for Psychical Research through Jackson's contemporary moment and the Duke Parapsychology Laboratory. With her extensive reading for *The Haunting of Hill House* and her interest in the occult, Jackson was likely aware of these developing theories. Predominant theories of hauntings usually focused on ESP or telepathy, or the reaction of a subjective mind to overwhelming psychical residue in certain places. This idea of ghosts as the results of "thought-transference" repeats throughout the report on Ballechin House that was part of Jackson's research. In the late nineteenth century, the British Society for Psychical Research undertook an investigation into ghosts with mixed results. The first investigator, Nora Sidgwick, concluded that ghosts were "thready creations of foggy nights and fevered imaginations," but she had to admit that the people she interviewed were convinced that they saw ghosts or experienced hauntings. She suggested that this "'certain sense' of being haunted" should be investigated (Blum 94–95). In later investigations of "crisis apparitions," members of the society posited that telepathy could play a role (116). In the mid-1940s, investigators for the Duke Parapsychology Laboratory created a file titled "The Spontaneous Case Collection." Even though Professor J. B. Rhine refused to believe in ghost sightings, there were so many reports of ghosts sent to the laboratory that they needed to open a file and investigate the most promising situations. Like the members of the British Society for Psychical Research, Dr. Louisa E. Rhine concluded that ghosts were the products of telepathy: "When someone sees a ghost, he or she is essentially taking information gained via ESP and creating a visual drama in order to convey that information from the unconscious to the conscious" (Horn 79, 102).

These theories of the supernatural reported by the British and American Societies for Psychical Research and the Parapsychology Laboratory influenced fiction from the late nineteenth into the mid-twentieth centuries, much of which Jackson probably read. One of the most well-known fictional ghost hunters, Algernon Blackwood's "psychic doctor" John Silence, follows this theory of subjective experiences of residual energy. In the story "The Psychical Invasion" he explains,

> I have reason to believe that on the dissolution at death of a human being, its forces may still persist and continue to act in a blind, unconscious fashion. As a rule they speedily dissipate themselves, but in the case of a very powerful personality they may last a long time.
>
> (20)

In another story "Secret Worship," Silence describes the ghosts that appear in the victim's unconsciousness as "shells of violent men," and he cautions that "thought and emotion can persist in this way ... after the brain that sent them forth has crumbled into dust" (170–71). With her broad reading in supernatural fiction, and her interest in trends in psychical research, it makes sense that Jackson would be aware of these theories in literature and popular culture at large. Tellingly, Jackson refers in *The Haunting of Hill House* to the Duke Laboratory's ESP cards, which were popular at the time. Theodora's consistently high scores in ESP tests with these cards catch Dr. Montague's attention when he is looking for assistants for his investigation.[6] Moreover, Jackson would imbue Hill House with the powerful lasting psychic residue of Hugh Crain, the ultimate patriarchal figure and misogynist. The supernatural manifestations then come through Eleanor, a woman sensitive to such vibrations and uniquely positioned to be a perfect victim of these forces. The supernatural experiences in the house monstrously mirror its violent past for female inhabitants and Eleanor's marginalized position outside of it in the real world of 1950s America.

In addition to her interest in paranormal literature, Jackson also voraciously read mysteries, a proclivity she mentions in her story "The Night We All Had

Grippe" (*Come Along with Me* 205), and her thoughts about supernatural literature and its emphasis on subjective perception find echoes in the literary elements of the mode of occult detective fiction. According to Srdjan Smajić in his book *Ghost-Seers, Detectives, and Spiritualists*, if one of the basic tenets of detective fiction is the phrase "seeing is believing," then the fundamental basis of supernatural fiction questions that visual literacy (92–93). While detective fiction asserts that our surroundings are easily understood if one knows how to read clues that may include "footprints and fingerprints, facial expressions and body gestures, cigar ashes and stained articles of clothing" (93), ghost stories test the human tendency to trust one's vision – they play with the very practice of perception through their ambiguity and undecidability. Detective fiction uses visual clues to pinpoint the perpetrator and explain the crime, but supernatural fiction deconstructs this reliance on sensory interpretation. In ghost stories of the uncanny, it is never crystal clear if the ghosts that are witnessed truly exist or are caused by illusions or even delusions – none of the senses can be trusted to interpret reliably the observed events. Smajić goes on to point out that in Victorian ghost stories there is always a double current: "desire and reluctance to believe that ghosts are more than optical illusions or mental projections" (61). When detective fiction and the supernatural are combined into a hybrid of occult detection, or, as we more commonly know it today, ghost hunting, these concerns are present. There is a desire to discover proof of ghosts through rational or scientific methods with a concurrent reluctance simply to accept hauntings on the authority of communal stories and experiences. Just as in the long history of the ghost story, where we find, on the one hand, spiritualists who claim to interpret supernatural events through extrasensory means with second sight and séances and, on the other hand, pseudoscientific occult specialists who desire methodically to categorize and precisely explain extranatural phenomena through observation and recordings, we find the boundary between the explainable and the unknowable embraced and/or policed, depending on the method and the desired outcome. Usually, however, the spirits who are being pursued do not cooperate with either method and give the slip to human methods of understanding, thus showing how deceptive our senses can be.

Working in this hybrid genre, Jackson combined her interest in mystery and supernatural literature with her inspiration from reading reports of the Society for Psychical Research and focused not on the investigations but rather on the undercurrents of motive and character of the investigators. One of the aspects of Jackson's novel that confused initial readers and editors was this issue of identifying its genre, or mode. Darryl Hattenhauer describes reader reports of an early manuscript draft: "I can't figure out what she wants to do with the story. Mystery? Spoof? Psychomystery? Gothic horror?" (169). All of these are present. As a result, in *The Haunting of Hill House* strands of supernatural and detective fiction intertwine into a paranormal mystery.[7] Dr. Montague becomes the occult detective attempting to "explain" the inexplicable, but Jackson makes Eleanor, a woman out of place in society, the protagonist. She is not independent nor married; neither is she a mother. She is lonely, homeless, and lost. Through the interplay between

Montague's attempt at rational, scientific investigation and Eleanor's visceral, fragmented descent into madness, Jackson subverts the patriarchal tradition of detective and, ultimately, occult detective fiction.

Much as how Jackson's novel characterizes Montague as a patriarchal authority figure, in the course of the development of mystery fiction, the detective became a distinctly male figure who has the market cornered on knowledge, observation, and rationality. In *Sherlock's Men: Masculinity, Conan Doyle, and Cultural History*, Joseph A. Kestner posits that Conan Doyle's Sherlock Holmes, in the tales published from 1887–1927, not only influenced detective fiction to come and contemporary theories of detection and crime investigation, but also responded to a "crisis" of masculinity as British society struggled with rapid modernization, changing gender roles, the rising challenges of the United States and Germany, the cost of maintaining and expanding empire, and economic fluctuations (3, 11). Kestner argues that the Holmes tales become "modes of modelling manliness" for their contemporary moment. Holmes even becomes a prime example of proper behavior for young men in Robert Baden-Powell's 1908 manual *Scouting for Boys*. According to Kestner, "Baden-Powell could plausibly endorse the Holmes tales as constructing a masculine script, given that they confirmed qualities which were radically gendered as masculine in Victorian culture: observation, rationalism, factuality, logic, comradeship, daring and pluck" (2). In Holmes, the master interpreter of signs, "reason/masculinity/actuality" stands in stark contrast to the feminine qualities of emotion and subjectivity (28, 32). He becomes the symbol of the Victorian myth of "'masculinist logocentrism'" (Kathleen Gregory Klein and Joseph Keller qtd. in Kestner 38).

Besides serving as an example for boy scouts and various fictional detectives, the character of Sherlock Holmes also greatly influenced the heroes of occult detective fiction, the supernatural side of the mystery tale. In his introduction to *The Complete John Silence Stories*, S. T. Joshi remarks on the influence of Doyle's detective on Blackwood's development of John Silence. Silence keeps a consulting room for clients, he refers to cases outside of the published Blackwood stories in which he appears, and he has an assistant, who reports on Silence's adventures (vi–vii). In his introduction to W. H. Hodgson's *The Casebook of Carnacki the Ghost Finder*, David Stuart Davies also notes the influence of Holmes:

> There is something very Doylean and Sherlockian about the Carnacki stories, not the least being the fact that while some of his cases prove to have supernatural explanations, some prove to have rational solutions in which traditional detective methods, of the kind that Sherlock Holmes would apply, get to the root of the mystery.
>
> (9)

Even though occult detectives often deal with supernatural mysteries that are difficult, if not impossible, fully to explain, they often follow Holmes's methods by applying rationalism and logic linked with background knowledge of the paranormal to their clients' quandaries. Their assistants, who report on their adventures, often mimic Watson's hero worship of Holmes. In attempts to make occult detection into a Sherlockian science, famous fictional ghost hunters, including Dr. Martin Hesselius, John Silence, Flaxman Low, Carnacki, Aylmer Vance, and John Bell, to name only a few, study the supernatural through experiments in laboratories and deep study in psychology, science, and esoteric lore, and they use methods of the Psychical Research Societies and special technologies – for example, Carnacki's photography and his "Electric Pentacle."

Furthermore, like the Holmes stories, most early occult detective fiction focuses on a male figure as the interpreter-of-the-clues and the one-who-explains. Kestner notes that, for Holmes, women are often not to be trusted, and their emotions make them "inscrutable" and "puzzles" to his reason (35–36). This tendency is echoed in occult detective fiction. For instance, there are predatory and sexually aggressive, thus evil, women in Blackwood's "A Psychical Invasion" and "Ancient Sorceries." In his "The Camp of the Dog," a young woman is a victim, but part of the reason for the werewolf's appearance is her inability to make up her mind regarding a suitor and her latent desire for independence. The supernatural situation is ameliorated when she accepts marriage. Alice and Claude Askew's Aylmer Vance (1914) faces a female vampire, albeit an apologetic and unwilling one, in the appropriately titled story, "The Vampire." In another Vance story, "The Invader," a husband must murder his wife because she has been irrevocably possessed by an evil spirit. George knows that his wife has changed because of her wanton cruelty, strength, and aggressive sexual appetites:

> Why, he declared that Annie's face changed before his eyes – that a devilish expression came into it, and to add to the sickening horror of the whole scene, the woman who called herself his wife began to make violent love to him – fierce, unrestrained love, and he had to suffer her hot, burning kisses.
>
> (17)

Here, Annie's identity is supposed to be "the woman who called herself his wife," but the possession that makes her alien to her husband gives her a strength of personality and passion that she did not have as his wife. Her newly acquired passion and power mark her as unnatural and evil and give her husband the right to kill her. Ironically, the situation resulted from George's insistence on experimenting with the supernatural and hypnotism and using Annie as his test subject; she begged not to be involved.

A concern with women's positions in a patriarchal society – as displayed in the occult detective fiction listed earlier – is an undercurrent in practically all of Jackson's work, and numerous critics have applied feminist lenses to her novels. Lynette Carpenter has suggested that a recurring theme in Jackson's work revolves around the "causes and consequences of female victimization and alienation" (200). For Carpenter, Jackson explores in her fiction the danger of female agency in "a society where men hold primary power" (199). Similarly, in his analysis of *The Haunting of Hill House*, Dale Bailey discusses the importance of what he calls "the June Cleaver ideology" to Eleanor's destruction in Hugh Crain's house, a structure that has never been welcoming to women in its past. From its phallic tower housing the library to its centerpiece of Crain's cut-and-pasted and blood-signed book that mandates proper behavior for his daughters and threatens eternal damnation for any impurity, the house is a monstrous monument to patriarchal parenting. It also stood a silent witness to the losses of three of Crain's wives, the quarrelling of his daughters, and the demise of any possibility of a direct line of descendants, as all of Crain's hopes for a family dynasty crumbled in acrimony. While Bailey notes that "the June Cleaver ideology" "permitted greater autonomy than the imprisoning dogma women labored under in the nineteenth century," he posits clear links back to "The Cult of True Womanhood" and views it as "a decades-removed middle-class dilution of that primarily upper-class phenomenon" (33). This results in women becoming limited to homemaker roles as "nurturing mothers" and "devoted wives." According to Bailey, "[t]he June Cleaver ideology flourished in the two decades following World War II" and "placed the woman in the kitchen, highlighting her role as a domestic life-support system for family members who functioned largely outside the home" (33). These expectations, therefore, trap Eleanor, who cannot see a path for her life other than the "June Cleaver ideology" scripted for her by society. Unfortunately for her, this ideology forms Hill House's foundation, and the superficial ghost hunt becomes, for Eleanor, an intensely concentrated cauldron of her insecurities as the house calls to her to make a home there and subsequently destroys her.

Since Jackson read mysteries and copious amounts of supernatural literature as research for her fiction and lived as a woman writer in the stifling patriarchy of 1950s America, the influences of the mystery and the supernatural tale understandably would intertwine in her work and serve a very different purpose than they did in works of the past. Her focus would be an oppressed modern woman inadvertently at the mercy of a man who thinks he knows and can interpret all – but cannot. To Montague, Eleanor appears to be irrationally afraid, hysterical even, and he ignores her subjective experiences at the investigators' peril. Eleanor is doomed because of her obsession with society's conventions – love, romance, family and children, home – and because Montague cannot fathom the importance of her emotions and perceptions as fully fledged components of his objective search for the supernatural. The paternal and authoritative ghost hunter Montague cannot take Eleanor's struggles with gender roles and expectations into consideration, even as those struggles activate the haunting in the house and victimize her.

At its most basic level, *The Haunting of Hill House* is a ghost hunt, a kind of hybrid nineteenth-century summer haunted house party meets our contemporary conception of *Ghost Hunters* on the SyFy channel. Showing her awareness of her research and genre, Jackson has her characters deploy multiple research tools, scientific and extrasensory, to hunt their spectral quarry. The plot that maneuvers Eleanor into facing her demons and her demise in Hill House is set in motion by Dr. Montague, an ambitious academic hidden under a kindly paternal exterior.

Montague is a believer in the supernatural who is frustrated by the structure of academe. Because searching for ghosts is looked down upon in research circles, he takes a PhD in anthropology and bides his time waiting for a "haunted" house to try his hand at investigating. The degree is earned to shore up his "unscientific" interest in the supernatural – it lends him an "air of respectability, even scholarly authority" (*The Haunting* 4). His mission is to write "the definitive work on the causes and effects of psychic disturbances in a house commonly known as 'haunted'" (4). Immediately, readers can see other Jackson doctors in Montague. His ambition, single-minded interest, and desire for authoritative power are reminiscent of the psychiatrists in *The Bird's Nest* and the story "Colloquy" (both of whom dominate and misguide female patients). As Hattenhauer emphasizes, Jackson parodies Montague and his wife's efforts to explain paranormal phenomena (10–11, 156). Dr. Montague foolishly believes that he can document the haunting of Hill House. He soon learns that his efforts are useless, as are those of his wife, who conversely is a proponent of extrasensory methods that rely on séances, psychic sensitivity, and automatic writing.[8] Meanwhile, as a masterpiece of indeterminacy, Hill House remains an ambiguous signifier where inhabitants' perceptions become twisted physically, because of its carnival house dimensions, and mentally as it preys upon the one vulnerable member of the group, the lonely and passive Eleanor Vance.[9] Eleanor lacks a strong sense of agency, identity, home, and reality before Hill House, and the house exploits this confusion. While everyone else hunts for Hill House's ghosts, Eleanor finds within Hill House, and the ambiguities of haunting, a "convenient shorthand" (Oppenheimer 125) for her inability to live a successful life within the strictures of patriarchal society – the "real world" outside of the house's walls.

Dr. Montague, the Sherlockian figure, believes that one can rationalize and control fear, a human emotion: "Fear ... is the relinquishment of logic, the *willing* relinquishing of reasonable patterns. We yield to it or we fight it, but we cannot meet it halfway" (*The Haunting* 159). In his mind, only unreasonable people without logic and willpower succumb to fear of the supernatural. Yielding means that one is overly emotional and weak. His strength is in rationally explaining the supernatural. Of course, by the end of his experiment, he has failed: Eleanor is dead, and he leaves Hill House disgraced, his grand study in question of ever being published. Hattenhauer describes Montague as having "a patina of empiricism and objectivity [that] deflect[s] any penetrating view of his underlying commitment not to investigate reports of ghosts, but to endorse them" (155). Montague comes to Hill House already believing that it is haunted because of stories he has heard; his investigation is not as objective as he claims it is. Indeed, Hattenhauer places some of the blame for Eleanor's demise on Montague's faulty reasoning and his fear of her fragmentation, a fear that he would deny. Hattenhauer writes,

> For Montague, to uphold reasonable patterns is to keep doing the same thing even when logic dictates otherwise. ... If he would handle [Eleanor's] anxiety with less of his own, she would not kill herself in the end. But he has to rid

Hill House of this foul contagion of irrationality, no matter how irrationally he does it.

(156)

Jackson undercuts the patriarchal occult detective figure by showing that he does not have all of the answers. He pretends to knowledge that he simply cannot possess, and he hides behind his credentials and his position in society.

Subsequently, as if to spite the "rational" Montague, nothing supernatural in Hill House can be concretely documented. Every time the team encounters something that they believe to be supernatural, they cannot prove its otherworldliness. All four investigators are rarely present for a supernatural episode, and if they are, it is still unclear whether their experiences are identical. By creating an unreliable narration that takes place partially in Eleanor's mind, Jackson makes it clear that the team is attempting to compartmentalize scientifically something that cannot be contained by human observation and measurement. Dr. Montague completely misses Eleanor's slow deterioration into a merged subjectivity with the house. He is surprised by her collapse, while the reader sees it coming from the beginning.

If we look at the supernatural events in Hill House, we directly notice their dependence on perception. Often, these manifestations test the adage that "seeing is believing." The notes that Montague asks his guests to complete become useless: "Each of them had written – carelessly, and with little attention to detail – an account of what they *thought they had heard and seen* so far in Hill House" (149, emphasis added). Theodora rails against the futility of them: "I *hate* writing these notes. . . . What are you saying about those noises last night? *I* can't describe them" (209). When the team first encounters the cold spot outside of the nursery, a spot that every person can feel, they disagree over *how* they experience it. Each member of the group describes the cold slightly differently. When they return to document the cold spot, they cannot measure it with any instrument. The chill makes it impossible to hold a measuring tape long enough to note the spot's dimensions. When they drop a thermometer into the spot, it "refused to register any change at all." The doctor "fumes wildly" about investigators at Borley Rectory who documented an eleven-degree drop in temperature. He "noted his results in his notebook," even though there is no real proof of the cold spot that can be recorded (150). Hill House defies explanation and observation. At one point in the investigation, Theodora's room is described as covered in a substance like blood, and the investigators close the room so that Montague can document it later. At the end of the novel, when Luke mentions that he never wants to see that room again, Mrs. Montague reveals that she checked it, and that "[t]here's nothing wrong with it," except that it needs dusting. Mrs. Montague's sessions with her planchette reveal little beyond information about her partner Arthur, and the supernatural events that she does describe are stock Gothic and ghost story narratives that do not apply to Hill House. The investigators cannot use measuring tape, chalk, thermometer, automatic writing sessions, or notes to pin down and prove their shared *experience* of a haunting. Everything becomes a subjective narrative within Jackson's narrative of Hill House's effect on Eleanor. This subjective outcome is reminiscent of Jackson's comment about the Ballechin House investigators:

> They thought that they were being terribly scientific and proving all kinds of things, and yet the story that kept coming through their dry reports was not at all the story of a haunted house, it was the story of several earnest, I believe misguided, certainly determined people, with their differing motivations and backgrounds.
>
> (*Come Along with Me* 200–1)

Eleanor's experiences and her fragmented perceptions filtered through her imagination form the bulk of the novel for the reader. In his obsession with proving the existence of ghosts, Montague misses the effects of the supernatural on the most vulnerable of his assistants, primarily because he does not value her experience. Smajić asserts,

> Occult detective stories are narratives about invasion, possession, obsession – about confrontation not just with external supernatural forces but also with what lies within: unexcavated layers of the psyche, buried selves that challenge the conviction that we are in possession of ourselves and that the self is a coherent, consistent, rational thing.
>
> (198)

Here, Smajić could very well be describing Eleanor's terrors during the investigation. While Dr. Montague and his wife work feverishly at proving there are ghosts in Hill House, the reader learns that, for all intents and purposes, Eleanor *is* the ghost.[10] She deals with the fear that "the self [is not] a coherent, consistent, rational thing" as she tries on new personas and new friends, and finally merges with the house itself. Hill House becomes her space of dissolution. It adds her to its pantheon of isolated and destroyed women, victims of the house's designer and patriarch, Hugh Crain. Eleanor has no place in the outside world other than in subservience. Her life has been paused since she had to be her mother's caretaker; she has no career; she has no home; she feels that she has no future outside of the fairy-tale narratives that she daydreams, which all involve a caring maternal figure and a dashing romantic prince to rescue her. During the investigation, Eleanor is confusing dreams and reality, she is losing time, and she is feeling targeted by the house, often telling the others that she wants to surrender to its influences. Dr. Montague never vacillates, though, from his observation of presumed "ghosts," and Mrs. Montague cannot even remember who exactly Eleanor is. For all of the Montagues' attempts at explanation, Hill House stands at the end of the novel exactly as it stood at the beginning, unchanged and unexplained, and Eleanor is left exactly as she was in life – placeless and following another's script.

Along these lines, approaching the novel as occult detective fiction emphasizes Jackson's masterful use of the supernatural to trouble traditionally solid binaries, thus calling into question our very methods of "knowing." Jodey Castricano takes this approach in her article "Shirley Jackson's *The Haunting of Hill House* and the Strange Question of Trans-Subjectivity," in which she argues that the entire book is about intersubjectivity as the characters' consciousnesses overlap through Theodora's telepathic abilities. Castricano argues that Jackson's aim is to investigate "the issue of what 'separates one mind from another'" (88), and she explores how "telepathy, clairvoyance, and the sentience of objects are tropes that combine in Jackson's novel to challenge certain classical models of human consciousness and subjectivity" (89). Hill House becomes a space in which the boundaries between characters' minds are almost imperceptible. This situation makes Hill House fertile ground for questioning the coherence of the self and its place in the larger society. I would posit, however, that Eleanor has the potential to be as sensitive as Theodora. After all, Eleanor was chosen for this experiment because she was the center of poltergeist phenomena when she was an adolescent (an experience she fears and vehemently denies). Therefore Eleanor's consciousness and her struggles to define her place in society and in Hill House become the focus for the reader, while Montague's experiments, ironically, occult this information. Because Jackson's narration is filtered through Eleanor's consciousness, her perceptions color those of readers, and we become just as confused as she is about what is real and what is supernatural, or if these two categories even are mutually exclusive.

While Montague pursues his "objective" mission, the reader is immersed in Eleanor's imagination and dreams. Questions about the relationship between dreams and reality flood the book from the first page, where the narrator imagines that even "larks and katydids . . . dream," to the end during Eleanor's bizarre moment of alert fear behind the wheel when she suddenly "realizes" that her car is crashing (*The Haunting* 1, 245–46). Because of her loneliness, Eleanor daydreams a new life for herself during her drive to Hill House, and these possibilities indicate her desires for romantic love and a family; she awakens in the midst of dreams of her mother's death to find herself experiencing supernatural events; she has a nightmare that she seems to believe actually occurred; and toward the end of the novel she becomes confused as to what constitutes reality. Most telling are those moments where the characters' minds interpenetrate based on Eleanor's dreams and perceptions, consequently suggesting that she is becoming the nexus of the haunting. Theodora, Luke, and Montague either mention aspects of Eleanor's dreams or discuss her thoughts out loud without her prompting them. Most of the conversations in Hill House seem to originate in Eleanor's daydreams and nightmares. Moreover, the other three investigators embody aspects of Eleanor that she dreams for herself: Luke as the courtly lover, Theo as the independent woman of emotion and passion, and Montague as the caring father figure. The entire novel could be read as a series of waking dreams, transforming the house and its occupants into metaphors for Eleanor's disturbed mind. Once she joins her consciousness to Hill House, she has permanently severed ties to her old life, the present, and even reality itself. Ultimately, through these recurring dream states, Jackson shows the characters' minds intertwining and merging, perspective becoming unreliable and murky, and the house itself invading human consciousness, as it preys on Eleanor's lonely hopes and dreams for a home.

Eleanor's lack of agency and disconnection from reality are evident during her drive to Hill House, a journey that she believes constitutes her first choice in life. She defies her sister's imperious order to stay home and believes, as she says, that something is finally happening to her. During this drive, she whiles away the time by daydreaming. She imagines elaborate narratives for her life, using the different homes and scenes that she passes. These fairy-tale fantasies boil down to her playing the role of a dutiful daughter in a functional family and waiting for a Prince Charming to come sweep her away. After the loss of her father and a lonely childhood, Eleanor's adult life has consisted of being the caretaker for her ill mother until she died as well, waiting on the woman's every need all day, and reading her romance novels in the evening. Later, she will mold even her experience at Hill House into one of a happy family, and she repeats the refrain "Journeys end in lovers meeting," expecting a romance to blossom during her stay. Eleanor has bought into scripts delineating how her life should be, rather than taking control and actually living it. She tries to live through her dreams and wishes for a "spell" to change her drab reality. Once she arrives at Hill House, aspects of her daydreams recur in her conversations with the other investigators. Eleanor is ashamed of her solitary life, so she creates a life for herself with details from her journey: she lives in a cottage with stone lions on the porch and oleanders in the yard. Interestingly, each character participates in this charade of playing a role rather than disclosing personal information. The group decides that Eleanor is a courtesan, Theo is a princess in a fairy-tale realm, Luke is the brave bullfighter, and Montague is a pilgrim. Theo and Luke continue this courtly banter any time Eleanor is present, and Theo elaborates on her princess story with details that Eleanor did not share. One example is Theo's flight to the "woodcutter's hut" to escape her enemies (*The Haunting* 123). Any time Eleanor is present, her dream world seems to entangle and overlap with the surrounding reality. There is no way that these subjective perceptions can play a role in Montague's formal investigation of Hill House.

The characters keep up this playacting and their comments on Eleanor's state of mind and her concerns until specific moments when she seems to awaken in the midst of a conversation, thus creating a moment where everything changes, as if she had come awake from a deep dream. Since Eleanor often is readers' only conduit of knowledge about what is occurring, we are just as shaken as she is. In the first moment, the conversation of the evening begins with Luke's regaling the party with detailed stories of executions. While he is describing ways of killing people, it is notable that Eleanor is thinking about how much she hates Theo and wants to kill her. Then, when Eleanor begins to explain how she feels when she is afraid, each of the characters chimes in with a new perspective on fear: according to the doctor, we fear ourselves; according to Luke, we fear seeing ourselves for what we truly are; and for Theo, we fear knowing what we want (159–60). All of these suggestions could apply to Eleanor. When Eleanor suggests that she could survive if she "could only surrender," the others cut her off sharply, and she jolts into consciousness. She does not even know what she was saying: "I was just talking along, she told herself, I was saying something – what was I saying?" The others are horrified because, as Luke says, "She has done this before" (160). They stare at her, making her more uncomfortable. This scene also makes readers uncomfortable because we realize that we are as confused as Eleanor. Perhaps the entire preceding scene was a product of Eleanor's dream world. Since Jackson has a limited third-person narrator dependent on Eleanor's perceptions, readers are as much in the dark as to who is speaking to whom about what as Eleanor is. In this situation, how can we truly *know* anything? This moment is our first indication that Eleanor has been spacing in and out of conversations since she arrived.

Reminiscent of the questionable supernatural episodes of the investigation, this problem for the reader simply to know objectively the happenings at Hill House sharply comes into question during the brief scenes when Eleanor is spying on the other characters. As we see her comrades interacting, the differences from what we have previously observed are astounding. Instead of childish banter about cottages and woodchoppers, courtesans and courtly favors, we hear Theo and Luke discussing the investigation and speculating about the professor's book. The most shocking change is in Mrs. Dudley, who, rather than being a horrifying automaton of the house warning others that no one in town can hear you when you scream, is shown to be a kindly woman. In a conversation with Mrs. Montague, she says nothing about the dark or screaming; instead, she offers her companion more coffee and defends Theo and Luke as young people having a fun summer fling (221–22). With Eleanor out of the way, the reader sees a much different picture of Hill House and the people inside of it. There are two levels: one contains Montague's investigation, and the other Eleanor's shifting perceptions during the investigation. This layering calls into question the possibility of a single way of perceiving the situation, and it helps to dismantle Eleanor's fragile reliability.

As Eleanor believes that she is joining Hill House, her consciousness meshes more fully with the house, and she moves further away from her companions. During her last night at Hill House, she realizes that she can hear everything inside and outside of the structure (206). She hears everyone in every room, and she hears the crickets on the lawn. She proceeds to run through the house and recreate the elements of the earlier paranormal events. She beats on the doors, dances and sings, and then leads everyone on a wild-goose chase into the library. Illustrating her twisted connection to the house's dark history, she climbs the spiral staircase from which the companion committed suicide. For her, every structure of consciousness and existence has collapsed and is fluid. She is one with the house, so she thinks, "Time is ended now" (232). She has no separate identity or place in time. She is in a flux within Hill House's time and space. At the precipice of self-dissolution, she looks down at the others in a confused liminal state of consciousness:

> For a minute she could not remember who they were (had they been guests of hers in the house of the stone lions? Dining at her long table in the candlelight? Had she met them at the inn, over the tumbling stream? Had one of them come riding down a green hill, banners flying? Had one of them run beside her in the darkness? and then she remembered, and they fell into place where they belonged) and she hesitated, clinging to the railing. They were so small, so ineffectual.
>
> (233)

At this moment Eleanor cannot distinguish between her imagination and reality. For her, the time before and after Hill House has merged. There is no difference between what she actually saw and people that she actually met on her trip and the people that she met in Hill House, and there is no distinction between real people and elements of her daydreams from her drive.

Eleanor's ultimate disturbing descent into unreality occurs when she is forced to leave Hill House for her own good. She strenuously refuses to go and finally admits to the others that she has no home of her own. Even though she begins to drive away, since she has nowhere to go and has linked her dream desires to the house, she continues to assert her right to stay. Apparently, she commits suicide, a tradition at Hill House, by driving her car into a tree that is just off of the driveway, but readers only reluctantly can ascribe agency in this act because Eleanor appears to be in yet another dream state. As she is driving toward the tree, she thinks, "I am really doing it, I am doing this all by myself, now, at last; this is me, I am really really really doing it by myself," but this triumph of choice is soon undercut at the moment of impact. In a final instance of coming to her senses amid a state of confusion, Eleanor suddenly questions what is happening: "In the unending, crashing second before the car hurled into the tree she thought clearly, *Why* am I doing this? Why am I doing this? Why don't they stop me?" (245–46). Seemingly, Eleanor has nodded off at the wheel and then jerked awake to a shocking end. Moreover, she does not gain the connection and comfort that she sought at Hill House because "whatever walked there, walked alone" (246). The other consciousness in Eleanor's head leaves her at impact, and she dies as alone as she was in life.

According to Castricano, Jackson manages to blur all structural oppositions in this novel, and I believe that she does so by revisiting and revising the conventions of mystery and supernatural stories, or occult detective fiction. She took that kernel of inspiration from the report on Ballechin House and created her own house, with her own people, and saw what she could make happen (*Come Along with Me* 200–201). Thus she follows her own suggestions that hauntings are more about perceptions than apparitions, and she continues her concern with women's agency by exploring whose perceptions ultimately matter. Smajić notes that occult detective tales often involve "trauma, psychological collapse, and violent

Perception and supernatural detection 51

death" (183), and *The Haunting of Hill House* contains all three, only the focus is on the occulted experience of women. Jackson presciently anticipates future feminist movements and escapes easy critical categorization as a popular genre writer by addressing concerns with women's place in society through an adept blending of multiple traditional modes of fiction.[11]

Notes

1 Since the 1990s, there has been a resurgence of scholarly interest in Jackson's work. In addition, since 2010, more of Jackson's fiction has come back into print, including a Library of America volume that collects *The Lottery and Other Stories*, *The Haunting of Hill House*, and *We Have Always Lived in the Castle*, and Penguin Classic editions of *The Road Through the Wall*, *Hangsaman*, *The Bird's Nest*, and *The Sundial*.
2 S. T. Joshi discusses Jackson as a writer of weird fiction, and he focuses on the supernatural aspects present in her domestic stories/family sketches. Darryl Hattenhauer examines Jackson's "belief" in the supernatural and its role in criticism of her work. He notes, "Jackson did not literally believe in the supernatural, for example, witchcraft and psychic phenomena. After her career was firmly established, she admitted that using anecdotes about her witchcraft and magic were promotional ploys" (8–9). In a similar vein, I am arguing that for Jackson, the supernatural is a metaphor that she deploys to interrogate very real issues, especially for women.
3 Similar to Jackson's attempts to avoid being summed up with one label – a "housewife," who happens to write – but rather be a writer and a wife and a mother in her biographical blurbs (and domestic sketches), another 1950s writer, Grace Metalious, faced a similar conundrum, only in her case over a publicity photograph, known as "Pandora in Blue Jeans," for her novel *Peyton Place* (1956). Alongside of the photograph, which shows Metalious dressed casually in jeans and sneakers pensively looking at a typewriter, her publisher decided to stress her marriage and family in her biographical blurbs. Emily Toth comments, "The appeal of *Peyton Place* would be the contrast between the respectable author – who, as small-town mother and schoolteacher's wife, fit perfectly the image of fifties' conformity – and the shocking contents of her book" (116–17, 121).
4 Jackson's knowledge of and interest in the lore surrounding Borley Rectory and Ballechin House are confirmed in the essay "The Ghosts of Loiret," recently published in the collection *Let Me Tell You* (249).
5 According to Tricia Lootens, Jackson promised her publisher "some dandy ghosts" and that "it may turn out that different people see different things; see, in fact, just exactly what they are expecting to see" (156). Even though there may not be a traditional specter in Hill House, Eleanor certainly encounters a personalized haunting that, as Lootens argues, plays on her position in society and the ways in which women can be "destroyed by the nuclear family, sexual repression, and romantic notions of feminine self-sacrifice" (152).
6 Stacy Horn cites this appearance of the Duke ESP cards in *The Haunting of Hill House* as an example of the contemporary public's fascination with the laboratory's work and Jackson's own awareness of this phenomenon (155–56).
7 While the investigators of Hill House fall asleep on their first night in the haunted building, Luke's aunt is mentioned as, three hundred miles away, she "closed her detective story" (92). This is one of many mentions of books and stories that are folded into Jackson's novel. Hattenhauer calls *The Haunting of Hill House* a "heteroglossic novel" and traces the many references in it to writing, including, to name a few instances, ghost stories, legends, fairy tales, mentions of other novels, and the importance of the library (169).

8 Deborah Blum describes how a large amount of the work of the British and American Societies for Psychical Research focused on debunking fraudulent mediums. Jackson's decision to play Mrs. Montague's methods against those of her husband may have issued from her awareness of this conflict.
9 Eleanor Vance's last name is an intriguing call back to Alice and Claude Askew's early twentieth-century occult detective Aylmer Vance.
10 See Anderson for a discussion of Eleanor as the ghost of Hill House.
11 Thank you to Benjamin F. Fisher, Amy K. King, and Lisa Kröger for offering comments on drafts of this essay and to Alida Moore for a helpful conversation about gender concerns in detective fiction.

Works cited

Anderson, Melanie R. "'Whatever Walked There, Walked Alone': What Is Haunting Shirley Jackson's Hill House?" *Journal of the Georgia Philological Association* (2009): 198–205. Print.

Askew, Alice and Claude Askew. *Aylmer Vance. 1914. Supernatural Detectives*. Volume 2. Landisville, PA: Coachwhip Publications, 2011. Print.

Bailey, Dale. *American Nightmares: The Haunted House Formula in American Popular Fiction*. Bowling Green, OH: Bowling Green SU Popular P, 1999. Print.

Blackwood, Algernon. *The Complete John Silence Stories*. Ed. S. T. Joshi. Mineola, NY: Dover Publications, 1997. Print.

Blum, Deborah. *Ghost Hunters: William James and the Search for Scientific Proof of Life After Death*. New York: Penguin Books, 2007. Print.

Carpenter, Lynette. "The Establishment and Preservation of Female Power in Shirley Jackson's We Have Always Lived in the Castle." *Shirley Jackson: Essays on the Literary Legacy*. Ed. Bernice M. Murphy. Jefferson, NC, and London: McFarland and Company, 2005. 199–213. Print.

Castricano, Jodey. "Shirley Jackson's *The Haunting of Hill House* and the Strange Question of Trans-Subjectivity." *Gothic Studies* 7.1 (May 2005): 87–101. Print.

Crichton-Stuart, John Patrick (Marquess of Bute) and Ada Goodrich-Freer, eds. *The Alleged Haunting of B – House*. 1899. Project Gutenberg, 2005. E-book. http://www.gutenberg.org/files/16538/16538-h/16538-h.htm.

Hattenhauer, Darryl. *Shirley Jackson's American Gothic*. Albany: SUNY P, 2003. Print.

Hodgson, W. H. *The Casebook of Carnacki the Ghost Finder*. London: Wordsworth Editions, 2006. Print.

Horn, Stacy. *Unbelievable: Investigations into Ghosts, Poltergeists, Telepathy, and Other Unseen Phenomena from the Duke Parapsychology Laboratory*. New York: Harper Collins Publishers, 2009. Print.

Jackson, Shirley. *The Bird's Nest*. 1954. New York: Penguin Books, 2014. Print.

———. "Colloquy." *The Lottery and Other Stories*. 1949. New York: Farrar, Straus, and Giroux, 2005. 145–47. Print.

———. *Come Along with Me: Part of a Novel, Sixteen Stories, and Three Lectures*. 1968. Ed. Stanley Edgar Hyman. New York: Penguin Books, 1995. Print.

———. *Hangsaman.* 1951. New York: Penguin Books, 2013. Print.

———. *The Haunting of Hill House*. 1959. New York: Penguin Books, 1999. Print.

———. *Let Me Tell You: New Stories, Essays, and Other Writings*. Eds. Laurence Jackson Hyman and Sarah Hyman DeWitt. New York: Random House, 2015. Print.

———. *The Sundial*. 1958. New York: Penguin Books, 2014. Print.

———. *We Have Always Lived in the Castle*. 1962. New York: Penguin Books, 2006. Print.
Joshi, S. T. "Shirley Jackson: Domestic Horror." *Shirley Jackson: Essays on the Literary Legacy*. Ed. Bernice M. Murphy. Jefferson, NC, and London: McFarland and Company, 2005. 183–98. Print.
Kestner, Joseph A. *Sherlock's Men: Masculinity, Conan Doyle, and Cultural History*. Aldershot: Ashgate, 1997. Print.
Lootens, Tricia. "'Whose Hand Was I Holding?': Familial and Sexual Politics in Shirley Jackson's the Haunting of Hill House." *Shirley Jackson: Essays on the Literary Legacy*. Ed. Bernice M. Murphy. Jefferson, NC: McFarland and Company, 2005. 150–68. Print.
Murphy, Bernice M., ed. *Shirley Jackson: Essays on the Literary Legacy*. Jefferson, NC, and London: McFarland and Company, 2005. Print.
Newman, Judie. "Shirley Jackson and the Reproduction of Mothering: The Haunting of Hill House." *Shirley Jackson: Essays on the Literary Legacy*. Ed. Bernice M. Murphy. Jefferson, NC: McFarland and Company, 2005. 169–82. Print.
Oppenheimer, Judy. *Private Demons*. New York: Fawcett Columbine (Ballantine Books), 1988. Print.
Smajić, Srdjan. *Ghost-Seers, Detectives, and Spiritualists: Theories of Vision in Victorian Literature and Science*. Cambridge and New York: Cambridge UP, 2010. Print.
Toth, Emily. *Inside Peyton Place: The Life of Grace Metalious*. 1981. Jackson: UP of Mississippi, 2000. Print.

4 Speaking of magic
Folk narrative in *Hangsaman* and *We Have Always Lived in the Castle*

Shelley Ingram

Syracuse University professor H. W. Herrington once wrote to Shirley Jackson, congratulating his former student on the success of her short story "The Lottery." Jackson wrote back, saying that "it had all originated in his folklore course" (Oppenheimer 131). Though Jackson would remain steadfastly mercurial about the origins or meanings of "The Lottery," this exchange tells us that Jackson had been, at least at one time, a student of folklore. And how could she not be? Her husband, Stanley Edgar Hyman, was a prominent, outspoken folklorist and literary critic. The consensus seems to be that Hyman was "her greatest influence" and that theirs was a relationship of deep mutual respect and, at times, loathing: codependent and destructive, but also sustaining and crucial. His was one of the loudest voices in one of the most divisive theoretical debates of the time, that of the role, meaning, function, and origin of myth. It seems inevitable, then, that Jackson would have had a great deal to say about her husband's mythic view of the world. But it is not enough to argue, as Darryl Hattenhauer does, that Jackson "disables" Hyman's theories of myth and ritual and "increasingly undercuts" the "mythy modernists," that she "subverts myth" by rooting it in "traces of the public" and "devalorizes myth" by placing it alongside folklore (46; 186–87). Jackson's engagement with the ideas of Hyman and his cohort of "mythy modernists" is more complicated than that, her definition of folklore more sophisticated. She was not simply subverting or undercutting Hyman's views; she was dynamically interacting with them.

In her novels *Hangsaman* and *We Have Always Lived in the Castle*, Jackson consciously and playfully manipulates myth, ritual, fairy tale, legend, and other folk narrative forms, wrenching them from their myriad "traditional" contexts and reconstituting them in the text.[1] By making estrangement from and oppression by folk and "pseudofolk" communities analogous to psychic despair, Jackson is moving within a critical discourse that positions belief, myth and folklore, and individual psychology as virtually inextricable. At the end of *Hangsaman* and *We Have Always Lived in the Castle*, Natalie and Merricat, the novels' respective protagonists, must each confront suppressed knowledge of a traumatic event. This confrontation leads to a conscription into folk narrative – myth for Natalie, legend for Merricat – which fixes them in discourse and alienates them from their lived communities. Natalie's and Merricat's stories are now communally shaped by the forces and functions of folk belief. But the different iterations of folk narrative we see in the texts suggest slightly different outcomes for each character, showing Jackson's facility with the conventions of traditional storytelling and her deep engagement with the era's debates about the quality and function of folklore. In these novels, Jackson not only casts doubt on the authenticity of modern folk culture, but also questions its ability to provide narratives from which her protagonists can construct psychically whole identities.

Hyman once argued that "without exception folk art" was "of very ancient communal origin . . . never the record of a historical personage or event," but "always a development out of primitive fertility ritual"("Some" n2). While some scholars were looking for historical or cosmological antecedents for myth, Hyman, drawing primarily from Jane Harrison and George Frazer, saw all myth deriving from ritual. He felt that ritual theory worked "for all areas of myth and folk literature," and he praised contemporary works on folk drama, folk tale and legend, customs, children's games, and music as exemplars of applied ritual theory ("Myth" 466). He believed myth to be ritual's "spoken correlative," which then broke down into other units of folklore as the original rite was forgotten or as new social needs arose. In short, Hyman tended to see in most "authentic" folklore a mythic, and therefore ritual, origin (McCullen 283).

Hyman's views were clearly influenced by both the broadly evolutionary ideals usually credited to the British anthropologist E. B. Tylor and the theories of Freud. Tylor and his cohort, like Hyman favorite Andrew Lang, posited an evolution of human culture through three distinct stages: savagery to barbarism to civilization. The dominant belief at this time was that "in savagery, people's lives were guided by myths; in barbarism, people wove the vestiges of the myths into folktales." These folktales survived in "civilized" society, but only if "the educated" turned "to peasants and to children" in order to find these "quaint remnants of the past" (Zumwalt, *American* 77). What survived from the earlier stages into more "evolved" culture was thought to be folklore. Hyman felt this view of folklore "dovetailed best" with "the classical psychoanalysis of Freud" ("Myth" 472).

Freud's theories of the unconscious were appealing for folklorists because Freud himself mapped the evolution of the individual psyche onto the evolution of culture. Freudian folklorists therefore held fast to the evolutionary theory of culture because it offered a model fitted to their beliefs that "neurotic symptoms are . . . vestigial remains from infancy just as Tylor's survivals were seen as vestiges from society's primitive past" (Schmaier and Dundes 143).[2] The most persistent Freudian folklorists felt that the folk did not need psychotherapy because they still had folklore, that folklore was where "the folk" worked out, through sublimation or expression, the conditions of the mind that psychotherapy sought to cure.[3] Hyman time and again linked "folk work" to "dream work," arguing that "folk material is analogous to the dream as a disguised fulfillment of repressed wishes" ("Anthropological" 238). For example, Hyman laments the degradation of the British traditional ballad in part because "like magic and the supernatural, sex, incest, and kin-murder tend to disappear or diminish" in "a folk process very like individual repression" ("Child" 236).

Thus the dominant framework for interpreting folklore in the Jackson/Hyman household saw the unconscious expressing itself through folklore, a process deeply related to primitive rituals and myths of past societies. We see, for example, in *We Have Always Lived in the Castle* that Jackson was "quite consciously splitting herself into" the sisters Merricat and Constance, representing "the same person, both Shirley." According to her first biographer Judy Oppenheimer, Jackson "had written the truth of what it was like for her" in their town in Vermont in order to examine "one of the central questions of her life – her own identity" (234, 236). Oppenheimer argues that there was always a "very direct link for Shirley between the book she was writing at any moment and the life she was then living" (236). Such ethno-autobiographical readings link Jackson's ideas about "truth" to a view of folklore that would see expressions of folklore, especially folk narrative, as expressions of the unconscious.

But folklore often asks us to believe in things that scientific rationalism insists cannot, in fact, be true. Such rationalism engenders the "attitude that many of the cultural expressions identified as folklore, especially folk belief, [are] pathological" (Mullen 120). We see this in Hattenhauer's vehement objections to both Hyman's marketing of Jackson as a witch and his interpretation of Oppenheimer's claim that "when Jackson saw and heard things that others did not, such phenomena were actually there" (9). Such assertions, Hattenhauer argues, "are not just laughably illogical. They are reactionary. They enable the sentimentalizing of Jackson as the purveyor of 'private demons' and the erasure of Jackson as the complex political writer who compares with the best of her generation" (9). Despite Hattenhauer's (or even Oppenheimer's) decisive claims, though, we cannot actually know what Jackson believed. Because belief is a cognitive, subjective process, we can never have access to it. All we can access are *expressions* of that belief (Pimple 51). Or, as Jackson once wrote, "being impossible, an abstract belief can only be trusted through its manifestations, the actual shape of the god perceived, however dimly" (*Sundial* 3). In his critique, Hattenhauer divides the world into believers/sophisticates, echoing the earliest scientific ventures of folklore studies itself, which posited "folk belief" as the domain of the uneducated and irrational and "disbelief" as the neutral, objective, rationalist stance.[4] Hattenhauer seems to deny the rationality and complexity of those who believe in or experience the numinous. But imagining the relationship between rationality and irrationality, whatever that is, as dichotomous misses the point of Jackson's representations of humanity and misreads, I believe, the "manifestations" of her belief.

In the past, folk belief was often interpreted as either, on the one hand, nonmainstream spirituality, superstitions, and "mistaken beliefs" (Pimple 52) or, on the other, "pathologies that advancing people had to leave behind" (Mullen 122). But there was a paradigm shift in the academic study of folklore toward the end of Jackson's life and Hyman's career that led to the redefining of folklore as not only something that is but also something that is done at a particular time in a particular place – folklore as process and performance. The shift from text to context in folklore studies, combined with the radical reconceptualizing of a folk group as *any* group with a common trait that fostered common expressions, also forced the creation of a new definition of folk belief. Current folkloristics situates belief outside of the binaries of true/false or superstition/ knowledge. Instead, it starts with the seemingly simple, and wholly human, notion that belief is "the certainty that something is true" (Hufford, "Beings" 19). Folk belief came to mean "beliefs that members of a (folk) group hold because they are members of that group" (Pimple 52), or more simply, "unofficial knowledge," a "way of knowing" (Motz 339).

This definition of folk belief is critical in the study of folk narrative (i.e., stories with currency in the vernacular discourse of a folk group) because it is not form or content that primarily determines how narratives are categorized. Instead, it is "the *attitudes* of the community toward them" (Oring 124). While Hyman saw all verbal and customary folklore as deriving from the myths that existed as the "spoken correlative of rites," William Bascom, a frequent target of Hyman's ire, offered up a typology of folk narrative that centered belief as the key component of their categorization; he classified folk narratives according to the beliefs of their tellers and their groups. Myths are sacred stories, believed by their audiences to somehow tell a truth, while folktales are clearly fantastical and meant to be unbelievable. Legends fall somewhere in between. That is, legends can be considered true, false, or possibly either, as they "often depict the improbable within the world of the possible" (Oring 125). What makes a legend is that "at the core" of the narrative "is an evaluation of its truth status" (Oring 125).[5]

Despite the emphasis on belief, however, narrative conventions came to exist as markers of genre. It is difficult to tell a fairy tale in our culture that is recognizable *as a fairy tale* without a "once upon a time," a damsel in distress, or a troll under a bridge, because folk narratives are communally interactive and reactive. It is within this dynamic tradition that Jackson works. She explores the connections between myth, ritual, and all of their descendants, including legends, tales, ballads, and rhymes, and she plays with the boundaries between belief and disbelief. Perhaps most importantly, she exploits the tension that exists between communal and individual iterations of folk narratives. Jackson situates Natalie and Merricat within worlds filled with folklore. Sometimes, the folklore compels them, speaks to them and to their conceptions of their own identity. Other times, the folklore serves as a tool of alienation, a way for Jackson to render concrete what she saw as a stultifying oppression by "the folk." But ultimately, Jackson complicates the notion that folklore can fully work for her particular protagonists and suggests that it can provide them only with an uneasy means of coping with psychic trauma.

In a 1958 review essay, Hyman singled out *Hangsaman* as a novel which positively represented the trend toward "myth and ritual" in American literature, as it was structured by a "series of ceremonial initiations leading to maturity" ("Some" 5). Because Hyman defined myth as the "spoken corollary to rite," it follows that he was reading the novel within the framework of sacred ritual. Hyman endorsed Arnold van Gennep's deceptively simple formula for ritual, a now familiar paradigm which proposed that all ritual followed a relatively stable tripartite pattern: a separation from the known world followed by a period of liminal existence, during which the ritual participant undergoes a kind of transformation that makes possible the final stage – a reintegration of the self into a new, refined social order. The subsequent critical reception of *Hangsaman* has been a variation on that theme, with *Hangsaman* often being read as "a novel of initiation into the adult word" (Lyons 63), an "initiation story" that leads to Natalie "finally emerging ... literally as well as figuratively, to a new self-understanding and a new approach to tangible reality" (Parks 19). It is no surprise, then, that the novel can be divided into three sections, each representing a stage in the ritual process and each establishing, as Hattenhauer astutely argues, a "metonymic chain of signifiers in [Natalie's] unconscious" from her father, Arnold, to his various substitutes (7). But while we would like young Natalie Waite to have reached a maturity that will help her repair her damaged psyche and reintegrate into her social order, her last words are fraught with ambivalence. After rejecting the advances of the female friend-turned-phantom Tony and returning to the seemingly solid safety of her university, Natalie realizes, "as she had never been before, she was now alone, and grown-up, and powerful, and not at all afraid" (218).

Hangsaman begins with Natalie living at home with her overbearing academic of a father and a retreating, resentful mother. Natalie is waiting to begin college, "desperately" fearful but ultimately determined to leave, as the thought of living the rest of her life with her parents was "a prospect so horrible" that she found herself "almost enjoying her fear of going away" (4). And go away she does, to a university clearly modeled after Hyman's Bennington College. Here Natalie struggles to fit in, unable to connect with the other women on campus or to distinguish herself in her studies. It is while she is caught up in the bickering marriage of her professor, Arthur, and his wife, Elizabeth, that Natalie discovers Tony. Read, alternately, as a real, flesh-and-blood person or as a manifestation of schizophrenic psychosis or as Natalie's "braver, more self-sufficient alter ego," Tony presents Natalie with her ultimate test: give in to the irrational promise of her seduction, or reject her and accept reality and adulthood (Rubenstein 313).

Folklorists often view folk narratives as especially powerful tokens of resistance, as folklore in general exists outside of ideologically sanctioned conduits of knowledge and outside of the notice of traditional power structures. But while folklore has great capacity for subversion, it *also* "informally teaches by supporting and reifying belief systems – as well as by controlling people," since they "learn from their culture's folklore what is proper and possible for them" (Stewart 54). The first two-thirds of *Hangsaman* highlights this alienating and oppressive dimension of folklore and folk narrative, as Natalie continually resists being incorporated into the competing folk and pseudofolk discourses that surround her. This resistance contributes to Natalie's increasing insecurity and the crumbling of her autonomy into a mess of disengaged pieces. It is not until she goes with Tony into the woods at the end of the novel that she stops resisting folk narratives, and the ambivalence inherent in this last line becomes key to a newly constructed mythic identity for Natalie, one that relies on the primordial fertility rite at the root, according to Hyman, of all folk culture.

Natalie's home life before she leaves for college is dominated by the autocratic Arnold, who I agree is as close to a literary representation of Hyman as we see in Jackson's work (Hattenhauer 103). He and Natalie engage in a ritualistic tête-à-tête each morning, where she hands him her previous day's writing, always with a profound "moment of dismay" (10). That moment also always passes, and she never fails to give him her notebook for his assessment. All the while, she is simultaneously composing various counternarratives that run as the *un*spoken corollary to this rite. Counternarratives are stories that ideally work to "identify" and "make visible" the "fragments of master narratives that have gone into the construction of an oppressive identity" (Nelson 7). I say "ideally" because counternarratives do not always succeed, and Natalie's have differing levels of success. The dominant counternarrative in the first section of the novel is a pulp detective story, in which Natalie imagines herself interrogated about the murder of her ambiguously unnamed lover, whose body is found on the floor of her father's study. Interspersed with the details of the morning spent with her family, this is a story that, as Wyatt Bonikowski points out, suggests violence against both her father and herself (79).

But Natalie invokes other counternarratives as well, including folk tales, ballads, rituals, and legends. Natalie is estranged from them all, and though she tries, she can never quite use them to resolve the nascent troubles of her unconscious. The garden at the Waite home had "belonged exclusively to Natalie;" it was here that her younger self "had delighted in playing pirate and cowboy and knight in armor" (22). Jackson does not situate Natalie as the princess in these stories, waiting to be rescued, just as she chooses for the novel's epigraph a stanza from the ballad "Maid Freed from the Gallows" that presents at least the possibility that the maid frees *herself* from a hanging. Natalie's play with legends of outlaws and heroes attempts to enact a counternarrative to the demands of the father, as legends are stories that could conceivably happen. Their power is in their possibility, and their meaning often resides in their "exploration[s] of social boundaries" that "challenge in some way . . . what the world is or should be" (Ellis 11). Other times, when Natalie feels overwhelmed by the horrors of growing up female – that is, when confronted with the possibility of marriage and children – she disengages by "her usual method – imagining the sweet sharp sensation of being burned alive" (10). Such an image connects her again to the punished maid at the gallows and perhaps to the witches of Salem. Natalie uses legendary narratives of women's suffering as a type of silent refusal of her society's narratives for women. The alternative narratives that she imagines are all, in one way or another, negotiating the fate of the subject: the maid bargaining for her life, the witch claiming power through death, the refusal of the princess in favor of the cowboy or the pirate.

Natalie's engagement of these legends fails, though, because something, which was "only remotely connected with knights," made the forest beyond the garden "dark and silent and unprovocative" (22). At a weekend party hosted by her father, the central event of the first section of the novel, it is strongly suggested that Natalie is sexually assaulted by one of Arnold's friends. This unnamed man leads her into the woods at the edge of the property, where awaited a "great terrifying silence," with trees which pulled darkness "about her with silent patient hands"

(42). The man tells her to sit on a fallen tree trunk, and she does. The use of free indirect discourse seamlessly intertwines the various competing narratives of this section:

> "Come along," the man told Natalie. "This I intend to hear more about." "And the blood?" the detective said fiercely. "What about the blood, Miss Waite? *How* do you account for the blood?" "*One is one and all alone and evermore will be so.*"
>
> (41)

Within the space of three lines, Jackson writes three competing narratives with the margins between them so fine as to be almost indistinguishable.[6] The first is the inscribing word of the father, spoken by the unnamed man functioning as Arnold's double. The unnamed man seems to be angry that Natalie made "a perfectly outrageous statement" in describing herself as "wonderful." Erupting into this dominant patriarchal discourse, and in turn being disrupted by the unnamed man, is Natalie's interior fantasy, drawing from pulp fictional narratives of interrogating detectives and blood-soaked carpets. This fantasy allows her the power to murder the father/lover but does not provide a clear escape from being fixed by the interrogatory male authority.

The third narrative is folk. The lyrics of the folk ballad "Green Grow the Rushes, O" disrupt both the reality of the father and the fantasy of the daughter. This is a communal voice, a "swell of sound" made up of the voices of the party with "everyone singing," the "people's voices" masking the conversation of Natalie and the stranger (37). The song's "stacking" method is both mnemonic and forcefully participatory, each stanza building on the one before. The critical interpretation of these lyrics, which had been much discussed in the pages of the *Journal of American Folklore* in the decade prior to the publication of *Hangsaman*, is that the "one" was the godhead, a celebration of "the original singularity, and the singular originality, of the divine source of life" (Kertzer 224).[7] In this instance, however, the song, performed by a faceless group of suburban intellectuals, offers no restitution of the divine, only a grotesque parody of communal performance. Its pseudofolk nature serves as backdrop to trauma – Natalie's presumed rape during her parents' party. The man, a family friend, sits Natalie down under "indifferent" stars, where no narrative can provide protection for her as she thinks, "Oh my dear God sweet Christ . . . is he going to *touch* me?" (43).

After this attack in the woods, Natalie creates a rite of repression, chanting, "I will not think about it, it doesn't matter," using ritual as a way of actively suppressing her trauma (43). We see again the importance of ritual when Natalie is later forced to participate in a dorm initiation where first-year students are roused from their beds in the middle of the night, sat on a stool, and then forcefully questioned by upperclassmen about obscene jokes and sex. Natalie thinks that the upperclassmen do not care too much that not all of the freshmen were present: "Another instance, she thought regretfully (or at least remembered later that she had so thought), of ritual gone to seed; the persecution of new students, once passionate, is now only perfunctory" (60). This scene has been treated lightly by critics, read as Jackson's mocking of empty gesture – but it is *not* empty, not for the other women and thus, by comparison, Natalie. As each girl steps down from the stool, after facing inquisition by her peers, she returns to "oblivion among her friends; she had passed," having clearly demonstrated that "she was not in any way eccentric, but a good, normal, healthy, American college girl, with ideals and ambitions and looking forward to a family of her own; she had merged" (61). The ritual, for most of the women, was successful.

In the essay "The Symbols of Folk Culture," Hyman suggests that the "Greek symbols never seem conventional or allegorical, but always the literal picturing of objects full of *mana*, magical power." He continues: "the absence of a folk culture in America seems to be precisely the absence of these *mana* experiences." One elusive site of *mana* is "the experience of ritual communion," a "temporary merger of individual identity in a collective whole that is larger than the sum of its parts," which "at its conclusion releases its individual units purged and fulfilled, as though they had been cast up from the belly of the whale" (307–8). It is Natalie's inability to be part of this collective release, largely because the event in the woods makes it impossible to answer the question "are you a virgin," that robs the moment of its *mana*: "What a silly routine, Natalie thought, not realizing . . . [that] worse than the actual being a bad sport was the state of mind which led her into defiance of this norm, this ring of placid, masked girls" (62). This is not a ritual "gone to seed" so much as it is a ritual out of reach for Natalie. Like at the party, where Natalie is separate from the pseudocommunal voice of the song and the patriarchal discourse of the father, she cannot participate in the rituals of her peers, because she has no way to believe in the *mana* they are attempting to claim. Natalie remembers "so clearly" the moment she began to question *mana*, when she rejected the possibility that wishing on a "wishing stone" would bring her a bicycle. This leads her to lament, some "cynical years later," that "it was less important . . . to allow her father's humor to be transmitted to his children than to keep alive her mother's faith in magic" (108). If she had just waited for the right moment, when she knew that she could, in fact, get a bicycle, "magic would have been sustained, and cause and effect not violated for that first, irrecoverable time" (108). Choosing her father's narrative, one rooted in a seemingly rational "cause and effect," over her mother's made the rituals of her peers impossible.

And yet, it is in her father's study that she finds books on "demonology" and, more important, "an abridged *Golden Bough*" (25).[8] Later, in a letter from Arnold to Natalie that Jackson clearly (and humorously) positions as Oedipal, Arnold fancies himself a knight and Natalie his princess. He writes, "It is as much as any knight can do, these days, to keep in touch with his captive princesses, let alone rescue them." He is interpellating her into the romance of the fairy tale, offering to "attack the dragon" that guards her, for she is "surely not confined only by magic" (137). Arnold seems to dismiss household magic while embracing, even if ironically, grand mythic narratives. But Natalie has spent much of the novel resisting all levels of interpellation into folk culture. Natalie *fights* knights in armor in her woods, until the nameless man attacks her. She does not add her voice to the chorus singing "Green Grow the Rushes, O," and she avoids being subsumed by the rituals of her classmates. She rejects the magic of her mother, and she resists the rescue of her father/lover. All around her are competing narrative discourses that would move her into the world of the pseudomagic; but it is her letter responding to Arnold, in which she links him to a suitor "caroling lustily under my window," that she finally crosses into the most mythic section of the novel. The narrative thus moves from clear non-belief, since fairy tales exist purely in the world of imagination, into the more truthful world of myth. It is, "speaking of magic," in this letter that Tony is first mentioned (138).

The "last erotic object in the metonymic chain that begins with her father" (Hattenhauer 108), Tony emerges from the woods, and Natalie, "going across the grass under the trees," sees "in the moonlight a figure coming toward her," the "girl Tony" (Jackson 141). As contemporary critics have pointed out, Tony's connections to trees are numerous, from her creation story to her sudden appearance one night, when Natalie at first mistakes Tony for a tree that "was not rooted and perhaps not completely indifferent" (148). Natalie's own indifference toward both her schoolwork and her family grows as she and Tony become closer, and Natalie feels that she has finally found a true friend, someone with whom she can enjoy "the feeling of being together without fear" (181). The weekend after Thanksgiving provides them a moment of respite from college and family life, and the two head out together on an odyssey that propels them further and further from campus.

Along the way they buy drinks at a drugstore, meet a one-armed man, spin vampire stories based on film posters, and stop to stare at a toy "hanged-man" in a shop window, a "tiny figure on a trapeze which turned and swung, around and around, endlessly and irritatingly" (193). "A tree of sacrifice is not living wood," Natalie says. Their "antirational and antisocial exhilaration" during this journey is alienating for the reader, as they move quickly from one venue to another, seemingly losing grasp on reality as they go (Lyons 63). This is, as Stevens argues, where Jackson begins to "trust the patient rather than the doctor," as the third-person narrator loses its objective neutrality, its disbelief (225). Natalie and Tony eventually catch a bus and ride to the end of the line to a closed-up amusement park called "Paradise Park," a grotesque Eden barren on this late November weekend. Tony pulls Natalie with siren-like power to a small copse of trees, where Natalie "saw with complacent pleasure a fallen tree across the small clearing and, as she knew she was expected to, sat down upon it" (212). Tony joins her there, and

> with Tony's hands on her face, on her back, holding her, Natalie shuddered. *One is one and all alone and evermore will be so;* "I will *not*," said Natalie, and ripped herself away. She *wants* me, Natalie though with incredulity, and said again, aloud, "I will *not*."
>
> (214)

This moment is often read as Natalie's reintegration into the outside world, where she deals with the trauma of abuse and irrevocably rejects magic for adulthood. In one of the earliest readings of the novel, John O. Lyons insists that, quite simply, "Tony (unknown to Natalie) is a Lesbian," and her intended seduction of Natalie leaves her "revolted," so much so that she "shakes herself awake from the world of childish imagination which has ended in horror and returns to the solid reality of the college" (63). Lyons dismisses the probable rape at the beginning of the novel as simply a case of Natalie "los[ing] her composure" at the "harmless" touching of her arm. But subsequent critics quickly corrected Lyons's early misreading, making clear the deep connections between the forest, the father, the rapist, and Tony. As Natalie follows Tony around the park, she notices that it "was indeed very dark and that ahead of her the figure she had mistaken for Tony was only another tree" (210). Tony is now usually read as a manifestation of Natalie's fractured consciousness, either as "schizophrenic episodes that result from her growing fear that she has no internal self" (Hague 80) or, in Wyatt Bonikowski's convincing argument, as representative of "the nature of the destructive *jouissance* within her, the claim of the Real outside of the Symbolic order" (83). But I am not so sure that it is entirely clear that Tony is an imaginary alter ego, invisible to all but Natalie. After all, Elizabeth (at least, according to the novel's third-person narrator) does say to Natalie "I saw you with someone" (149). What *is* clear is that Tony is not entirely of the world.

Throughout the novel, Natalie tries out different identities – a murderer, a pirate, a waitress, and a mental patient, a regent mapping the boundaries of her country. These repeated and unsuccessful attempts to construct effective counternarratives all lead her to Tony in the woods. This journey actually begins before the incident with the unnamed man, when, presumably surrounded by the books on demonology and *The Golden Bough*, her father leafs through her notebook and says, "'This has always been a favorite of mine, Natalie' . . . 'This one about the trees. "Lined up against the sky" is good, very good'" (10). It is easy to see, then, how the misplaced forest in "Paradise Park" can be read as the inevitable setting for the novel's conclusion, echoing that first conversation with Arnold and representing a "locale where the laws of conventional reality can be easily breached and where, as a result, the unwary traveler is all too vulnerable to demons both real and imagined" (Murphy 109). That she is expected in the grove of trees at *this* moment of reckoning is even less of a surprise, however, if we read *Hangsaman* as Hyman suggested, as myth, for next to the fairgrounds is a lake, and next to the lake are the trees, and Tony says, "We have to be here first," before they can run away from the world to a place where "no one is alive but us" (209). Tony is offering Natalie a world outside of time, carried away by a "he" who would "take us wherever we wanted to go," finally landing in a place where

> sitting we can rule the world, where the stars are around our feet and the sun rises when we glance down and beckon, where far below there are contests to make us laugh and above us there is nothing but our own crowns.
>
> (208–9)

In short, Tony is offering Natalie the chance to be a god.

Bonikowski argues that Natalie "has recreated and relived the trauma of the sexual assault in the garden" through the "repetition of a primordial crime that lies at the heart of relationship with her father" (83, 81). Adding the lens of Hyman's myth-ritual theory weaves together the two concurrent strands of criticism in a way that would be intimately familiar to those in Jackson's literary circle. The central "primordial crime" that is at the heart of Hyman's myth-ritual theory is the murder of the dying king. Hyman says that "the key image of *The Golden Bough*, the king who slays the slayer and must himself be slain, corresponds to some universal principle we recognize in life" (*Armed* 439). The slayer becomes "King of the Woods," Diana's priest, who guards her sacred grove next to the lake at Nemi. Here he waits, until the next runaway slave finds and breaks the golden bough, signaling his intent to challenge the sitting king. The winner's triumphant strength and health assure the continued strength and health of his community. Because Hyman believed that "rites, and only rites, have myth-engendering power," because he "subsumes all folk narrative under that term" (Fontenrose 28), and because he calls *Hangsaman* a mythic novel, I want us to see what he saw: Jackson seizing as a powerful site of meaning-making the primordial crime at the heart of his particular brand of myth and folklore.

The "King of the Wood at Nemi," according to Frazer, "was regarded as an incarnation of a tree-spirit," who "had to be killed in order that the divine spirit, incarnate in him, might be transferred in its integrity to his successor" (iii. 205). Frazer imagines "a dream-like vision of the little woodland lake of Nemi, 'Diana's Mirror' as it was called by the ancients" (i. 1). Jackson creates in "Paradise Park" a type of funhouse mirror version of Diana's sacred grove. It is late fall instead of spring, and the park is crowded with remnants of its secular nature, like the "faint, almost undetectable odors of wet bathing suits, and stale mustard, and rancid popcorn" (206). While Natalie at first rejects an anthropomorphic rendering of trees, saying that "a tree is not a human thing, with its feet in the ground and its back hard against the sky," eventually her "feet went without sound on the path," and she "knew surely that the trees bent over her, trying, perhaps, to touch her hair" (209–10). She "came out at last, almost crying . . . onto a smooth bare place where the dusk, or the light of the lake far behind reflected from the clouds overhead, fell with a brazen and ghastly clarity" (212). The reflection from "Dianna's mirror" is grotesque, an inversion of the sacred realm of myth.

Though promised the chance to live as a god with nothing above her but her crown, Natalie knows that this promise is a lie and that only "one and one and all alone" can emerge from this confrontation. She looks, hopes, for "a weakness in the traitor to make this an equal battle," while Tony "her head back against a tree trunk" says, "'It's good to be here at last; it's the only possible place'" (213). Jackson is deliberately playing with the anthropomorphic imagery of the tree spirits and sacred groves, reconfiguring the traditional myth to highlight its inadequacy as a viable narrative for Natalie. Natalie rejects Tony, slaying the father/rapist only to take Tony's place in a world of ambivalence, where "everything's waiting" for her, where she expects a "hand or branch to pull her rudely down again" (214).

This victory is ambivalent because, in the myth, such a victory cannot promise peace. The winner does not move into a life of luxury; he now takes his place a watcher of the grove, constantly fearing the appearance of a challenger, for the new priest will have "only escaped the fire to fall by the sword" (Frazer, *Abridged* 816). It is a life defined by surveillance. Natalie has perhaps bested her trauma and achieved some peace, but at a price. She has not been fully reintegrated into the world around her; instead, she is rewritten and subsumed by its mythology. Natalie has been taken up by the mythic process and is now simultaneously part of the narrative of the folk and always separate from it, for "no crowned head ever lay uneasier, or was visited by more evil dreams," than the slayer of the king (Frazer, *Abridged* 1–2). She is now Natalie "waits," her identity prescribed by the ambivalence of the primordial myth, and she waits for her own inevitable sacrifice.

Merricat Blackwood begins *We Have Always Lived in the Castle* in a similar state of suspended animation, still venturing into the village but always vigilant of threats to her carefully maintained world. Hattenhauer argues that in *Castle*, Jackson "places myths and rituals alongside fairy tales, legends, and nursery rhymes" as part of her "nascent postmodern subversion of myth criticism." He goes on to say that what is "even more important" is that "she devalorizes myth criticism by breaking the opposition of myth and ritual on the one hand, and magic and witchcraft on the other," thereby "demystifying" the "myth critics' tendency to obscure ideology under valorized canonical myths and to separate those privileged myths from other beliefs and practices they called 'folklore'" (187). But this is not actually how Hyman defined folklore. Hyman believed that all folk work and folk art derived from myth. The "other hand" of myth and ritual was not folk culture but what Hyman called "pseudo-folk" culture – that is, that which passed as folklore but was really popular or mass culture or idiosyncratic creations of an individual artist.

Hyman instead argued that artists "are not creating in a folk or primitive tradition, but are using the myth and legend, the magic and ritual, of these cultures with some degree of ironic adaptation to their own needs," so that their "art can furnish us with meaningful and moving symbols that can bring *mana* back into a culture sadly deficient in it" ("Symbols" 312). He suggested that the only truly mythic folk culture left in the United States, aside from small pockets of immigrant culture, belonged to "children at play," who expressed "true folk culture, age old and magical, in their games and songs," and the "full ritual communion – collective, purgative, and overwhelming" of the lynch mob (311). In *Castle*, Jackson continues to engage with various folk forms in order to exploit the tension between the individual, the unconscious, and the community. Jackson represents both these sites of "true" folklore in an "ironic adaptation" that is quite comfortably in line with Hyman's views. What she does question, though, is the possibility or viability of *mana* at all in modern society, because the reification that results from the inclusion of the Blackwood sisters into narratives of folk culture also, like in *Hangsaman*, makes permanent their alienation.

We Have Always Lived in the Castle begins by intimately situating the reader in Merricat's mind: "My name is Mary Katherine Blackwood. I am eighteen years old, and I live with my sister Constance. . . . Everyone else in my family is dead" (1).

That Merricat poisoned her father, mother, younger brother, and aunt is not fully revealed until the last third of the novel, and it is Constance, the elder sister by a decade, who stood trial and was ultimately acquitted for the murders. The unmarried sisters live together in Blackwood Manor, surviving quite well on the money and goods that had been accumulated by their parents and the Blackwoods before them. Constance is agoraphobic, unable to leave the grounds of the Blackwood manor, closing herself off from almost all interaction with the outside world. Merricat loves Constance, yes, but Constance is not the sole remaining member of Merricat's family. They live with their incapacitated Uncle Julian, who managed to survive his attempted murder, and Jonas the cat.

When the novel begins, Merricat is away from the manor on her weekly errands, travelling through town terrified of being tormented by the villagers, the "ugly people with their evil faces," their "flat grey faces with the hating eyes" (2). She is accosted by these villagers, pinned by their vicious stares, constructed through their gossip, and taunted by their children. Readers so acutely feel her terror that we find it possible to empathize with her as she says, "I would have liked to come into the grocery some morning and see them all, even the Elberts and the children, lying there crying with the pain and dying" (9). Merricat's fear permeates the book and is seemingly justified when, near the end of the novel, the townspeople stone the Blackwood manor and gleefully destroy much of house's first level, breaking dishes and windows, emptying food onto the floor. The moment they spy Merricat and Constance huddled together, waiting for a chance to flee, is truly frightening, and it is a relief when the sisters get to hide away in Merricat's secret grove, a womb-like enclosure from which she and Constance emerge the next day as a postlapsarian Adam and Eve. It is only after this event that Merricat confesses, and the reader gets confirmation, that, yes, at twelve years old Merricat murdered her family.

The major conflict in the novel is set in motion with the arrival of Cousin Charles, come to lay claim to Constance and thus the Blackwood fortune. Merricat both detests and is deeply afraid of Charles, for she fears that he will disrupt the seemingly Edenic life she fights so hard to maintain. When Merricat sets the Blackwood manor on fire as a way to drive out the "demon" Charles, the fire draws the villagers to them. It is only then, after the fire is extinguished, that the villagers stone the house. When Merricat and Constance return to the ruins of their home the morning after, they begin the new normal of their lives, drinking from the two surviving handled cups and hiding from the world. Charles makes one last attempt to win Constance, but despite a moment of hesitation, Constance ultimately chooses Merricat. The sisters now live together in Merricat's fantasy world on the moon: "We are so happy," Merricat says (146).

We see an immediately recognizable form of folklore in the first chapter, when the children of the town shout taunts at Merricat:

> Merricat, said Connie, would you like a cup of tea?
> Oh no, said Merricat, you'll poison me.
> Merricat, said Connie, would you like to go to sleep?
> Down in the boneyard ten feet deep!
> (16)

The study of children's lore at first fits comfortably within familiar evolutionary ideology carried over from the nineteenth century, the prevailing theory being that a child "recapitulates the development of the race" because "survivals of the primitive" were "preserved in children's folklore" (Zumwalt, "Complexity" 25). Children were seen as incubators in civilized society for the folklore of the past, joining "savages" and "primitives" and the human unconscious as sites for folklore's preservation. Children's folklore often relies on parody and inversion of recognizable narratives found in the adult world, and such refractions allow children the space to try out different epistemologies of power. Rhyming is one of the most recognizable forms of children's folklore since its formulaic structures make the rhymes fairly easy to remember and allow creative energy to be focused on adapting local or specific language and content (Mechling 109). Most importantly, children are simultaneously members of several different folk groups, through which they learn to "use stylized communication to create the sense of a shared, meaningful world" (Mechling 94). Folklore is one of the most powerful tools in the acculturation of children.

Fieldwork done with children's taunting behavior shows that, across cultures, "the person insulted is depicted as deviating from culturally defined values," so that "the children's estimations of the extent to which cultural values are implicit in the insults were close to those of the adults" (Jorgensen 224). Taunts are reversals of the cultural imperative to be polite, but because the targets of taunts often turn out to be those individuals of whom adults also implicitly or explicitly disapprove, they are safe receptacles for "malicious intentions and negative emotions," like revenge or hatred or domination (Jorgensen 222). Taunts are not about "kids being kids"; they are about children becoming adults and the way in which play helps them learn who and how to hate. Taunts allow children to probe the boundaries of the adult community that they are one day going to enter, and in *Castle* the children's taunts are clearly defined moments of border-controlling logic that are crucial to the textual construction of folk groups. The Blackwoods are outsiders because of their wealth and because of how they use their wealth against the people of the town. The taunts reverse that power dynamic, turning it on itself in a moment of carnivalesque joy. Merricat's hatred of the townsfolk is not benign, and it *is* part of the Blackwood legacy. The Blackwood sisters get away with murder, free to live with their riches in the big castle beyond the "wire fence" constructed "to keep the people out" (53). The taunts correct the mistakes of the institutions – in this case, the courts – and they allow the children to exert control over figures of whom they are afraid. In short, though this particular taunt cannot be found in any ethnographic collection of children's folklore, it is an accurate representation of the performance of folklore, both in function and in form. Here are the folk, expressing through folklore what they might otherwise repress.

Likewise, Hyman suggested that "the only culture trait" citizens in the United States "possess which might fairly be called a full ritual communion – collective, purgative, and overwhelming" is "the lynch mob" ("Symbols" 311). In *Castle*, that trait manifests when Chief Jim Donell, after putting out the fire at the Blackwood manor, despite the repeated chants of the townspeople to "let it burn," bent down and "took up a rock," and "in complete silence ... turned slowly and then raised his arm and smashed the rock through one of the great tall windows." Soon "a wall of laughter rose and grew behind him and ... they moved like a wave" toward the house (105–6). The stoning of the manor is punctuated with lines from the children's taunts, such as when the family doctor runs in and asks, "Where is Julian Blackwood," to be answered with a shout of "Down in the boneyard ten feet deep" (107). The joy of the mob reaches an apex when Jim Donell says, softly and politely, "Oh, no, said Merricat, you'll poison me," while "over it all was the laughter" (109). That these two folk cultural traits, highlighted by Hyman as signifying presence in a culture otherwise marked by absence, converge in this moment suggests that Jackson was pointedly engaging folklore to make manifest the darker communal impulses of human society.

Thus readers are forced to confront early on the consequences of folklore being used as a tool for conscription, suppression, and expulsion. Oppenheimer insists that Jackson saw *Castle* as the "truth" of what life was like, that Constance and Merricat were herself, split in two. Jackson's daughter agreed, saying that her mother "told me that's what Constance and Merricat are about ... they are the same person, both Shirley" (235). This may be, but Merricat is nonetheless an invented person, and invented people have invented folklore; Jackson manipulates recognizable narratives of folklore in order to heighten the creativity of Merricat's own insular world-building. Merricat's invented folklore, though, like that of *Hangsaman*, is uncanny, a type of funhouse mirror inversion of traditional forms.

Merricat's childhood is atypical, and not just because she murdered her family. She lacked a folk community within which to create that "shared, meaningful world" (Mechling 94). With no Tony to usher her into the world of myth and ritual, Merricat has to make do on her own. She had fairy tales she read and myths she learned from her cat and, most prominently, rituals she invented. Merricat buries and nails a mixture of protective tokens around the Blackwood property that represent patriarchal, economic, and epistemological power on the one hand and a patently infantilized feminine world on the other. There are a "box of silver dollars buried by the creek" and "a little notebook" phallically nailed to a tree, where her father "used to record the names of people who owed him money, and people who ought, he thought, to do favors for him" (53). But she also buries a doll, her baby teeth, her marbles, and other "treasures" given to her by Constance, like "a penny, or a bright ribbon" (41). These are all artifacts of realms in which she does not and cannot belong, and they function as a way for her to make contact with worlds outside her of understanding and to harness, she believes, their power in the interest of bringing concrete stability to her lived reality.

These rituals are structured as superstitions, verbal expressions with conditions and results often followed by a conversion ritual. If salt is spilled (condition), bad luck will follow (result) unless some of the salt is thrown over one's shoulder (conversion ritual) (Mullen 126). But despite the tendency of critics to read Merricat's beliefs about the power of her sympathetic magic as superstitions, they are not. Ritualized superstitious behavior acts outside of reason; the "compulsive act" of superstition is performed in *spite* of rationality, not as replacement for it (Hufford, "Response" 105). If a person performing a ritual believes the ritual to work because of clear cause and effect, it is not a superstition, because the performer believes they are acting rationally. Merricat's rituals may be unrecognizable to anyone but her, and they may not have any easily recognizable ethnographic corollary, but Jackson makes it clear that Merricat believes they will work.

But do they? The rituals and talismans are meant to keep Constance in and Charles out. As this is ultimately what happens, what is to keep us from accepting Merricat's magic as true, other than an expected scholarly stance of disbelief? James Egan argues that Merricat's magic "fully" fails, that "Merricat's 'magic' rituals and her elaborate, insular fantasy world . . . substitute for a normal morality," allowing a "monstrous" and "total, horrific inversion of the domestic ideal" (22, 23). Egan's use of scare quotes around the word "magic" makes his view of Merricat's rituals clear. The rituals *have* to fail if we are to read the novel as a cautionary tale about monstrous children, and if we are to see it as a perversion of the midcentury American family. And for many ritual theorists, rites "cannot exist in an aesthetic or formalist vacuum; they require the context of community." They "convey the sense of satisfaction peculiar to them alone in the intense experience of community that is their chief reason for being" (Hardin 847). Merricat's rituals are practiced outside of a human folk group, bringing about no communion. Indeed, they specifically reference a world in which she has no place. Merricat has repressed her act of familicide, but unlike the villagers she has no outlet through which to express that repression, no traditional community from which to learn the coping mechanism of folklore. Jackson, then, does not construct Merricat's rituals as a reflection of any so-called authentic folk experience, but as a testament to the needs of an individual alienated, or exiled, from a traditional folk culture.

We see similar disconnects between Merricat and what scholars at the time would have considered "traditional" folk communities in reference to folk narrative. While Merricat tries to stop the change promised by Charles's arrival, for instance, she turns to her cat Jonas for myth: "All cat stories start with the statement," Merricat hears Jonas say, "my mother, who was the first cat, told me this" (53). Merricat thus is able to believe for a moment that "there was no change coming," that she was "wrong to be so frightened" (53). Merricat constructs an etiological myth and endows Jonas with the ability to share it, using the language of myth as a conduit of communion with a community uncomplicated by murder and ghosts and "ugly people with their evil faces" (11). Much as the tokens of her rituals are fetishistic totems signifying lack, so too is the claiming of a mythic history through her cat. The language of myth shows Merricat's need to believe that the power of her magic will hold.

Perhaps most telling is Merricat's linking of her own narrative to the fairy tale. She "likes fairy tales" best, tales preserved in books found in the library. At the beginning of the novel, the conventions of the fairy tale are tellingly used to flatten Constance (20). She describes Constance as "a fairy princess," saying, "I used to try to draw her picture, with long golden hair and eyes as blue as the crayon could make them . . . the pictures always surprised me, because she *did* look like that" (19–20). Merricat's fairy-tale view of Constance comes from the literary (rather than oral) tradition, and her corporeality is described only by the transfer of crayon to paper. This is a singular, exiled, rather than plural, communal characterization. It is through the solitary acts of reading and drawing that Merricat imposes the narrative of the fairy tale onto her reality. This singularity continues when Merricat says that

> I had buried all my baby teeth as they came out one by one and perhaps someday they would grow as dragons. All our land was enriched with my treasures buried in it, thickly inhabited just below the surface with my marbles and my teeth and my colored stones.
>
> (41)

The repetition of the singular possessive – "my teeth," "my marbles," "my treasures" – also marks Merricat outside the realm of folk tradition, as an agent acting *on* it rather than *within* it.

The fixing of the narrative of *We Have Always Lived in the Castle* as a fairy tale is beguiling, because it can resolve much of the tension around the end of the novel and recoup a morally ambiguous narrative. Being able to frame the story's plot as "happiness/ disturbance/ happiness restored" or "Lack/ Lack Liquidated"[9] gives us a pattern for reading the text that is comfortable and ameliorates some of the unease brought about by Merricat's murderous revelations. It allows the reader to believe Merricat when she says that she and Constance are "so happy," without having to take a seemingly unreliable narrator's word for it. Jackson herself asks us to consider this when she writes that, after returning home following their night in the woods, Merricat and Constance had "come back through the wrong gap in time, or the wrong door, or the wrong fairy tale" (114). Merricat says, "I could not allow myself to be angry, and particularly not angry with Constance, but I wished Charles dead. Constance needed guarding more than ever before and if I became angry and looked aside she might very well be lost" (79). Merricat here is cast as the dragon protecting the princess. That Charles neatly fulfills the traditional role of the prince, seeking a princess and her father's wealth, lends credence to this reading, as he attempts from the moment of his arrival to vanquish Merricat. But as Honor McKitrick Wallace argues, "Merricat's narrative also places her in the role of Propp's hero, questing after the princess Constance," besting the false hero Charles (179). Merricat's rituals now have a certain pragmatism, as her "new magical safeguards were the lock on the front door, and the boards over the windows, and the barricades along the sides of the house" (145–46). She even contemplates finally "mending the broken step." These are protective acts, ones that can be read as prescriptively masculine. By the end of the novel, though, Merricat drapes herself in tablecloths while Constance dons Uncle Julian's suits, presenting perhaps a third option for the *dramatis personae* of the fairy tale: Merricat presenting herself as a princess, living in her castle with her prince, Constance.

But it is the "wrong fairy tale," because the novel is not meant to be read as a fairy tale at all. A fairy tale is not meant to be believed. It is wholly fantastic, thought to exist in a world outside of our own. Instead, the novel takes on the characteristics of myth and, finally, legend in order to ask its readers to believe in the truth of Merricat. We once again see a young female protagonist who both refuses and is refused participation in any community that would have been considered traditional, venturing into the sacred woods with her closest companion. In *Hangsaman* this is Tony; in *Castle*, it is Constance, who is also, like Tony, often read to be a manifestation of the protagonist's "other half" (Oppenheimer 234). But where Natalie slays, Merricat embraces. Natalie refuses seduction, while Merricat seduces, leading Constance to the "entrance of [Merricat's] hiding place" where she "pushed [Constance] gently" down onto a bed of leaves and blankets (110). But both choices deny Jackson's protagonists full participation in the civilizing world of adulthood, and neither reintegrates them fully into "normal" society but instead into a world of heightened surveillance: while "all the strangers could see from outside, when they looked at all, was a great ruined structure overgrown with vines," every day Merricat and Constance sat and looked out, "watched the children playing, the people walking past" (140).

Merricat and Constance, however, do not become moribund in an ancient myth, fixed by its unchanging universality. The remains of the Blackwood manor have been incorporated into local lore. As one visitor remarks, "It used to be a lovely old house, I hear. . . . I've heard that it was quite a local landmark at one time," an appeal to credibility mixed with distancing from the source ("I've heard") as a negotiation of belief (140). The sisters live in the ruins of their once magnificent house, subsisting in part off of the offerings of food cooked by the village women. The motives for these ritual offerings are a mixture of guilt, penance, and, finally, fear: "You can't go on those steps," the children warned each other; "if you do, the ladies will get you." This time, when children taunt, "Merricat, said Constance, would you like a cup of tea," it is followed by an offering of "a basket of fresh eggs and a note reading, 'He didn't mean it, please'" (146). The taunts of the children are now mediated by Merricat and Constance's status. They are living alone, absent a traditional patriarch, certainly challenging the "boundaries of what the" villagers thought the "world is or should be" (Ellis 11). While in *Hangsaman* Tony offers Natalie a chance to live above the world, "where the stars are around our feet" and people exist only "far below," the women of the Blackwood manor, though sacralized through ritualistic offerings, are firmly part of the everyday, a horizontal rather than vertical separation from the community. As such, in *Castle* Jackson has created legend – a powerfully dynamic narrative form that forces its audience to confront the fantastic and sacred in the world of the mundane, to test their belief in that which seems unbelievable.[10] In *Hangsaman* and *We Have Always Lived in the Castle*, then, Jackson connects negotiations of belief to the narratives of folk communities and to the depths of the human unconscious in a way that shows deep engagement with the era's discourses of folklore, signifying in many ways on her husband's full immersion into theories of myth and ritual. Jackson does not destabilize myth by equating it with folklore; instead, she unmoors folk narratives from their traditional contexts and reimagines them for a world in which her damaged women refuse interpellation into a folk community.

Nonetheless, when repressed knowledge erupts, folk narratives take over. Natalie and Merricat had resisted, rejected, and been rejected by traditional folk communities, only to at last become rescripted through them and their narratives. For Natalie, that narrative is mythic; for Merricat, it is legendary. This difference is more than categorical – it is perhaps essential to the way the texts make meaning. Legends are fragmentary, unstable narratives, lacking the rigid formulaic structure of myths and fairy tales. They involve an active audience who negotiates and tests their belief, offering the possibility for truth in a way that myth and fairy tales do not; as such, there is agency in legend for the teller of the tale and for the character being constructed. This gives a dynamism and adaptability to legend that separate it from traditional myth narratives. In that way, no, Merricat's magic does not fully fail. She is, like Natalie, still conscripted by folk narrative, but she and Constance are now important to the town's knowledge of itself, upheld through the ritual actions of the community and nourished, quite literally, by the power of its belief. Jackson has disrupted the primordial myth by creating a legendary space in which her protagonists, while not completely healthy or whole, can at least reject the solitary anxiety and the overdetermined identity that come from the slaying of the king. They are indeed utterly and completely happy in their "life on the moon." At least, that is, according to Merricat.

Notes

1. See DeCaro and Jordan for more on the process of "re-situating" folklore.
2. A large part of the appeal of Freudian psychology as a method for understanding folklore was that Freud himself had expressed a deep interest in it, arguing that "we derive our knowledge from widely different sources: from fairy tales and myths, jokes and witticisms, from folklore, i.e., from what we know of the manners and customs, sayings and songs, of different peoples, and from poetic and colloquial usage of language. Everywhere in these various fields the same symbolism occurs, and in many of them we can understand it without being taught anything about it" (188).
3. The psychological branch of the myth-ritual school felt that "myth embodies man's unconscious feelings," that "the psychic and biological growth of the individual reenacts the stages of the psychic and biological growth of the human race," which is expressed through a group's folklore (Ferris 255).
4. See Hufford, "The Scholarly Voice and the Personal Voice: Reflexivity in Belief Studies."
5. The categories of "myth," "folktale," and "legend" go back to the earliest days of folklore study. The Grimms' categories of *mythen*, *märchen*, and *sägen* were revised in Bascom's prose typology, which still serves as a foundational text in the study of folk narrative.
6. Indeed, Stevens claims the novel to be "solely from Natalie's point of view," leading to his primary argument that the novel "lets the patient speak for herself" (225).
7. The version cited in *Hangsaman* is English, but the ballad itself is widely diffused and can be traced back to at least the fifteenth century. The debate in the *Journal of*

American Folklore was concerned, among other things, with whether the song was of Christian or Jewish origin, as it is part of both Christmas and Passover traditions. See Yoffie.

8 James Frazer's *The Golden Bough* was a cornerstone of Stanley Edgar Hyman's ideas about the world. It was a book that connected magic and religion, myth and ritual, and Hyman was as famous for his dogmatic adherence to Frazer's ideas as he was for any of his own writing. Yet it is an *abridged* version we find in Arnold's possession. Hyman was insistent that any critique of Frazer (numerous by the time Hyman was writing) be centered on the full thirteen volumes of *The Golden Bough*.

9 Alan Dundes, in *The Morphology of North American Indian Folktales*, extrapolates from Propp's *Morphology of the Folk Tale* what he calls the "motifeme" – the plot motivation of lack (L) and lack liquidated (LL). Similarly, fairy tale scholar Max Lüthi argues that "the structure of the fairytale is characterized by the basic framing tension [of] Lack / Striving for remedy, behind which stands that pattern Happiness/ Disturbance/ Happiness restored" (56).

10 I see this as an act of ostension, or "legend-tripping," which refers to a physical, bodily engagement with the subject of legend – for example, reenacting the plot of legends or visiting legend sites. There is a wide span of emotional engagement possible with such ostensive events, ranging from "thrill-seeking play to humbled reverence," which can lead to "legend as pious thrill" and a "legend-trip as a religious experience" (Lindahl 174). Visits to sites of legend, like, I would argue, Blackwood Manor, realize "all the playful, scary, and sacred dimensions of ostension" (Lindahl 165). Furthermore, Donald Holly and Casey Cordy link the involvement of material objects, like offerings, to the moment when ostension shifts from disbelief to belief, when it comes to act more like religion than vicarious play (336). We see Jackson representing a full range of ostensive action outside Blackwood Manor, from the women who make offerings of food as if to a deity to the children who fearfully but gleefully trespass on the grounds to the tourists who stop to picnic and take pictures. These are all elements of legend ostension, in which meaning is negotiated from the profane to the sacred so that it can function in a variety of ways for individual pilgrims.

Works cited

Bascom, William. "The Forms of Folklore: Prose Narratives." *The Journal of American Folklore* 78.307 (1965): 3–20. JSTOR. Web. 5 Jul. 2014.

Bonikowski, Wyatt. "'Only One Antagonist': The Demon Lover and the Feminine Experience in the Work of Shirley Jackson." *Gothic Studies* 15.2 (2013): 66–88. Web. 5 Jul. 2014.

De Caro, Frank and Rosan A. Jordan. *Re-situating Folklore: Folk Contexts and Twentieth-Century Literature and Art*. Knoxville: U of Tennessee, 2004. Print.

Dundes, Alan. *The Morphology of North American Indian Folktales*. Helsinki: Suomalainen Tiedeakatemia, 1964. Print.

Egan, James. "Sanctuary: Shirley Jackson's Domestic and Fantastic Parables." *Studies in Weird Fiction* 6 (1989): 15–24. Print.

Ellis, Bill. *Aliens, Ghosts, and Cults: Legends We Live*. Jackson: U of Mississippi, 2003. Print.

Ferris, William R., Jr. "Myth and the Psychological School: Fact or Fantasy." *New York Folklore Quarterly* 30.4 (1974): 254–66. Print.

Fontenrose, Joseph. *The Ritual Theory of Myth*. Berkeley: U of California, 1971. Print.

Frazer, James George. *The Golden Bough: A Study in Magic and Religion*. 1922. New York: Macmillan, 1951. Print.

———. *The Golden Bough: A Study in Magic and Religion.* 1922. Abridged Edition. New York: McMillan, 1963. Print.

Freud, Sigmund. "Symbolism in Dreams." *International Folkloristics: Classic Contributions by the Founders of Folklore.* Ed. Alan Dundes. Lanham, MD: Rowman & Littlefield, 1999. 177–96. Print.

Gennep, Arnold Van. *The Rites of Passage.* Chicago: U of Chicago, 1960. Print.

Hague, Angela. "'A Faithful Anatomy of Our Times': Reassessing Shirley Jackson." *Frontiers: A Journal of Women Studies* 26.2 (2005): 73–96. JSTOR. Web. 15 Nov. 2013.

Hardin, Richard F. "'Ritual' in Recent Criticism: The Elusive Sense of Community." *PMLA* 98.5 (1983): 846–62. JSTOR. Web. 17 Jun. 2014.

Hattenhauer, Darryl. *Shirley Jackson's American Gothic.* Albany: State U of New York, 2003. Print.

Holly, Donald H., Jr. and Casey E. Cordy. "What's in a Coin? Reading the Material Culture of Legend Tripping and Other Activities." *The Journal of American Folklore* 120.477 (2007): 335–54. JSTOR. Web. 25 Aug. 2015.

Hufford, David J. "Beings Without Bodies." *Out of the Ordinary: Folklore and the Supernatural.* Ed. Barbara Walker. Logan: Utah State UP, 1995. 11–45. Print.

———. "Response: The Adequacy of Freudian Psychoanalytic Theory." *Journal of Folklore Research* 40.1 (2003): 99–109. JSTOR. Web. 22 Jun. 2014.

———. "The Scholarly Voice and the Personal Voice: Reflexivity in Belief Studies." *Western Folklore* 54.1, Reflexivity and the Study of Belief (1995): 57–76. JSTOR. Web. 2 Jul. 2014.

Hyman, Stanley Edgar. "The Anthropological Approach." *The Journal of American Folklore* 66.261 (1953): 237–38. JSTOR. Web. 29 Jul. 2014.

———. *The Armed Vision: A Study in the Methods of Modern Literary Criticism.* New York: Vintage, 1955. Print.

———. "The Child Ballad in America: Some Aesthetic Criteria." *The Journal of American Folklore* 70.277 (1957): 235–39. JSTOR. Web. 17 Jun. 2014.

———. "Myth, Ritual, and Nonsense." *The Kenyon Review* 11.3 (1949): 455–75. JSTOR. Web. 24 May 2014.

———. "The Ritual View of Myth and the Mythic." *The Journal of American Folklore* 68.270, Myth: A Symposium (1955): 462–72. JSTOR. Web. 17 Jun. 2014.

———. "Some Trends in the Novel." *College English* 20.1 (1958): 1–9. JSTOR. Web. 7 Jun. 2014.

———. "The Symbols of Folk Culture." *Symbols and Values: An Initial Study.* Ed. Lyman Bryson. New York: Cooper Square, 1964. 307–12. Print.

Jackson, Shirley. *Hangsaman.* 1951. New York: Penguin, 2013. Print.

———. *The Sundial.* 1958. New York: Penguin, 2014. Print.

———. *We Have Always Lived in the Castle.* 1962. New York: Penguin, 2006. Print.

Jorgensen, Marilyn. "Teases and Pranks." *Children's Folklore: A Source Book.* Eds. Brian Sutton-Smith, Jay Mechling, Thomas W. Johnson, and Felicia R. McMahon. New York: Garland, 1995. 213–24. Print.

Kertzer, Jon. "The Course of a Particular: On the Ethics of Literary Singularity." *Twentieth-Century Literature* 50.3 (2004): 207–38. JSTOR. Web. 7 Jun. 2014.

Lang, Andrew. *Cock Lane and Common-Sense.* 1887. New York: AMS, 1970. Print.

Lindahl, Carl. "Ostensive Healing: Pilgrimage to the San Antonio Ghost Tracks." *The Journal of American Folklore* 118.468, Emerging Legends in Contemporary Society (2005): 164–85. JSTOR. Web. 1 Sep. 2015.

Lüthi, Max. *The Fairytale as Art Form and Portrait of Man.* Bloomington: Indiana UP, 1984. Print.

Lyons, John O. *The College Novel in America.* 1962. Carbondale: Southern Illinois UP, 1968. Print.

McCullen, J. T., Jr. "Review: The Ritual Theory of Myth." *Western Folklore* 26.4 (1967): 283–84. JSTOR. Web. 2 Jul. 2014.

Mechling, Jay. "Children's Folklore." *Folk Groups and Folklore Genres: An Introduction.* Ed. Elliott Oring. Logan: Utah State UP, 1986. 91–120. Print.

Motz, Marilyn. "The Practice of Belief." *The Journal of American Folklore* 111.441, Folklore: What's in a Name? (1998): 339–55. JSTOR. Web. 14 Aug. 2013.

Mullen, Patrick B. "Belief and the American Folk." *The Journal of American Folklore* 113.448 (2000): 119–43. JSTOR. Web. 2 Jul. 2014.

Murphy, Bernice M. "'The People of the Village Have Always Hated Us': Shirley Jackson's New England Gothic." *Shirley Jackson: Essays on the Literary Legacy.* Ed. Bernice M. Murphy. Jefferson, NC: McFarland and Company, 2005. 104–26. Print.

Nelson, Hilde Lindemann. *Damaged Identities, Narrative Repair.* Ithaca: Cornell UP, 2001. Print.

Oppenheimer, Judy. *Private Demons: The Life of Shirley Jackson.* New York: Putnam, 1988. Print.

Oring, Elliott. "Folk Narratives." *Folk Groups and Folklore Genres: An Introduction.* Ed. Elliott Oring. Logan: Utah State UP, 1986. 121–45. Print.

Parks, John G. "Chambers of Yearning: Shirley Jackson's Use of the Gothic." *Twentieth-Century Literature* 30.1 (1984): 15–29. JSTOR. Web. 28 Jul. 2014.

Pimple, Kenneth D. "Folk Beliefs." *The Emergence of Folklore in Everyday Life: A Fieldguide and Sourcebook.* Ed. George H. Schoemaker. Bloomington, IN: Trickster, 1990. 51–56. Print.

Rubenstein, Roberta. "House Mothers and Haunted Daughters: Shirley Jackson and Female Gothic." *Tulsa Studies in Women's Literature* 15.2 (1996): 309–31. JSTOR. Web. 28 Jul. 2014.

Schmaier, Maurice D. and Alan Dundes. "Parallel Paths." *The Journal of American Folklore* 74.292 (1961): 142–45. JSTOR. Web. 22 Jun. 2014.

Stevens, Jason W. *God-Fearing and Free: A Spiritual History of America's Cold War.* Cambridge, MA: Harvard UP, 2010. Print.

Stewart, Polly. "Wishful Willful Wily Women." *Feminist Messages: Coding in Women's Folk Culture.* Ed. Joan Newlon Radner. Urbana: U of Illinois, 1993. 54–73. Print.

Wallace, Honor Mckitrick. "'The Hero Is Married and Ascends the Throne': The Economics of Narrative End in Shirley Jackson's *We Have Always Lived in the Castle*." *Tulsa Studies in Women's Literature* 22.1 (2003): 173–91. JSTOR. Web. 17 Nov. 2013.

Yoffie, Leah Rachel Clara. "Songs of the 'Twelve Numbers' and the Hebrew Chant of 'Echod Mi Yodea.'" *The Journal of American Folklore* 62.246 (1949): 382–411. JSTOR. Web. 28 Jul. 2014.

Zumwalt, Rosemary. *American Folklore Scholarship: A Dialogue of Dissent.* Bloomington and Indianapolis: Indiana UP, 1988. Print.

———. "The Complexity of Children's Folklore." *Children's Folklore: A Source Book.* Eds. Brian Sutton-Smith, Jay Mechling, Thomas W. Johnson, and Felicia R. McMahon. New York: Garland, 1995. 23–48. Print.

5   *The Road Through the Wall* and Shirley Jackson's America

Richard Pascal

In recent years readers who are aware of Shirley Jackson's recurring concern with some of the dominant sociopolitical patterns of her era have uncovered, even in her more Gothically oriented texts, a keenly discerning social critic. The later novels, *The Sundial*, *The Haunting of Hill House*, and *We Have Always Lived in the Castle*, teasingly deploy elements of the Gothic in order to comment obliquely upon the domain of suburban realists, such as John O'Hara, Richard Yates, and John Cheever. And her most famous work, "The Lottery," though disturbingly set somewhere in the rural America of her time, ordinarily strikes readers and commentators as a grim fable or parable about the tragic consequences of adherence to damaging traditions and social conventions rather than a realistic dramatization of life in the modern era. Her brilliance as a fantasist of the uncanny is, of course, justly admired. Traces of the occult, or at least of obscure forces that lurk in shadows, are indeed the defining features of much of Jackson's work, as the titles of several of the most prominent critical studies of it readily indicate: Darryl Hattenhauer's *Shirley Jackson's American Gothic*, Roberta Rubenstein's "House Mothers and Haunted Daughters: Shirley Jackson and Female Gothic," and John G. Parks's "Chambers of Yearning: Shirley Jackson's Use of the Gothic," to cite only a few examples.

Unfortunately, however, that categorical frame, appropriate with regard to much of Jackson's fiction, has apparently had the effect of distorting critical analyses of her excellent first novel, *The Road Through the Wall*, and perhaps of discouraging scholarly interest in it. As a Gothic critique of aspects of modern America, she was not concerned to focus directly upon the very secular everyday world inhabited by most of her likely readers.[1] Yet *The Road Through the Wall* presents itself as a narrative that is grounded within and focused upon a mid-twentieth-century suburban setting notably devoid of Gothic shadows or hints of malignant presences.[2] Heavily laden with details of a specific time and social milieu, it adheres to social realist conventions, and it seeks, overtly in places, to contextualize its characters and narrative events by indicating the social and economic forces that have largely determined them. Only the dire Old Testament recitations of a minor character, an elderly recluse who addresses them to her dog, are suggestive of even a figuratively occult dimension to latent powerful forces affecting the people and events related in the narrative. But the relevance of her mystical mutterings to the actual state of the community is vague at best, and their direness is rendered hollow by portions and aspects of the narrative that call attention at significant points to contrastingly prosaic socioeconomic determinants that press upon the lives of the residents of Pepper Street. These are embodied discreetly, as I will argue, in the figure of another elderly woman, a wealthy and worldly-wise nonresident who appears to own much of the property in the area. She is seemingly the most minor of all the characters in the narrative, easily overlooked by readers; Pepper Street people appear to be unaware even of her existence. Yet her importance to the fate of the community, and to the concerns of the novel, stands in ironically inverse proportion to the small amount of textual attention that is directed to her. In her very facelessness and worldliness she is, so to speak, the blank face of the secular Powers that preside over them.

The Road Through the Wall, in short, not only openly invites a historicizing approach but also demands to be read as a work of mimetic fiction. My argument here, in brief, is that the small community of "Pepper Street" scrutinized in the novel is intended to be representative of much of middle-class suburban life in the postwar era. Modernity's wistful, sentimentalizing memory of the feudal village as a community of citizens who live in fellowship with one another as social equals is the mythic paradigm for leafy suburban areas such as the novel's "Pepper Street," but its applicability is perpetually undermined by the society's still more intense veneration of another idealized remnant of feudal society, that of the landed estate. For an actual "estate" in the modern sense of the term, an exclusive, walled community, lies adjacent to the small neighborhood in which the events of the narrative transpire. This estate overtly incarnates the conspicuously consumed privacy bought by worldly success – privacy that signifies not merely privilege but also social purity, isolation from polluting contact with social Others; and its tantalizing proximity is also figurative, suggestive of the pervasive myth that social grandeur on that scale, though by nature exclusive, may be a realizable aspiration for some who are as yet outsiders. The result of modern society's jostling juxtaposition of the two romanticized preindustrial institutions has been to make ostensibly village-like suburban communities fundamentally uncommunal sites of suspicion, isolation, and instability such that even the ancient practice of mobbish victimization, the very basis of social bonding in the grim vision of "The Lottery," can only faintly and sporadically inspire residents to congregate into a collective whole that is greater than any single one of them.

Their forgotten village green

Oddly, but significantly for what is in most respects a conventionally conceived narrative, there is no focalizing protagonist or group of characters that can be regarded as "major" in *The Road Through the Wall*. Rather, the action ranges freely among eleven households, and the focus frequently shifts from one character to another of the more than two dozen residents of Pepper Street in Cabrillo, a small town that lies within easy commuting distance of San Francisco. The effect is to foreground the neighborhood itself as the narrative's major "character," as though to enforce our sense of the street's holistic communitarian aspect. Initially, it seems that the small community is imagined as a site of idyllic rural retreat from a perhaps unsettling wider world. Thus, in the beautifully conceived prologue, a panoramic introductory tour of each house and household on Pepper Street climaxes in an evocative account of an ordinary spring day in which the doings of schoolchildren and parents are virtually apotheosized by the image of a "bedroomish arch" of tree blossoms presaging timeless fine times for "the roots of growing things," human as well as vegetable (12). In this opening section, it is as though the inclinations of individuals and families to cluster together into a close-knit community are regarded as no less rewarding and fundamental than the rhythms of the natural world. The privacy afforded the neighborhood appears to offer an optimal climate for participation in a small and highly interactive social group.

The impression of such communal amity and complacency is subtly undermined from the very start, however, with the opening sentence's declaration that "The weather falls more gently on some places than on others, [and] the world looks down more paternally on some people" (3). The subtle conflation of "weather," or natural forces, with a "world" that in playing favorites can be understood only as the social realm, establishes Pepper Street as a fabricated natural environment ("place") that cloaks its hapless dependence upon powerful outside economic interests in sylvan garb – and, importantly, signals that it is but one of a multiplicity of communities thus paternally blessed. What applies there applies much more widely, in other words, to most if not all other "charming and fairly expensive" (4) socially constructed places; it may serve, the text has discreetly insinuated, as a specimen suburb. A subsequent, less subtle narratorial comment hints more baldly at socioeconomic determinants in observing interpretively that "No man owns a house because he really wants a house," and Pepper Street's residents live there "because they were able to afford it, and none of them would have lived there if he had been able to afford living elsewhere" (3).

As the narrative progresses and episodic glimpses of convivial individuals and families accrete, the pattern established in the initial paragraph is repeated and amplified. While the reader is on one level encouraged to imagine the community as a harmonious social entity, a counteractive undertow of suggestions emerges to indicate that the neighborhood's cohesiveness and sense of communal identity are at best transitory and frail because impersonal forces determine where and how individuals reside. The most emphatic indication is a lengthy narratorial aside strategically situated at the approximate midpoint of the text. It announces that a great transformation of the literal and social structures of the area is imminent: the wall enclosing the adjoining "estate" is to be altered so that an apartment block may be constructed. As will be discussed ahead, the alterations are portentous for the residents of Pepper Street. Of significance here, however, is the narrative's concern to ensure the reader's awareness of the economic imperatives that condition the lives of those who "called themselves upright American citizens" (180). If the lives of their forefathers had been "quietly governed" for them by forces of nature, such as the sky and the earthworm, modernity has created

> other unseen governors: the prices in a distant town, regulated by minds and hungers in a town even farther away, all the possessions which depended on someone in another place, someone who controlled words and paper and ink, and who could by the changing of a word on paper influence the very texture of the ground.
>
> (178–79)

Such impersonal governors – such *governance*, more precisely – require that the very "hungers" of citizens be regulated for the sake of prices in that distant town. "Even the very chair on which Mr. Desmond sat in the evenings," we are told, "belonged to him on sufferance . . . and Mr. Desmond, although he had not known it, had chosen it because it had been presented to him as completely choosable" (179). The passage rattles on in similar vein, echoing Veblen's turn-of-the-century notion of "conspicuous consumption" as well as anticipating in some degree William H. Whyte's conception of the "organization man." From an aesthetic standpoint it seems somewhat intrusive, a brief jeremiad that distracts attention from the characters and their interactions. Its import, though, has thereby been amplified: the residents of all the Pepper Streets, all the middle-class suburban communities of America, are hardly more than counters to be manipulated and shifted as deemed necessary or desirable for the sake of profit. And under such conditions, community in the traditional sense, which values stability, permanence, and neighborly affiliation, is not a viable possibility.

Even so, the narrative suggests in various ways that the impression of a latter-day village community offered in the early pages is not entirely without foundation. A certain amount of sociable activity does take place: street games played by teenagers and children provoke occasional amicable conversations between onlooking adults; some of the wives meet weekly in different homes for a chatty sewing circle; the most respected man in the neighborhood conceives a plan to involve the street's youngsters in a drama group; a neighborhood garden party promotes a mood of camaraderie among those who attend and drink freely; and most significantly, the everyday familiarity enforced by residences situated in close proximity to one another leads, in several instances, to the striking up of friendships. It is largely the neighborhood's young people whose interactions create a semblance of communal feeling. The kids and adolescents often gather on the street, in pairs or larger groupings. Their games and group activities are derived, it is implied, from an atavistic desire to coalesce into an assemblage wherein individual autonomy may be justifiably rendered subordinate to the claims of the larger group. An evening of "tag and hide-and-seek and long involved games with a line across the street from curb to curb and elaborate systems of bases and penalties," for example, is said to involve the playing out of "some ancient ritual of capture and pursuit" (38). The point is conveyed emphatically in a subsequent episode that sees several of the children playing a word game called "Tin-Tin":

> Tin-Tin is probably as old as children. . . . Wherever children congregate they will probably have their own version of Tin-Tin, its elaborate ritual determined by the children and their fathers and their grandfathers operating individually on an immutable theme. Pepper Street's Tin-Tin was as nonsensical as most; the entire introductory ritual had lost its meaning and probably its accompanying dance.
>
> (138)

This musing narratorial comment, tellingly digressive, stresses the nonsensicality of the game, even while imputing to it residual traces of a meaning that is immutable, although long forgotten or possibly sublimated. The apparent contradiction hints at the significance of Tin-Tin and games similar to it: their rituals, irrespective of meanings forgotten, instill in each participant a sense of the rudiments of their communal association. Tin-Tin involves the assigning to each player of a secret nonsense name that is subsequently disclosed to all in response to an interrogation process that sanctions "any personal or outrageous or hilarious question." There are, the game instructs, rules that must be complied with and patterns that must be adhered to rigorously, and expressions of individuality are encouraged but closely monitored. "The whole procedure," the narrator goes on to observe, "filled some deep undefined need in neighborhood life" (139). Like the lottery in the famous story, if less brutal, the "procedure" is a bonding ritual whose original significance has been forgotten but which calls unto the neighborhood *as* a neighborhood.

Those few commentators who have analyzed *The Road Through the Wall* at any length have found in the text's presentation of the community's pastoral pleasantness an underlying "Edenic" myth of innocence (and ultimately innocence lost). This is the reading advanced by Joan Wylie Hall, who extracts from the narrative's occasional references to gardens and dying plants an implicit metaphorical reference to the Garden of Eden and its "fall": "The dying flowers and the crushed grass of this first novel speak unmistakably of the loss of the innocence of Eden" (269). The effect, and the stated intent, of this reading is to de-emphasize the novel's sociohistorical context and foreground rather a "more universal" (263) thrust. But the textual justification for inferring an "Eden" metaphor is speculative at best, as there are no explicit references to the Old Testament story, and the biblical Eden was hardly, in any meaningful sense, a community as well as a garden. Pepper Street's garden-like environs and its appearance of communal harmony hark back rather to a different mythicized historical site that is implicitly alluded to by the children's games, and explicitly signaled in subsequent portions of the narrative: the preindustrial village. In the most significant such passage, thirteen-year-old Marilyn Perlman confides to her newfound friend Harriet Merriam her cherished daydream fantasy of a former life. "'I *know* who I was'" (152), she tells her closest friend, and on being pressed for details she conjures up an idyllic "village green" community within which her own individuality was assured, as well as her sense of group affiliation. In part it is a reverie designed to render in greater depth the personality of the dreamily introspective character who articulates it. Marilyn, sensitive and different, occupies a rather tenuous position among her peers in the neighborhood. Yet it is clear that the narrative accords Marilyn, by virtue of her sensitivity, a degree of imaginative clairvoyance lacking in most of the other characters. Thus, while her friend's corresponding fantasy of a past incarnation as a bejeweled Egyptian priestess is given only cursory narrative attention and is openly deflated by the narrator's catty observation that she is "trying to look inspired" (154), Marilyn's vision of a prior incarnation is recounted in lengthy, respectful detail:

> "I *remember*," Marilyn said emphatically. "I really do." Her voice became softer, as though she were describing a scene familiar and lovely. "There's a very *very* blue sky, and the hills and grass are so green they almost hurt your eyes and the road is white and it curves around the hill and there are flowers and trees and everything is so *soft-looking*, and far away beyond the hill you can see where the road leads into a little town. . . . I can see the town, too," she added, never looking at Harriet. "It has houses with low roofs and a bridge over a little river and all the houses are white and they have brown wood trimmings and there's a village green in the center of the town."
>
> (153)

The implication is that she envisions, with almost mystical second sight, the pastoral paradigm that subliminally informs the modern suburban imagination. When she further elaborates upon her vision, the static scene is activated into a lively scenario in which an approaching *commedia dell'arte* troupe becomes the town's populace. And the spectacle of Pantaloon and the rest, stock characters who traditionally exemplify diverse personality types, "talking and laughing and singing" in evident enjoyment of the company of one another (153), encourages the previously distant dreamer, not a popular child in her actual neighborhood, to come running toward them in exhilarating anticipation of being welcomed and invited to join in. In the embracing softness of that town there is only *commedia*, because there is no sense of divisive Otherness – only a subsuming acceptance of individual peculiarities.

The full significance of Marilyn's reverie doesn't become apparent until the closing portions of the novel, which recount the efforts of the people of Pepper Street to band together collectively in accordance with a shared sense of purpose. As the garden party enters its dying stage, it is discovered that three-year-old Caroline Desmond is missing and has not been sighted for hours. When subsequent hasty searches fail to locate her, a sense of crisis settles upon the neighborhood, and the neighbors gather, "almost everyone, on what was traditionally their forgotten village green – the sidewalk in front of the Donald house" (252). The ground underfoot is asphalt, not a greensward, and like the meanings of the street games the significance of a village green has been largely lost to communal memory;

only the dreamy Marilyn can still summon it to the forefront of consciousness. On occasion even so, as though in response to a pattern deeply engrained in an inaccessible but influential region of their psyches, these suburbanites may assemble on its nearest contemporary equivalent, the quiet street. The "occasion" related in the novel turns grim, with implications to be explored ahead. But the horrible nature of the incident should not obscure the fundamental point that the suburbanites' sporadic displays of community spirit derive from an atavistic and never entirely subdued impulse to reside communally as well as domestically.

Enviable privacy

Increasingly, as marketplace-oriented modernity has its way, the allure of the forgotten village green in the modern suburban unconscious is more than counterbalanced by the desire to inhabit another dimly remembered preindustrial social site, that of the medieval landed "estate." The desire for a grand and secure domain of one's own points away from the public concourse. Where the image of the village green is suggestive of openness and (to a degree) of egalitarian commonality, that of the estate signifies triumphant individuality and autocratic exclusiveness to the point of regal isolation. There are in the novel's "Cabrillo" actual estates – of a sort. The narrative is careful to specify that the town is situated upon formerly secure class and ethnic borderlines that are in the process of being redefined. In the period between the two World Wars – the novel is set in 1936 – the suburbanization movement in the United States that would accelerate greatly in the post–World War II era was beginning to burgeon, for many previously discrete towns not far from cities had become satellite residential communities (Beauregard 41–42). Cabrillo is presented as a virtual case study of such a town in that period of transition. Formerly a locale in which the very wealthy resided in magnificent mansions bounded by private parklands – a classic nineteenth-century suburb, in other words – it has recently broadened its social base to incorporate a number of middle-class families of more ordinary means, as well as a few lower-class residents. It is located "perhaps thirty miles from San Francisco . . . halfway between a suburban development and a collection of large private estates" (9) on a main highway that leads to the city.

"Fairly expensive" (4) Pepper Street, where houses were constructed in the recent past on property originally encompassed by a large nearby estate, is "on the borderline between these two" (19). The young neighborhood's position ensures that it is possessed of what is termed, in a key phrase, "an enviable privacy" (9–10), in that it is "rarely troubled with invasions" (10) from the nearby main highway. In stressing the degree to which the area affords its occupants a high degree of such privacy, the text insinuates that a desire to be insulated from the diverse urban population of America partly motivated the quite recent migrations to Pepper Street. Therefore, for example, an encounter between two teenage girls and an "excellently dressed" (68) Chinese man points toward racist attitudes that underlie the residents' cheery communal interactions. After accepting his invitation to tea, they are surprised when he tells them that the apartment isn't his. "'Not in this neighborhood,'" he tells them; "'They wouldn't rent an apartment to me'" (116). The girls' relative obliviousness of the racism endemic to the area is an indication of its ideological unobtrusiveness in the larger society. Clearly, it is a powerful social undercurrent that is not often acknowledged openly as such. Contrastingly, the belief that those engaged in menial occupations are lower orders in the fullest sense is a very prominent aspect of the community's set of shared assumptions and values. When the man further explains that he works in the apartment as a servant, the girls are appalled at having socialized with "help" and depart abruptly. Further underscoring the implication that such shared ethnic and class bigotry is rife in the community is the treatment, both in behavior and gossipy innuendo, directed by several of the street's social stalwarts at a Jewish family, at two lower-class families who inhabit (sequentially) a frowned-upon "house-for-rent," and at serving girls who work in one of the middle-class households. The neighborhood strives to perpetuate and refine its status as an enclave reserved for white middle-class citizens, and members of nonmainstream subgroups are regarded as potential advance agents of invasions from the main highway.

The enclave mentality that enshrines privacy as a sacred right in the neighborhood and, by implication, the entire town and many others like it is operative in relation to an even more circumscribed area, that of the individual residential site. The reputedly witchlike behavior of the street's oldest resident, "crazy old Mrs. Mack" (5), presents a parodic extreme of the widely shared obsession with defining one's house and its immediate environs as an exclusive private fiefdom. Mrs. Mack sees almost no one, and the children of the neighborhood believe that she spends all day in her home "peering out at them through the boarded-up windows, putting spells on anyone who entered her yard" (87). The spells aren't known ever to have harmed anyone at whom they were directed, but they do achieve their purpose of reinforcing neighborhood respect for the property line that demarcates Mrs. Mack's territorial imperative. The aim of asserting domain over a separate home site in a "nice" area composed of many such is to establish the right to hex away, at will, any intruders – even when the latter are your neighbors and class peers. It is decidedly not village green behavior.

While crazy old Mrs. Mack simply wishes to establish territorial domain in order to banish the surrounding community totally, most of her neighbors face a more complicated challenge. Modern suburbanites must achieve a similar though less extreme result by inhabiting homes that are at once attractive and exclusionary. Important though it is to secure the home against invasion, the irony implicit in the phrase "enviable privacy" is that privacy thus ensured has become an enshrined mode of exhibitionism. The walls and hedges and lawns of the nicer homes on Pepper Street serve not only as obstructions to public scrutiny but also as fetishistic inducements to it. Passersby are meant to notice grounds and facades in order to behold the elegant secretiveness that veils from full view the internal space of familial and personal intimacy. Thus the prologue's house-by-house survey of the Pepper Street community subtly specifies the extent of visual exclusiveness afforded most of the residences, in the forms of fences, facades, lawns, and gardens, and calibrates the degree to which commodified privacy has been effectively flaunted by each. Next to Mrs. Mack's house, for example, "successfully hid" by an orchard, is the rented residence of the Byrne family, a "recent regrettable pink stucco" (5). The Roberts family, situated economically somewhere between the Byrnes and the more affluent Desmonds, inhabits a house "thickly surrounded with bushes which were inadequate to disguise the fact that the roof was colonial, the windows modern, and the whole a gaudy yellow" (5). They are of relatively modest means, so cannot (or do not know how to) conceal their shameful vulgar taste more than partially from the prying eyes of passersby. By contrast, it is the Desmond family who, above all, instantiate the socially endorsed aspiration to be conspicuously private. Theirs is the quintessential modern middle-class suburban house – one that is "designed," as Catherine Jurca phrases it, "to manufacture one's credentials for inhabiting it" (36). They are "the aristocracy of the neighborhood" and their impressive home, "richly jeweled with glass brick" (4), is simultaneously eye-catching and opaquely resistant to fully effective gazing. Its privacy teases.

The desirable higher state of splendorous private space would be residence in what Mr. Desmond envisions for his children in the not too distant future: "a house not visible from the street" (72). An enormous expanse of pastoral terrain between the household and the public area, more effective by far as both impediment and display than are walls constructed of glass bricks, is the exceptionally coy exhibitionism reserved for the very affluent – an "arrogant veil of gated privacy" (12), as Baxandall and Ewen concisely put it. And it is such a site of discreetly advertised privacy that the neighborhood beyond the tall brick wall represents to Pepper Street residents. Significantly, the wall's importance is purely symbolic, for it is not a literal barrier to access; there is a gated entry, but the gates are "square piles of brick . . . with no bars between." Nonetheless, it is regarded by all on Pepper Street as a venerable socioeconomic borderline that is not to be transgressed: "an effective end to Pepper Street life" (11), for the exclusiveness signified by the wall, while it elicits middle-class envy, is felt not as an affront but as a source of inspiration, pride, and security. Proximity to it engenders in some of the street's residents a belief in their own capacity to relocate someday within the elite neighborhood, but even those who entertain no such aspiration appear to regard the adjacent buildings and grounds subconsciously as grandly proportioned images of their own domestic sites. This is explicitly said to be so of the Merriam home, "modeled originally after someone's grandfather's manor-house" (9), but it clearly pertains to others, at least figuratively. The privacy that is held to be enviable and worthy of emulation is infused with the romantic aura of a social configuration derived from preindustrial times that lingers in modernity's appropriation of the term "estate." Kate Flint has observed that the connotations of "suburb" in modern times have included "buying oneself . . . into the tradition and culture of the aristocracy," even for homeowners of modest means. As one 1920s suburbanite cited by Flint reflected, "'We felt like we were living rich in miniature'" (114).

It is not commodity fetishism solely that motivates the public displays of affluence common in upscale suburban areas such as Pepper Street, however. The widely prevalent feeling of affiliation with the more exclusive nearby neighborhood is insinuated strikingly in the reaction of an elderly resident, Mr. Martin, to news of a planned demolition of the wall and concomitant redevelopment of a portion of the grounds presently enclosed by it into a new apartment block:

> [O]nce the wall was broken into, the fields of the estate, the sacred enclosed place which harbored the main house, the garages, the tennis court and the terraced gardens as well as Mr. Martin's greenhouses, would be exposed to intrusions from the outside world, perhaps small boys with stones, perhaps curious trespassers gathering flowers, perhaps all those people with large feet who trample down tiny growing things.
>
> (185)

In his senility, Mr. Martin blurs the distinction between his own modest domain and the much grander one on the other side of the wall. The significance of his reverie of vicarious possession must be understood in the light of a further point of confusion that the text subtly indicates. Mr. Martin envisions an "estate" in the original, premodern sense of the term, which denotes a large landed property dominated by a mansion, rather than the modern derivation, which refers to an upmarket suburban housing development. Early in the novel it is made clear, however, that a substantial portion of the "large estate" that once encompassed the property on both sides of the wall "had been sold off lot by lot" (10). Subsequently, even though the exclusive neighborhood is still referred to as an "estate," with connotations derived from the older usage, there is no longer one main house presided over by one wealthy family: it has become (although the term is never specifically invoked) a prestigious and expensive "housing estate." Where formerly there was the venerable oneness of an aristocratic domestic model, there is now plutocratic plurality.

And plurality is itself debilitating in Mr. Martin's mind. The "enclosed spaces" of modern households and communities are "sacred" primarily insofar as they look inward upon themselves. The only communality that is sacred begins and ends at home, and in the extreme consists in monadic isolation and differentiation even from one's neighbors. As Kenneth T. Jackson has argued, from its beginnings in the nineteenth century the suburban movement imbued even the most modest of houses with "the values once accorded only the ancestral house, establishing it as the temporary representation of the ideal permanent home" (51). Those middle-class houses may mimic the trappings of wealth by way of material display in varying ways and degrees, as we've seen. But their most valued attributes are those of "permanence," or the appearance of such, and – perhaps more importantly – "detachment" from the wider society, as Peter G. Rowe suggests when he observes that "the dominant feature in the American middle landscape is the single-family home. No other artifact is as pervasive or carries the same emotional charges as the detached house in its suburban garden" (67). Modern suburbs, howsoever smitten with nostalgic references to neighborly village living, are checkerboard agglomerations of manifestly detached and inward-looking households. With or without the showy trappings of a miniature manor house, they pointedly advertise their detachment.

That is why Mr. Martin doesn't wish to acknowledge that the original estate has already been torn apart and reconfigured, albeit into lesser facsimiles of itself: it represents not merely wealth and privilege but also the impregnable integrity of a stronghold. The vision of small boys with stones, and of trespassers who might pick some flowers or walk on one's lawn, seems an unlikely catalyst for grave foreboding; such petty transgressions of territorial imperative are to be expected in any small neighborhood community that functions as such. But the redevelopment portended by the destruction of the wall brings with it the probability of even *more* "neighborhood" in the modern sense: more demographic diversity, higher population density, and the disruptiveness of an economy that feeds on the "disregarding abandoned battering tearing-apart of things permanent" (186) in order to convert them into marketable real estate. If the nearest concrete embodiment of the prevailing residential dream has fallen victim to disruptive social and economic forces, the prospect for one's own home site appears to be bleak. Demolition and fragmentation seem, literally, to be just around the corner. But the point is less that the homes of people such as Mr. Martin are to become more vulnerable to redevelopment schemes in the area than that the mere introduction of the possibility of change renders faith in "things permanent" – such as enclave households and holistic small communities with village green mentalities – untenable: "what with tearing down walls and selling land, who could tell what would follow?" (186).

Barbarity and dirt: Privacy transgressed

Although the old man's excessively grim forebodings may not precisely reflect the feelings of other Pepper Street residents, it is clear that his distress over the impending destruction of the wall is in some degree shared by most of them. In articulating the community's reaction to the news, the narrator employs rhetoric and imagery suggestive of a doomsday scenario: "a breach was to be made in the northern boundary of the world. Barbarian hordes were to be unleashed on Pepper Street" (180). Apprehensiveness about the construction of the "road through the wall" of the novel's title takes the form, initially, of irritation with the dust raised by the demolition process. "The idea that placid Pepper Street was being deformed by workmen and dirt and great foul machines was almost as bad," the narrator observes, "as the prospect of being shortly on a direct road with the rest of the world" (185). Neighborhood outsiders, and class or ethnic Others, are particularly to be shunned, for their strangeness is extremely apparent, and may rub off the more readily. A dirty street presages a body politic befouled, because when the literal dust has settled, the socioeconomic defilement is likely to commence in earnest. The immediate threat is that more barbarians – more workmen, more outsiders, more class and ethnic Others – may be on the way. But greater numbers of residents of any kind whatever augur badly. On Pepper Street, as we've seen, social interaction, even with likeminded neighbors, is to be engaged in only fastidiously and diffidently, for in varying degrees all who are Other in even the most basic sense are barbarians, invasive foreign particles, "dirt." The community's presentiment of all that impinging, discomfiting, sweating multiplicity construes it as barbaric otherness sufficient to "put the first wedge into the Pepper Street security, [a security] so fragile that, once jarred, it shivered into fragments in a matter of weeks" (182).

The fragility of "Pepper Street security" is a measure of the degree to which the community valorizes insularity and homogeneity at all levels: communal, domestic, and personal. Security thus rigidly conceived is an inherently precarious state in a community that is not wealthy enough to construct homes so distant from the public thoroughfare that neither neighborhood nor household can be a world utterly unto itself. Nonetheless, the prevailing, if unattainable, domestic ideal is to remain emotionally chaste, unaffected by social intercourse, and the exemplary family in this regard is, predictably, the Desmonds. Their high status, evident, as discussed earlier, in their showy house, is even more apparent in the care they lavish upon their golden-haired three-year-old daughter. A much-admired child who is never seen to interact with any of the other children, Caroline is kept immaculately clean by her obsessive mother. When a lower-class seven-year-old girl from the street's so-called rented house presses upon Caroline the gift of a "grimy rag doll," Mrs. Desmond hastens her daughter home for a wash (84). And when workmen arrive in the neighborhood to demolish the wall, the dust thereby aroused compels Mrs. Desmond to change Caroline into clean clothes three or four times a day and eventually to move to a summer resort until the street work is completed.

But more is implied by the adulation of the pristine Caroline than the prevailing communal attitude toward class hierarchy and the desire to maintain an impermeable boundary between the privileged and those less advantageously positioned. Just as Mrs. Mack's sense of territorial imperative indicates fear and loathing of all outsiders, irrespective of their class affiliations, Mrs. Desmond's efforts to isolate Caroline's body within a virtual halo derive from a distaste for personal contact with anyone – anyone at all! In the extreme, physical cleanliness signifies not only class or ethnic superiority but also a state of inviolate self-containment that seems all but metaphysical. When Mrs. Desmond's acquaintances in the sewing circle refer to Caroline as an "angel," it seems more than a casual term of endearment. Caroline's purity does not connote Christian sanctity or even Victorian innocence so much as social virginity. She is viewed as an especially rarefied being because her appearance suggests that, throughout the charmed course of her early childhood, contact with persons outside her household has been minimal and has left no lasting impression. Certainly no dust raised by contact with class or ethnic Others who inhabit "the rest of the world" beyond Pepper Street has tarnished her angelic composure, and neither has she been affected in any discernible manner by contact with her peers. Neighboring Hallie Martin, nine years old, has become accustomed to feeling herself to be "lean and dirty and wet-faced" upon sighting the "little and delicate and clean" Caroline. In an early incident, Hallie is seen to be aware that were she to stand outside the Desmond yard, Mrs. Desmond would "come out on the side porch to sit quietly until Hallie was gone away; if

Hallie stayed Mrs. Desmond would finally take Caroline indoors" (31). That is why, sensing such an attitude on the part of Mrs. Desmond, and fearing that the immaculate Caroline may almost be the superior creature that her appearance is fashioned to embody, Hallie then wanders down the street, saying to herself, "old Caroline wets her pants" (31). To the resentful earthling an angel sullied is an appealing thought, the articulation of which, even inaudibly, may besmirch the luminous being with telltale commonness.

The association of dirt with debasing personal contact resonates with a closely related concern in the novel: the interrogation of the notion of what is "dirty" in the familiar slang sense of the term that connotes sexual vileness. An early series of episodes focuses upon the neighborhood's scandalized reaction to the revelation that among several of the schoolgirls there has been, recently, a fad for composing love letters to local boys. Although the text makes it clear that in most cases the activity is not indicative of sexual precocity, the responses of some of the parents and one of the boys suggest that they presume otherwise. Of particular significance is the fretfully antagonistic behavior of fourteen-year-old Pat Byrne toward his younger sister Mary: "'You cut out all this dirty stuff,' Pat said. He put his face close to his sister's and said again almost helplessly. 'You just *cut it out*, that's all'" (30).

Pat has been receiving letters from his own sister, a comical indication of her unawareness of the construction that might be placed on what she has been doing. Only twelve years old and swept along by the tide of peer group enthusiasm orchestrated by an older and more knowing teenager who lives down the street, she, like the others, is motivated by a desire for the feeling of group affiliation that derives from engaging in such a clandestine activity. Her brother's squeamishness about this innocuous fantasy game reflects the society's attitude toward sexuality or anything even faintly connoting it. Even the mere thought of sex has the power to befoul and humiliate anyone it brushes against.

While Caroline incarnates purity, another child comes to embody dirtiness. The association of sexual desire and dirt is established most strikingly in an episode in which thirteen-year-old Tod Donald, whose alleged personal deficiencies have established him as a pariah among the children in the neighborhood, sneaks into the Desmond home while its inhabitants are away. In a protracted act of voyeurism he investigates various rooms in the house, and the climactic phase of his trespass occurs when he ventures into the bedroom shared by the mother and daughter, both of whom he reveres. To Tod's young male imagination the softly textured chamber with its curtains gently stirring is a space that exudes feminine softness, delicacy, and beauty; it is "so pretty that even the presence of Mrs. Desmond would have been superfluous" (93). An "overpoweringly sweet" whiff of some perfume he has dabbed on himself then renders that impression so palpable that he finds himself creeping into her clothes closet:

> Half-shutting the closet door behind him, he wormed his way in through Mrs. Desmond's dresses and negligees until he reached the most hidden part of the closet, and he sat down on the floor, his perfumed hand over his face.

There, far back in the closet in Mrs. Desmond's room, he said, quite loudly, all the dirtiest words he knew.

(95)

Tod's behavior in this instance is that of an adolescent boy who is confused about sexual longings that have no socially acceptable outlet even on the verbal level. Unmistakably, he is simulating a transgressive sexual act. Yet, while striking, the sexual implication of his verbal ejaculations in the "most hidden part" of a feminine enclosed space is secondary in significance to what the incident implies about his need to impress something of himself upon Mrs. Desmond. He articulates words intended to demystify her as a living incarnation of pristine, insular selfhood by chanting it into a state as base as that which he believes his own to be, and thus to render her assailable.

On the intimately personal level no less than on the domestic and social levels, then, enviable privacy deters transgression even while coyly inciting it. The metonymic paradigm is in this instance distinctly gendered and sexual. But the text's primary concern is not to suggest that all amorous negotiations between men and women conform to a pattern in which the female is passive and the male is aggressive; the schoolgirl love letter affair is one of a number of incidents in which conventional notions of gender behavior are at least partly overturned. The significance of Tod's desire to violate Mrs. Desmond's personal space is not simply sexual but, so to speak, residential. The important implication is that the conventional conception of male-female romantic interplay, which projects female virtue as an insular state that arouses male desire for transgressive contact, encodes society's dominant model for communal, familial, and personal fulfillment: triumphant occupancy. Suburb, home, self, and even body constitute, in this vision, areas within which insularity flourishes by flaunting itself and proclaiming its imperviousness to invaders who are filth-ridden with their Otherness.

Bonding ritual: The "stoning" of Tod Donald

In the narrative's climactic sequence of events the figures of Caroline and Tod, embodying respectively the idealized insider and the despised domestic outsider, insularity and transgressiveness, purity and dirt, are positioned in sharp contrast to one another. Often rejected and mocked by the other children, Tod has been the neighborhood's domestic pariah throughout the novel. Earlier the narrative has recounted incidents in which the harsh treatment meted out to him by other children has provoked in return aggressive efforts to gain attention. On one occasion, for example, in order to attract notice he throws stones at another child in full view of a group that has been treating him with unconcealed contempt. Therefore it is no surprise when the spreading awareness of the disappearance of Caroline at the neighborhood party causes suspicion to gravitate toward the dirty little nuisance despised by all. Residents' ordinarily dominant inclinations to retreat into the private strongholds of home and self as the party winds down are set aside, but less out of concern for the missing child than because the occasion has provided them with an experience of shared exhilaration: "The prevailing mood was one of keen excitement; no one there really wanted Caroline Desmond safe at home" (253–54). Death, or serious harm to an innocent child, is in the offing – and the communal impulse, catalyzed by the prospect of shared horror, is reinvigorated. Subliminally, at least, the community is willing to sacrifice even its most iconic insider – as well as, even more readily, her somewhat despised antithesis. There is a touch of mob frenzy in the responses of this polite modern neighborhood. In the impressionable eyes of the frightened Frederica, a teenager of extremely marginal status on the street as she lives in its one rented house,

> The people in the street . . . had gathered closer together so that it was impossible to single out any one of them . . . [T]hey were so close together that there were no names for any of their faces, and the hands might be clasped tight in the hands of strangers.
>
> (257)

Thus it is that, on a village green summoned for a short time from the otherwise forgetful collective unconscious, insular modern suburbanites affiliate into a semblance of leveling, blanketing crowd anonymity. Pressure is brought to bear upon the homegrown agent of subversion and pollution by the residents' adrenalin-charged closing of ranks. They do not have to stone Tod literally, as their counterparts in "The Lottery" do to their annually designated victims. It is enough that he be made to squirm with shame and fear. An extensive search of the area finds Caroline's dead body in a ravine that is sometimes incorporated into the play activities of neighborhood children, and a bloodstained nearby rock is taken as evidence that she has been murdered, and probably violated. (Significantly, "No-one had ever seen Caroline as dirty as she was then" [258].) The prevailing suspicion is then fueled by another youngster's account of a visit paid him by a strangely behaving Tod somewhat earlier. When Tod finally does return home, after having hidden for a while in incredulous awareness that most of the neighborhood's residents were out in the night looking for him, he is interrogated by an intimidating policeman in whom he sees several other authority figures – a dentist, a doctor, "the man at the movie theater who wanted to know how old you were before he let you in for half price" – who have had the power to make him feel tarnished with sin. Insinuating interrogation by the policeman reactivates the rejection anxiety he has been subjected to throughout his childhood. And subsequently, left alone for nearly an hour under harsh instruction to "think about all this" (263), he hangs himself to death with a piece of clothesline.

As though openly reflecting the impression given by the narrative's positioning of the incident – it is related near the end of the novel – the policeman's response is a "great, gusty breath" of closure: "'Well . . . that settles *that*'" (263). And so it seems to, superficially, for as shown earlier, the reader has been primed to suspect strange little Tod and therefore to endorse the swelling communal verdict. While the narrative treatment of the closet incident is itself coolly sympathetic in tone, encouraging understanding of Tod's emotionally malnourished nature rather than dismissiveness or condemnation, what the climactic episode reveals seems in keeping with an incriminating behavioral pattern observable throughout the rest of the novel: he is an unhappy boy, not entirely in control of himself, and capable of forcible entry into, and desecration of, spaces deemed private. It seems particularly telling that upon exiting the Desmond home, Tod had plucked a blossom in the garden and crushed it in his hand "cruelly" (96).

Yet, while the circumstantial case against Tod appears compelling, in its concluding paragraphs the narrative expends considerable effort upon the raising of serious doubts about the verdict it had seemed previously to encourage. A conversation between Mr. Merriam and Mr. Perlman that takes place not long after the double tragedy, but long enough for the collective fervor to have dissipated and residents to reflect and respond as individuals, reveals that each has some doubts about the grounds for assuming that Tod was a murderer. And in a separate exchange Mrs. Byrne informs Mrs. Merriam of her son Pat's conjecture that Caroline wasn't assaulted but had fallen and hit her head fatally against a nearby rock, thereby panicking an accompanying Tod into his suspiciously evasive behavior. By the novel's end the matter remains murky. Nothing is said that exonerates Tod resoundingly, but neither is his guilt confirmed, or even rendered more probable than not. His suicide may or may not amount to a tacit confession on his part; possibly it signifies nothing more than his sad, passive-aggressive acceptance of his status as the neighborhood pariah. What is beyond doubt, however, is the implication that the sensational public spectacle of his death, and that of Caroline, has had a catalytic effect on the neighborhood. Normally diffident street residents had joined together to engage in guilty pleasures – voyeurism and scapegoating – and thereby thought and acted, for a brief while, as an old-fashioned community, a village, rather than a mere agglomeration of autonomous and discrete individuals.

The Road Through the Wall thus shares with "The Lottery" a vision of a small community in which the sanctioned victimization of designated domestic Others persists. To a significant degree, the figurative stoning of Tod parallels the literal stoning of Tess Hutchinson: both are village insiders turned Other so that the community can reinvigorate its sense of bondedness. In the novel, however, victimization is not ritualized or bound to a single calendar date, nor is it overtly violent. In most instances it takes the form of hurtful gossip and innuendo and, at times, exclusionary practices. Among the neighborhood's adult residents there is much demeaning of workers, menial help, and members of marginalized religious and ethnic groups; and their children are constantly on the alert for signs of weakness or Otherness in any of their number so that taunting and shaming may be crudely rationalized. What is most unsettling about both the story and the novel is their insinuation that communality is reinforced by the willingness of people who are in most respects peaceable, whatever their other petty failings, to persecute one of their own. For this reason, the claims of some commentators that these two narratives expose something amorphously metaphysical, such as the "wickedness in human nature" or "evil [that] lies within the human heart" (Murphy 19), fail to grasp the perhaps more unsettling implication that such acts of communal persecution are perpetrated by entrenched impersonal patterns of behavior that may be fundamental to the very process of social aggregation; individuals, as individuals, have very little control over their actions. Therefore the stoning in "The Lottery" elicits cruel acts from the crowd as a collective entity, but there is no indication that malicious impulses impel any of the townspeople as individuals; it is telling that even as the stoning commences there is nothing frenzied in their behavior. Similarly, while what happens to Tod in *The Road Through the Wall* exposes the readiness of the neighborhood residents to permit emotional pain to be inflicted through the sanctioned cruelty of its young, there is no indication that his violent end is what they had foreseen, desired, or required. For all their pettiness and narrow-mindedness, most of them are not cruelly inclined; they are modern suburbanites pursuing their separate paths who yet retain a desire for the rallying sensation of being a collectivity. They welcome the opportunity to participate in a faint, *ad hoc* approximation of the traditional village bonding ritual in which a designated Other is rendered *persona non grata*, even unto death.

The bonding experience in *The Road Through the Wall* differs significantly from that in "The Lottery," however, in that its effect is superficial and fleeting. The village in "The Lottery" seems not merely stable but also classless. There is not an estate to be seen in the vicinity of their village and none is referred to, and its inhabitants seem content with their small democratic polity. By contrast, the hierarchically minded people of Pepper Street appear to sense that their suburban street is a makeshift fabrication of community at best, a way station for some who are rising and an enclave for others who have nowhere better to relocate. The neighborhood is an unstable social compound and has been from the start. The closing portions of the novel mute the impact and significance of the deaths of the two children by highlighting the community's impermanence and social fragility. Several families are said to have moved away not long after the tragic block party, but not, with the exception of the Desmonds, in consequence of it. The emigrations of families and individuals are simply integral to the contemporary order of things; "from the 1940s to the 1970s," James T. Patterson has noted, "roughly 20 percent of Americans changed residence every year" (66). In quest of the showy veneer of stability, Jackson's suburbanites are ever willing to disrupt their lives by relocating. Though they are desirous of the aura of permanency associated with the village green and the landed estate, their veneration of antique social arrangements and institutions is belied by their reclusiveness and Sisyphean restiveness. Eventually the enlarged road through the wall is completed, signifying the transition to what will be a much altered neighborhood, but one that will be no more socially stable than it had ever been. Before a year has passed, the new pavement laid down in the reconfigured street betrays its inherent mutability (and by extension that of the community) despite one young citizen's effort to establish, in time-honored kid fashion, a transcendent connection with other eyes and future generations: "A wide break appeared in the sidewalk the first winter, near the spot where Jamie Roberts had left the print of his hand in the fresh cement" (271). What happened to Caroline and Tod, and the bonding effect it had on the residents, is in the process of becoming just as vague as the impression of Jamie's hand.

Yet the implication of the novel's closing pages is not merely that, as Catherine Jurca observes in her study of the suburb in modern fiction, "in the postwar period suburban house ownership and transiency were more frequently aligned than opposed" (145). The narrative's dispassionate account of the aftermath of the partial diaspora that transforms the neighborhood also highlights the suggestions advanced throughout the text that powerful, if obscure, socioeconomic forces dominate the lives of modern suburbanites. In the end, it is primarily the gnawing of estate envy and the marketplace mentality underlying it, not a battering influx of barbarians from the highway, that have rendered the traditional village green but a dimly remembered anachronistic model for the community. In *The Organization Man*, the classic study of middle-class life that appeared a few years after *The Road Through the Wall*, William H. Whyte observed that "On the one hand suburbanites have a strong impulse toward egalitarianism; on the other, however, they have an equally strong impulse to upgrade themselves" (287). In Jackson's novel the egalitarian impulse is the weaker force, although still a factor. The desire of some to secure their holdings in a safe suburban stronghold and the aspirations of others to relocate to a grander, more conspicuously discreet gingerbread castle together provoke the shifting social alignments of modern America. Those who can better themselves proceed to own bigger; they migrate outward and upward. Those who cannot advance hold fast, ever more inclined to secure their households against the public concourse; they migrate, so to speak, inward. In either situation, the ideal has been, as Kenneth T. Jackson put it, "no longer to be part of a close community, but to have a self-contained unit, a private wonderland walled off from the rest of the world" (58). Thus has estate envy invaded the superficially reassuring confines of America's village green suburbias.

And it is upon that note, ironic rather than tragic or melodramatic, that *The Road Through the Wall* closes. In quest of stability and permanence, much of the middle class has embraced transiency as its de facto way of life. America ever aspires to be on the make and on the move – primarily because those aspirations have become commodified. Modernity has subordinated the community to the marketplace, nature to business, and individual agency to impersonal socioeconomic forces. Nothing could be farther from Marilyn's idealizing vision of a holistic small community in which everyone has a standing invitation to be welcomed and embraced than the modern suburban configuration, which, inherently prone to the "disregarding abandoned battering tearing-apart of things permanent," detaches, dislocates, and isolates.

These sobering implications are conveyed most strikingly at the end of the narrative by the curiously congruent fates of two reclusive elderly ladies – the hermetic Mrs. Mack, by reputation a witch to the children on the street, and the woman whose financial dealing has in actuality brought "ruin" of a sort to the superficially stable neighborhood. As noted earlier, the gnomic Old Testament mutterings of Mrs. Mack offer a vaguely metaphysical commentary on the changes besetting her small neighborhood and, by extension, middle-class American communities generally. Near the end of the narrative, she quotes verbatim from the *Book of Habakkuk* (2:9–12), intoning aloud:

> 'Woe to him . . . that coveteth an evil covetousness to his house, that he may set his nest on high, that he may be delivered from the power of evil! Thou hast consulted shame to thy house by cutting off many people, and hast sinned against thy soul. For the stone shall cry out of the wall, and the beam out of the timber shall answer it. Woe to him that buildeth a town with blood, and stablisheth [sic] a city by iniquity.'
>
> (269)

Unmistakably – albeit with the thundering vagueness of prophetic discourse – the passage refers to the recent happenings in the community in which a wall has been tampered with for the sake of covetousness. But its inflated rhetoric and moralistic excessiveness are strong indicators of its inapplicability, in other than a very general sense, to the actual social phenomena it decries – as is, of course, the fact that the only audience for Mrs. Mack's scriptural outpourings is her dog, for the text itself is no more impressed than that dog presumably is, having shown that the "town" that is Pepper Street was not built by blood or evil, but by high finance. Nor was it by the wider Cabrillo, or American suburbia generally, established by iniquity in the biblical sense, but rather by the impersonal workings of the capitalist marketplace that treats home sites as commodities and foists an isolating ethos of individualistic possessiveness upon those who inhabit them.

A living prophecy at variance with the rhetoric she invokes, Mrs. Mack's fate has been clear throughout: she will end her days in nutty privacy in her fiercely defended stronghold, a sad instantiation of suburbia's obsession with walling oneself within one's personal territorial imperative. But at the very end, with a terse closing paragraph, the narrative summons to the forefront of the reader's attention an even more striking embodiment of the socially bereft state of life in modern communities: the nameless property-owning old lady who personifies, so to speak, the depersonalizing ethos that dominates the newer ways of communal life. As dispassionate and economical as she herself had been in her socially disregardful real estate manipulations, the final sentences provide a purposively flat denouement to the novel: "The old lady who had owned the wall and the property it enclosed passed away very quietly in her sleep. No one was at her bedside when she died" (271). Significantly, she remains nameless, and very, very private – more "detached," even, than any of the residents and households whose "bedroomish arch" she and the forces that empower her have irretrievably disrupted. Her reappearance at the critical curtain-closing stage of the narrative seems somewhat incongruous, superficially, for she has not previously seemed an important figure. Subsequent to her brief appearance midway through the text she has gone unmentioned until the final paragraph. But the implication of her belated prominence is that she – or what she represents – has been, all along, the one "major character" in the novel, for socioeconomic agency, the power of the marketplace to effect events and affect people, is unobtrusive, impersonal, and uncaring. Her covert centrality is not eerie or evil or psychologically deranged, but simply a prosaic fact of contemporary society. She is no witch, but her well-hidden, callous power is, in its modern way, very spooky.

Notes

1 This generalization may appear to overlook Jackson's amusing prosaic treatments of middle-class family life that appeared in such mainstream venues as *The Saturday Evening Post*, *Reader's Digest*, and *Woman's Day*. These chronicles were "realistic" only in the sense that family situation comedies on radio and television widely popular in their time can be said to inhere in verisimilitude. They were not regarded as "serious" literature by Jackson herself, however, nor have they been treated as such by latter-day commentators.
2 One reading of the novel that appears to suggest otherwise was offered, if Jackson biographer Judy Oppenheimer is to be believed, by Shirley Jackson herself. Oppenheimer cites her as having asserted that everything she had written expressed her sense of "great forces of destruction, which may be the devil," and that *The Road Through the Wall* "stated this in miniature." Oppenheimer hasn't offered a more precise reference for the quotation other than to record that it is taken from an "unpublished statement ... for publisher's publicity use" in the Shirley Jackson archive at the Library of Congress. While the analysis of the novel offered in this essay should serve, I hope, as an effective refutation of that way of understanding it, I will note here that Jackson is notorious for having promoted herself as a "practicing amateur witch," which she undoubtedly believed was a more attention-getting persona to put before the reading public than that of a social realist. See Oppenheimer (125, 287).

Works cited

Baxandall, Rosalyn and Elizabeth Ewen. *Picture Windows: How the Suburbs Happened.* New York, NY: Basic Books, 2000. Print.
Beauregard, Robert A. *When America Became Suburban.* Minneapolis: University of Minnesota P, 2006. Print.
Flint, Kate. "Fictional Suburbia." *Popular Fictions: Essays in Literature and History.* Eds. Peter Humm, Paul Stigant and Peter Widdowson. London: Methuen, 1986. 111–26. Print.
Hall, Joan Wylie. "Fallen Eden in Shirley Jackson's *The Road Through the Wall*." *Renascence* 46.4 (Summer 1994): 261–70. Print.
Hattenhauer, Darryl. *Shirley Jackson's American Gothic.* Albany: SUNY P, 2003. Print.
Jackson, Shirley. *Come Along with Me.* New York: Viking, 1968. Print.
———. *The Road Through the Wall.* New York: Farrar, Straus, 1948. Print.
Johnson, Bernice. *The Suburban Gothic in American Popular Culture.* Houndmills: Palgrave Macmillan, 2009. Print.
Joshi, S. T. "Shirley Jackson: Domestic Horror." *Studies in Weird Fiction* 14 (Winter 1994): 9–28. Print.
Jurca, Catherine. *White Diaspora: The Suburb and the Twentieth-Century American Novel.* Princeton: Princeton UP, 2001. Print.
Kosenko, Peter. "A Marxist/Feminist Reading of Shirley Jackson's 'The Lottery.'" *New Orleans Review* 12 (1985): 27–32. Print.

Kunstler, James Howard. *The Geography of Nowhere: The Rise and Decline of America's Man-Made Landscape*. New York: Simon and Schuster, 1993. Print.

Oppenheimer, Judy. *Private Demons: A Life of Shirley Jackson*. New York: Putnam's, 1988. Print.

Parks, John G. "Chambers of Yearning: Shirley Jackson's Use of the Gothic." *Twentieth-Century Literature* 30 (1984): 15–29. Print.

Patterson, James T. *Grand Expectations: The United States, 1945–1974*. New York: Oxford UP, 1996. Print.

Rowe, Peter G. *Making a Middle Landscape*. Cambridge: MIT Press, 1991. Print.

Rubenstein, Roberta. "House Mothers and Haunted Daughters: Shirley Jackson and the Female Gothic." *Tulsa Studies in Women's Literature* 15.2 (Fall 1996): 309–31. Print.

Whyte, William H. *The Organization Man*. New York: Simon and Schuster, 1956. Print.

6 "Laughing through the words"
Recovering housewife humor in Shirley Jackson's *We Have Always Lived in the Castle*

Andrea Krafft

Throughout her novels and short fiction, Shirley Jackson embraces tropes such as haunting, the feminized victim, and, most importantly, the dilapidated manor house. Accordingly, much of the existing scholarship about Jackson's final novel, *We Have Always Lived in the Castle* (1962), situates this work within the Gothic tradition and focuses on how Mary Katherine (also known as Merricat) and Constance Blackwood occupy a marginal position as the "witches" of their village. While the Blackwood sisters are undoubtedly monstrous, to focus solely on this novel's Gothic elements ignores its central relationship with strange laughter. I aim to recuperate the lighter side of *We Have Always Lived in the Castle* by building on James Egan's observation that Jackson fuses Gothic and comic elements in order to intensify "her vision of a flattened, empty world" ("Comic" 46). More specifically, I argue that Jackson parodies Cold War domestic life in this novel by combining horror and humor in order to lay bare the absurdity of a culture that limited a woman's interests to "her husband, her children [and] her home" (Friedan 18).

As not only a writer but also a wife and mother of four children during the post–World War II era, Jackson was quite familiar with how the demands of domesticity could lead to a sense of personal crisis. She often wrote about the difficulty of maintaining her professional identity when others treated her as "Mrs. Stanley Hyman," reducing her to the title of "housewife."[1] Her dissatisfaction with being diminished to her domestic role in many ways prefigures the issues that Betty Friedan catalogues in *The Feminine Mystique* (1963). Friedan notes how, during the late 1950s, women felt "a strange stirring," a sense of incompleteness in the midst of their homebound lives (15). She even describes the home in Gothic terms, as a "comfortable concentration camp" in which women found themselves trapped (307). Although the two women share a common interest in critiquing Cold War domesticity, Friedan distances herself from Jackson (in addition to Phyllis McGinley and Jean Kerr), claiming that her use of humor essentially betrays women and that "there is something about Housewife Writers that isn't funny – like Uncle Tom" (57). While Friedan would understandably disapprove of making light of women's problems, she overlooks how humor also might enable women "to subvert the very power that keeps" them "powerless" (Walker 9). Throughout *We Have Always Lived in the Castle*, humor very clearly becomes the primary mode of conflict between the villagers and the Blackwood sisters, as Merricat and Constance gain power through laughter and jokes and refuse the silence that the villagers attempt to impose upon them.

Ranch house, haunted house: The Gothic genre as a Cold War parody

Prior to examining the ways in which *We Have Always Lived in the Castle* explores the power struggle over humor, I want to acknowledge how this novel's Gothic genre caricatures the settings of domestic life. As Elaine Tyler May argues in *Homeward Bound: American Families in the Cold War Era* (1988), the cultural consensus during the 1950s was that the home "held out the promise of security" against outside threats, thus leading to the spread of "domestic containment" (16). However, like other writers in the female Gothic tradition who exaggerate domestic enclosure, Jackson reveals how the comforting home might also be potentially imprisoning and strange.[2] For example, she describes the Blackwood manor as "a castle, turreted and open to the sky," transforming the home into something "weird" and haunted (Jackson 120). As the site of Merricat's poisoning of her parents, brother, aunt, and uncle, the house is, even before the novel begins, aligned with fragmentation and violence rather than with the familial ideal of "togetherness" that originated in *McCall's* magazine in 1954 (Halberstam 591). Similarly, the "unchangingly grey" village does not provide the sisters with a comforting sense of community but instead reminds them of the pressures of conformity and their own marginalization, essentially parodying the paranoid suburbs of the Cold War era (Jackson 6). The Blackwood sisters are in many ways victims of containment, as the occupants of the village attempt to limit their mobility and usher them back into their isolated home.

Similarly to how she aligns the Blackwood manor and village with Gothic locations, Jackson characterizes Merricat and Constance Blackwood as monstrous in order to emphasize how their society views them as "other." As Hélène Cixous notes in "The Laugh of the Medusa" (1976), the woman is "the uncanny stranger on display," a figure that might become destructive if released from the margins (880). Merricat draws attention to the weirdness of women when she describes herself and Constance in the midst of their housework as "carrying our dustcloths and the broom and dustpan and mop like a pair of witches walking home" (Jackson 69).[3] In this fusion of domestic work with malicious magic, Merricat manifests Friedan's "schizophrenic split," in which women cannot reconcile domesticity with their desire for something more (46). Constance's apparent agoraphobia is a similarly grotesque exaggeration of the effects of domestic enclosure, as, ever-obedient, she represents how some women during the 1950s felt "like shut-ins" (Friedan 22). The Blackwood sisters, despite being warped and "witchy," garner the readers' sympathies, as domesticity becomes the more fearsome monster in this novel.

"Laughter, coming from all sides": The villagers and normalizing humor

Just as Jackson parodies the haunted house and the monster in order to criticize domesticity, she crucially alters the Gothic mob of angry villagers to examine the pressures of Cold War "normativity." In *We Have Always Lived in the Castle*, the villagers do not just "storm the hated castle" (which occurs later in the novel) but also, more importantly, alienate the Blackwood sisters by aggressively ridiculing them (Murphy, "People" 122). Lynette Carpenter notes that this kind of humor serves the purposes of patriarchy, for it threatens to dismantle the Blackwood sisters' dearly purchased "self-sufficiency" ("Establishment" 32). Jackson explicitly genders the villagers as masculine: "the men stayed young and did the gossiping" (3). Because the jokers enjoy a privileged social position, they have "the freedom . . . to enjoy, to joke, to criticize, [and] to question" Merricat without facing any repercussions (Walker 44).[4] Their laughter is constant and insidious, as Merricat, walking through the village, senses "the laughter, coming from all sides" (Jackson 6).

The omnipresent laughter of the villagers helps them to achieve two basic purposes: to deal with their fear of the Blackwoods and to mark the sisters as abnormal. With respect to the first purpose, Freud suggests that humor allows people to avoid the emotions "to which the situation would naturally give rise" by replacing the expected response "with a jest" (162). He argues that a criminal facing the gallows, instead of demonstrating his fear about his execution, could joke that "the week's beginning nicely" (Freud 161). The villagers similarly rely on the tactics of gallows humor because Merricat's mere presence in the grocery store terrifies them. For example, after letting out "a little horrified laugh," Mrs. Donell counteracts her fear of Merricat with a joke, noting that "the Blackwoods always did set a fine table" (Jackson 8).[5] Beyond demonstrating their fear of the Blackwoods, the villagers' laughter works as a corrective and singles out individuals who do not fit "what we ought to be" (Bergson 17). Henri Bergson, in his famous study of laughter, notes that humor serves the goals of a group by implying "a kind of secret freemasonry, or even complicity, with other laughers" (6). The villagers, by mocking the Blackwoods, thus attempt to enforce a sense of cultural normality that, according to Anna Creadick, became "most fully articulated and deeply inscribed into everyday American life" during the postwar years (2).

Because the Blackwood sisters have so far overstepped appropriate social boundaries, the villagers no longer try to befriend them, but rather use their jokes to aggressively excise Merricat and Constance from the town. Because "the people of the village have always hated" the Blackwoods, they use humor to express their rage, allowing it "to bubble up without restraint" (Jackson 4; Douglas 364). Jim Donell does this when he confronts Merricat in the coffee shop, claiming that he heard a rumor that she was "moving away" (Jackson 12). Laughing at his morbid punch line that "a good number of the Blackwoods are gone already," he indicates his desire to drive out the remaining members of the family (Jackson 13). Additionally, his physically threatening stance, as he crowds Merricat and stares directly at her, signifies the aggression that underlies his humor. In a similar gesture, the crowd of laughing children mirrors Jim Donell's confrontation of Merricat in the coffee shop. As she is leaving the village, a row of Harris boys line up and chant:

> Merricat, said Connie, would you like a cup of tea?
> Oh no, said Merricat, you'll poison me.
> Merricat, said Connie, would you like to go to sleep?
> Down in the boneyard ten feet deep!
>
> (Jackson 16)

Merricat's speculation that the children's parents taught them the nursery rhyme indicates its underlying social function: it mocks the crime of the Blackwood sisters and simultaneously attempts to shame them into leaving the village. Though the Blackwoods continue to live in their family estate, the laughter of the villagers succeeds in establishing a group whose language Merricat does "not speak" (Jackson 16).

While the alienating humor of the villagers creates a clear "in-group" and "out-group," Jackson demonstrates how this kind of laughter bleeds into physical aggression. This is evident toward the end of *We Have Always Lived in the Castle*, when the villagers combine their laughter with a physical assault on the Blackwood house. After the local fire brigade extinguishes the blaze that drew them to the property, Jim Donell initiates the destruction by smashing a "rock through one of the great tall windows" (Jackson 106). The physical attack on the home serves the same purpose as the villagers' humor, specifically targeting "the drawing room and the kitchen" in order to undercut the Blackwood gynocracy (Carpenter, "Establishment" 36). Merricat conflates this violence with the humor of the villagers, as they produce "a wall of laughter" that moves "like a wave," threatening to dismantle the property with the rocks (Jackson 105–6). As she describes the damages to the property, she claims that "above it all, most horrible, was the laughter" (Jackson 106). When the villagers finally find Merricat and Constance, their laughter again creates an aggressive boundary between themselves and the Blackwoods. Their chanting of fragments of the nursery rhyme pushes back the sisters, who respond to the villagers by retreating into domesticity (Jackson 108). Notably, only the death of Julian Blackwood ends the vicious laughter of the villagers, as their respect for patriarchy negates their desire to destroy matriarchy.

The aggressive humor of the villagers apparently succeeds in marginalizing the Blackwood sisters from the outside world. To some extent, the sisters opt into their position as outsiders, preferring their own community to that of the people who hate them. Although James Egan sees the Blackwood sisters as madwomen locked into "a Gothic dungeon," I see their movement toward domestic enclosure as a culmination of their attempt to reclaim the house as their own ("Sanctuary" 23). As Merricat notes early in the novel, she believes that property should pass down from mother to daughter. She takes offense that the Rochester house, where her mother was born, is now owned by a new family when "by rights it should have belonged to Constance" (Jackson 3). Likewise, Merricat's poisoning of her family ensures that the Blackwood house will pass on to her older sister rather than to her younger brother. Merricat's aggression effectively echoes an increasing sense of frustration among disenfranchised American women during the 1950s, when married women's property still became absorbed into the husband's and "many states still had 'head and master' laws, affirming that the wife was subject to the husband" (Coontz 5).[6]

"Frighten[ing] them more": Merricat's aggressive humor

"Silly Merricat" demonstrates how women can adopt an aggressive stance as a (sometimes preemptive) defense mechanism against a society that threatens to control and silence them (Jackson 73). Specifically, she morbidly teases people, reminding them of her potential for violence through her smiles. Merricat's dark humor aligns her with a larger tradition of female writers who value subversion and violence, such as Hélène Cixous, who celebrates the deadly figure of Medusa because "she's beautiful and she's laughing" (885).[7] Cixous claims that the main task of women writers is to embrace this chaotic figure, "to blow up the law, to break up the 'truth' with laughter" (888). Nancy Walker and Zita Dresner similarly point to humor as a means of expressing violence "in more covert and indirect ways than men do" (41). Because social expectations of feminine passivity discourage overt aggression, laughter allows a way for women to toy with violence. This kind of behavior is particularly fitting for Merricat, as her burial of aggression in humor reflects her poisoning of the Blackwood family dinner, in that she hides violence in apparently pleasant and domestic contexts. Through Merricat, we can see the "hint of Medusa's glare" that Joan Wylie Hall recognizes as a feature of Jackson's comedic writing (74).

Merricat frequently draws on aggressive humor in order to compete with the overwhelming laughter of the villagers. When she hears the awkward chuckling of the people in the grocery store, Merricat orders "a small leg of lamb" noting that it is a favorite dish of her Uncle Julian (Jackson 8). In response to her request, "a little gasp went around the store like a scream," as everyone knows that lamb was on the menu for the final Blackwood family dinner (except for the reader, who is initially left out of this joke) (Jackson 8). Merricat makes clear that her order is not accidental, as she immediately follows her mention of the lamb with a request for sugar (Jackson 8). Her relentless dark humor recalls that smiles and laughter function in similar ways to baring one's teeth and growling, presenting "visible weaponry to a possible opponent" (Barreca 75). Merricat notably buries her morbid allusions within domestic language: on the surface, she is simply gathering groceries, but underneath, she fantasizes about the villagers fleeing and dying in front of her. She calms herself by thinking about how she "could make them run like rabbits" if she "said to them what" she "really wanted to" (Jackson 8). Thus, Merricat's particular talent lies in masking her rage with a smile.

Just as she responds to the public laughter of the villagers with aggressive humor, Merricat teases visitors to the Blackwood estate in order to distance herself and Constance from the community. When Helen Clarke and Lucille Wright visit for tea, Merricat purposefully makes the women uncomfortable by alluding to the family murders. Even though everyone knows that the sugar bowl once contained arsenic, she repeatedly offers it to her guests. She also assures the shaky women that "everything my sister cooks is delicious" and happily encourages them to eat what they fear to be poisonous (Jackson 29). When the nervous women finally leave, Merricat acknowledges that she was teasing them because she enjoys "frighten[ing] them more" (Jackson 39). She delights in mortifying the other women, an activity in which Constance and Julian also participate by openly discussing the poisonings. Yet, Merricat initiates her dark jokes only after Helen and Lucille suggest that Constance should "come back into the world" (Jackson 27). Because she wants to preserve her isolated home, she becomes violent and smashes a milk pitcher before turning against those women who represent the threat of the impinging community. Merricat attempts to define the boundaries of her sister's world through her aggressive humor by keeping Constance laughing at her antics rather than seriously considering the appeal to return to the community.

Merricat's aggressive humor is her crucial weapon for defending her home against not only female visitors but also the threat of a patriarchal return in the person of her cousin, Charles Blackwood. She envisions Charles's entry into the house as an invasion, noting that "our wall of safety had cracked" as Charles begins to lay claim to the family's money and to live in her father's old room (Jackson 58). Because Charles disrupts her bond with Constance (and because he is unkind to Uncle Julian), Merricat confronts him with a darkly humorous recitation of the death-cup mushroom and its effects. Sitting at the dinner table, she notes that "the *Amanita phalloides* . . . holds three different poisons," and she enumerates the symptoms of "violent stomach pains, cold sweat" and "vomiting" (Jackson 72). Her mention of poison recalls her murder of the former Blackwood patriarchs, which Charles does not think is "very funny" (Jackson 73). Constance laughs at her sister's morbid reference, however, noting that her sister is "silly" (Jackson 73). Although the scene is not explicitly funny, Merricat and Constance clearly delight in the subversion of Blackwood men through imagined (or real) violence. In such moments of dark laughter, the sisters resemble what Avril Horner and Sue Zlosnik call "the empowered monstrous female" of feminist Gothic texts (117).

In a similar manner to his youngest niece, Julian Blackwood also experiments with aggressive humor as a means of counteracting the threatening presence of the patriarch. Lynette Carpenter notes that Julian is in a similar position to the Blackwood women, effectively feminized because he depends on the charity of his brother, John, and is thus "subject to his authority" ("Establishment" 33). Even after the murder of his brother, Julian never succeeds in accumulating his own wealth because the arsenic incapacitates him both mentally and physically. Remarkably, when he senses the return of his brother in the figure of Charles, Julian responds quite aggressively. He yells at Charles to "get away from my papers" and calls him a "damned impertinent puppy" (Jackson 92, 93). As with

Merricat's violent outbursts, the sisters find Julian's attack on Charles to be funny, as it undercuts the potential return of the father figure. Merricat observes that she "was laughing at Charles and [that] even Constance was smiling" because Uncle Julian caught his nephew off guard (Jackson 93). Though part of Julian's humor stems from his confusion of Charles with John and Arthur Blackwood, he shares Merricat's drive to remove the patriarch from the home through mockery.

Although Julian and Merricat both aggressively mock Charles, the Blackwood women find it necessary to shift from verbal to physical attacks against the male imposition of power in their lives. Merricat imagines the various ways in which she could punish her cousin for his invasion of her household. For instance, after he digs up her box of silver dollars (one of the various charms of protection she hides on the property), she imagines burying his head in a hole and scratching his face on "a round stone the right size," laughing at the thought of his funeral (Jackson 89). And yet, Merricat's threats escalate, just as the aggressive laughter of the villagers eventually intermingles with their destruction of the Blackwood home. Because her dark humor does not effectively remove Charles from the household, Merricat starts a fire in his room using his pipe and newspaper (Jackson 99). Constance responds to Merricat's violence with amusement and serenity: Charles runs screaming from the house, but she helps Julian up to his room to collect his papers (Jackson 101). This reflects Constance's earlier complicity in Merricat's dark violence when she "never called a doctor until it was too late" and "washed the sugar bowl," both ensuring that her sister's plan would be effective and destroying the hard evidence of the crime (Jackson 37). Constance is not simply a bystander to her sister's violence, but participates in it as "a passive-aggressive enabler," and perhaps even as a conspirator (Hattenhauer 177).

From smiling domesticity to liberated laughing ladies

While Merricat's aggressive humor provides the Blackwood sisters with a helpful way of defending themselves against the violence of the surrounding community, Constance offers a more positively charged mode of affective response. When she first appears in the novel, Constance, with her apparently permanent smile, reflects the idealized model of the feminine mystique, as she is "fluffy and feminine; passive; [and] gaily content in a world of bedroom and kitchen" (Friedan 36). Recalling her own experience during the 1950s, Nancy Weisstein similarly observes that women were encouraged "to laugh as much [as] possible, and when you can't manage a laugh, to smile" (132). In some ways, Constance seems to be merely placating her strange sister, babying her, and thereby adopting the role of ersatz mother. Her smiles and laughter serve, however, two important functions within the Blackwood house. First, Constance's embracing of Merricat's dark jokes is a kind of gallows humor: she laughs at reminders of the murders because she refuses to feel "compelled to suffer" (Freud 162). More importantly, Constance's participatory laughter with Merricat is "a means of communication" that strengthens the bond between the two sisters (Walker xii). Because nihilism may be the only alternative response for the marginalized sisters, laughter helps them to reconstruct a feminine community from the rubble of their family home.

The manner in which laughter gives way to a gender-exclusive community bound together with mirth is evident in the sisters' use of jokes that are primarily nonsensical to the reader (i.e., inside jokes). In response to Constance's observation that "furred leaves" could potentially grow on the moon, Merricat starts joking that Jonas is a kind of furry plant (Jackson 59). Merricat's response, though illogical, serves its purpose of making Constance laugh, as their in-joke is based on "a common pool of information and a shared perspective" (Barreca 85). Just as the secrets of the Blackwood murders join the two sisters together, their inside jokes unite them in a mutual bond. This communicatory role of laughter is especially crucial after the destruction of the Blackwood property, which more clearly separates the sisters from the remainder of the community. Because the brutality of the villagers demonstrates to Constance that a return to society is impossible, she consigns herself to a life within the home. Like the villagers' aggressive "wall of laughter," the sisters use humor to close themselves off from the world (Jackson 105). In addition to boarding up the house, Constance and Merricat constantly laugh and smile, turning inward on their relationship as a kind of safeguard (Jackson 128).

This communal laughter occurs after Charles Blackwood finally leaves the sisters to themselves, signaling their complete separation from the possible return of masculine control. After Charles departs for his car, Merricat notes that she and Constance "held each other in the dark hall and laughed . . . our laughter going up the ruined stairway to the sky" (Jackson 144). Merricat describes their laughter as something transcendent that transports the joined female voices to the level of the heavens. Furthermore, this characterization of the victorious female voices signals, as Carpenter has noted, a celebratory rejection of romantic love in favor of sisterhood ("Establishment" 34). The sisters delight in the fact that Charles fails to replace John Blackwood and that they retain possession of their "father's safe" and the family property (Jackson 119). Furthermore, with the departure of the patriarch, we see the transformation of female aggressive humor from an outwardly directed threat into a kind of in-joking. For example, Constance, mocking Charles's exaggerated despair, observes that he should have shot "himself through the head in the driveway" (Jackson 146). Unlike previous instances of aggressive humor, the main difference here is that Charles cannot hear Constance's mockery. Instead, Constance threatens Charles from a distance not to attack him but rather to bond with Merricat. Thus, the sisters turn to mirth as a way of protecting their "self-contained community of women" (Carpenter, "Establishment" 38).

It is difficult, however, to view this laughter as entirely positive, as the sisters sit in the ruins of their former home, mixing their giggles with tears (Jackson 144). Constance's final stance in the text is especially ambiguous, as she seems to be on the verge of hysteria. When dressing her sister in a tablecloth, she asks, "What have I done to my baby Merricat?" (Jackson 136). Similarly, Merricat notes that her older sister lives "in terror lest one of our two cups should break" (Jackson 145). Constance's precarious position between terror and laughter indicates the instability of the new feminine community, especially given the continuing threat of starvation. Because of the physical realities of their situation, the sisters are not entirely self-sufficient: they depend on the kindness of the village women, since they refuse to leave the house to purchase food. On the one hand, the food provides "a means of communication" between the Blackwoods and a larger society of women (Carpenter, "Establishment" 36). This expands the imagined feminine community that Constance and Merricat establish through laughter, while still sheltering them from the threat of the male villagers. On the other hand, the sisters become codependent on the community, indicating that their desire for marginalization and domestic enclosure does not completely triumph over the power of the community at large.

This calls into question how subversive their communal female humor really is, since they constrict their laughter to the home instead of turning to "an open rebellious humor" (Weisstein 136). Barreca notes that humor, if it remains "behind closed doors . . . stay[ing] among ourselves," is a socially permitted model for women's expression (196). Walker similarly argues that women can joke easily among themselves because they are "invisible to men," thereby posing no threat to existing power structures (85). However, these critiques of domestically enclosed female humor unfairly ignore what Merricat and Constance gain through their communal laughter. If the sisters remain committed to the aggressive model of humor, their constant confrontation with the villagers does not offer any possibility of resolution. Though Cixous complains that women "shouldn't be conned into accepting a domain which is the margin," Merricat and Constance quite consciously choose to separate themselves from these violent social relations (881).

The Blackwood sisters gladly participate in their own marginalization by embracing the creation of their own isolated community because of the fear and shame of the villagers. The villagers treat the Blackwood manor, "a great ruined structure overgrown with vines," as a kind of haunted house (Jackson 146).[8] The sisters mock the villagers for imagining that the monstrous witches who inhabit this crumbling house could inflict "some sort of preternatural vengeance" (Murphy, "People" 123). Furthermore, they embrace their newfound role as Gothic monsters, as their supposed mystical power ensures that the villagers will leave them alone (for the most part). The villagers, in turn, transform the Blackwoods into a tool for behavioral control by claiming that they "go hunting little children," especially the "little bad boys" who walk "too near that house" (Jackson 141). Although some "curious villagers" still gather "outside the house," they maintain a tense level of respect for the sisters (Jackson 146). Tellingly, they leave baskets of food for Merricat and Constance, apologizing for their behavior, but also asking the sisters not to respond in kind. Moreover, after a little boy shouts a fragment of a mocking nursery rhyme at the house, they find eggs and a note claiming that "he didn't mean it, please" (Jackson 146). The sisters not only pity the fearful villagers but also joke about their newfound role as witches, laughing about the idea that they eat children. In their Gothicized household, the sisters are fully enclosed from the threat of the aggressive villagers, which allows them to be (as Merricat claims) "so happy" (Jackson 146).

Ultimately, Jackson celebrates the monstrous women of *We Have Always Lived in the Castle*, as they break away from society and demonstrate the possibility of a female-determined community. However, it remains unclear if their containment within the home ends up confirming the power of their surrounding society to alienate subversive women and thus to maintain the normative structures of domestic life. At the very least, laughter provides a significant starting point for subversive feminine voices seeking more radical change. As Jackson emphatically and optimistically noted in her journals, "laughter is possible laughter is possible laughter is possible" (qtd. in Carpenter, "Domestic" 147). It is not surprising, then, that her final novel ends with the insistent laughter of the Blackwood sisters echoing in our ears, and the villagers quaking in fear as the witches cackle in their castle.

Coda: Getting the last laugh

I conclude by considering how *We Have Always Lived in the Castle* relates to Jackson's larger oeuvre, specifically *Life Among the Savages* (1952) and *Raising Demons* (1957). Like her final novel, Jackson's domestic memoirs combine the mundane with the imagery of horror, most noticeably in their titles. Yet, much of the existing scholarship about Jackson (with the exception of Bernice M. Murphy's "Hideous Doughnuts and Haunted Housewives: Gothic Undercurrents in Shirley Jackson's Domestic Humour") ignores the cultural critique that underlies her domestic writings. Her biographer, Judy Oppenheimer, characterizes *Life Among the Savages* as "sunny and peaceful" and Darryl Hattenhauer omits the memoirs from his book-length study of Jackson's fiction (169). I argue that this oversight stems from the fact that multiple critics and even "the Hymans did not take the [domestic] stories seriously," given that much of the content of *Raising Demons* and *Life Among the Savages* was originally published in women's magazines, such as *Mademoiselle*, *Good Housekeeping*, and *Woman's Home Companion* (Friedman 150). To reject writing directed toward housewives overlooks how even apparently optimistic domestic narratives can speak to a broader interest in renegotiating domesticity and motherhood. After all, women's magazines repeatedly sought out contributions from Shirley Jackson, published articles about divorce, printed editorials from anxious mothers, and so on. Furthermore, as Murphy has noted, Jackson published her memoirs contemporaneously with her "explorations of psychological breakdown," suggesting "the close relationship between two of her favourite subjects – madness and domesticity" ("Hideous" 231). In this brief examination of Jackson's domestic memoirs, I will demonstrate how she represents the home as a site of unpredictability, a critical tendency that also emerges in her more explicitly Gothic novels.

The primary source of anxiety and comedy throughout Jackson's memoirs is the sense of chaos that seems to prevent her from maintaining control over both the cleanliness of her home and the behavior of her children. *Life Among the Savages* begins thusly:

> Our house is old, and noisy, and full. When we moved into it we had two children and about five thousand books; I expect that when we finally overflow and move out again we will have perhaps twenty children and easily half a million books.
>
> (385)

This commentary on the apparent self-replication of both children and household objects serves a twofold purpose. First, Jackson imagines absurd domestic and maternal excess in order to amuse a likeminded reader. Second, this passage points to a more sinister suggestion that children might overpower the home, physically overwhelming the mother with their chaotic bodies. Like Merricat, Jackson's children frequently flout Dr. Benjamin Spock's promise that "your baby is born to be a reasonable, friendly human being" (42).

Jackson's belief in the dark potential of domesticity becomes fully evident when she describes her family's home in Gothic terms; in such moments she transforms the dream of housewifery and motherhood into the stuff of nightmares. In the beginning pages of *Raising Demons*, she describes the magnetic pull of the home as "the grip of something stronger than I was," a kind of inexorable force that overwhelms her (538). Likewise, she aligns the home with Gothic imagery in *Life Among the Savages*, which ends with a handbill (written by her husband, Stanley Edgar Hyman) describing their home as "a meeting-place, or nest, for demonic spirits" (529). Though Jackson includes this handbill as an illustration of a familial inside joke, it remains difficult to ignore how the language of horror signals her domestic frustrations, especially given that she similarly warps the home with the Blackwood manor. She even sarcastically notes, "I cannot think of a preferable way of life, except one without children," and she additionally describes her life as one of "back-breaking labor" (Jackson, *Savages* 386, 397). While she does not condone the abandonment of domestic life and at other times seems perfectly satisfied with her home and family, in such moments of complaint she seeks to elicit a dry chuckle from readers who also worry about losing their free will to housework and maternal responsibility.

The communal impetus of Jackson's humor emerges most clearly in an episode from *Life Among the Savages*, in which she and another mother share a laugh at the meat counter of the local grocery store (a site which is also central to Merricat's aggressive humor). Despite a previous squabble, Jackson and Mrs. Howell find common ground in commiserating about their children and describe them as "horrible little beasts" and "liars" (Jackson, *Savages* 414). By ending their confrontation with a shared laugh about the deceptiveness of children, Jackson demonstrates the potential of domestic humor to bring together "a community of women" (Neuhaus 121). This brief moment of bonding between Mrs. Howell and the narrator signals the greater relevance of Jackson's domestic comedy to the broader community of women readers, a topic that Jessamyn Neuhaus explores more thoroughly in "'Is It Ridiculous for Me to Say I Want to Write?': Domestic Humor and Redefining the 1950s Housewife Writer in Fan Mail to Shirley Jackson" (2009). Yet, I would like to add that the two women not only exchange a laugh about demonic children but also exchange recipe tips about cooking hamburger and liver. This demonstrates that comedic critiques of domestic life can exist alongside the very material of familial togetherness that one might find in the pages of a women's magazine.

Jackson's primary complaint throughout *Life Among the Savages* and *Raising Demons* is that she is living in an age that establishes unrealistic ideals for family life. As Nancy Walker says in *A Very Serious Thing: Women's Humor and American Culture* (1988), Jackson and other domestic comediennes like Jean Kerr ask us not to examine "ineptitude on the part of the homemaker but instead to [consider] the impossibility of the standards for performance" (186–87). Jackson's memoirs contain strains of the Gothic and moments of disruptive laughter that destabilize the notion of familial normativity and predictability by requiring us to reconsider the ideal portraits of family life that emerged in postwar sitcoms such as *Leave It to Beaver* (1957) and *Ozzie and Harriet* (1952). Likewise, her final Gothic novel, *We Have Always Lived in the Castle*, moves away from the postwar model of the nuclear family in favor of a more radical vision of a sororal community based on humor. Although Judy Oppenheimer puzzlingly claims that "Shirley was no feminist" (164), Jackson, in both her early nonfiction writing and her final novel, fuses the Gothic with the comic, thus calling into question the fantasy world of Cold War domesticity that continues to dominate the American popular imagination.

Notes

1 See both "Epilogue: Fame" (1948) and "The Third Baby is the Easiest" (an episode from *Life Among the Savages*) for Jackson's narratives about other women ignoring her role as a writer in favor of emphasizing her domestic identity.
2 Angela Hague similarly notes that homes in Jackson's writing "often function as places of entrapment and incarceration for the women who visit or live in them" (82).
3 In an earlier moment of monstrous identification, Merricat speculates that she "could have been born a werewolf" (Jackson 1).
4 Mary Douglas similarly notes that the joker in "a privileged position . . . can say certain things in a certain way which confers immunity" (372).
5 Although some of the villagers who joke are women, their humor still supports the goals of patriarchy. Mrs. Donell is a particularly striking example, as her husband, Jim, leads the charge against Merricat and Constance.
6 Merricat is by no means Jackson's only character who aggressively reclaims domestic space. In "The Story We Used to Tell" (unpublished until 1997), two women escape their entrapment in an aging portrait of a mansion by murdering the old man who owns it. Similarly, "Mrs. Anderson" and "What a Thought" (both also unpublished until 1997) feature women who violently turn against their husbands.
7 Similarly, Regina Barreca notes that "a woman who can make a man laugh when he doesn't want to is as dangerous as a Medusa" (19).
8 John G. Parks observes that the vines covering the house, in addition to lending it a Gothic significance, represent nature sheltering the sisters from "the assaults of a vengeful and violent world" (248).

Works cited

Barreca, Regina. *They Used to Call Me Snow White . . . But I Drifted: Women's Strategic Use of Humor*. New York: Viking, 1991. Print.

Bergson, Henri. *Laughter: An Essay on the Meaning of the Comic*. Trans. Fred Rothwell. New York: Macmillan, 1914. Print.

Carpenter, Lynette. "Domestic Comedy, Black Comedy, and Real Life: Shirley Jackson, A Woman Writer." *Faith of a (Woman) Writer*. Eds. Alice Kessler-Harris and William McBrien. Westport: Greenwood, 1998. 143–48. Print.

———. "The Establishment and Preservation of Female Power in Shirley Jackson's *We Have Always Lived in the Castle*." *Frontiers* 8.1 (1984): 32–38. JSTOR. Web. 29 Nov. 2010.

Cixous, Hélène. "The Laugh of the Medusa." Trans. Keith Cohen and Paula Cohen. *Signs* 1.4 (1976): 875–93. JSTOR. Web. 29 Nov. 2010.

Coontz, Stephanie. *A Strange Stirring: The Feminine Mystique and American Women at the Dawn of the 1960s*. New York: Basic, 2011. Print.

Creadick, Anna G. *Perfectly Average: The Pursuit of Normality in Postwar America*. Amherst: U of Massachusetts P, 2010. Print.

Douglas, Mary. "The Social Control of Cognition: Some Factors in Joke Perception." *Man* 3.3 (1968): 361–76. JSTOR. Web. 4 Dec. 2010.

Egan, James. "Comic-Satiric-Fantastic-Gothic: Interactive Modes in Shirley Jackson's Narratives." Murphy, *Shirley Jackson* 34–51.

———. "Sanctuary: Shirley Jackson's Domestic and Fantastic Parables." *Studies in Weird Fiction* 6.1 (1989): 15–24. Print.

Freud, Sigmund. *Humor 1927*. Scribd. Sean Springer. 19 July 2010. Web. 5 Dec. 2010.

Friedan, Betty. *The Feminine Mystique*. New York: Norton, 1963. Print.

Hague, Angela. "'A Faithful Anatomy of Our Times': Reassessing Shirley Jackson." *Frontiers: A Journal of Women Studies* 26.2 (2005): 73–96. JSTOR. Web. 14 May 2014.

Halberstam, David. *The Fifties*. New York: Villard, 1993. Print.

Hall, Joan Wylie. *Shirley Jackson: A Study of the Short Fiction*. New York: Twayne, 1993. Print.

Hattenhauer, Darryl. *Shirley Jackson's American Gothic*. Albany: State U of New York P, 2003. Print.

Horner, Avril and Sue Zlosnik. *Gothic and the Comic Turn*. New York: Palgrave, 2005. Print.

Hyman, Stanley Edgar, ed. *The Magic of Shirley Jackson*. New York: Farrar, 1966. Print.

Jackson, Shirley. "Epilogue: Fame." 1948. Jackson, *Ordinary* 386–88.

———. *Just An Ordinary Day*. Ed. Laurence Jackson Hyman and Sarah Hyman Stewart. New York: Bantam, 1997. Print.

———. *Life Among the Savages*. 1953. Hyman 383–530.

———. "Mrs. Anderson." Jackson, *Ordinary* 99–103.

———. *Raising Demons*. 1957. Hyman 531–753.

———. "The Story We Used to Tell." Jackson, *Ordinary* 179–85.

———. *We Have Always Lived in the Castle*. 1962. New York: Penguin, 2006. Print.

———. "What a Thought." Jackson, *Ordinary* 170–73.

May, Elaine Tyler. *Homeward Bound: American Families in the Cold War Era*. New York: Basic, 1988. Print.

Morris, Linda A., ed. *American Women Humorists: Critical Essays*. New York: Garland, 1994. Print.

Murphy, Bernice M. "Hideous Doughnuts and Haunted Housewives: Gothic Undercurrents in Shirley Jackson's Domestic Humour." *The Ghost Story from the Middle Ages to the Twentieth Century: A Ghostly Genre*. Eds. Helen Conrad O'Briain and Julie Anne Stevens. Dublin: Four Courts, 2010. 229–50. Print.

———. "'The People of the Village Have Always Hated Us': Shirley Jackson's New England Gothic." Murphy, *Shirley Jackson* 104–26.

———, ed. *Shirley Jackson: Essays on the Literary Legacy*. Jefferson, NC: McFarland and Company, 2005. Print.

Neuhaus, Jessamyn. "'Is It Ridiculous for Me to Say I Want to Write?': Domestic Humor and Redefining the 1950s Housewife Writer in Fan Mail to Shirley Jackson." *Journal of Women's History* 21.2 (2009): 115–37. JSTOR. Web. 23 Nov. 2010.

Oppenheimer, Judy. *Private Demons: The Life of Shirley Jackson*. New York: Putnam, 1988. Print.

Parks, John G. "Chambers of Yearning: Shirley Jackson's Use of the Gothic." Murphy, *Shirley Jackson* 237–50.

Spock, Benjamin. *Baby and Child Care*. 1945. New York: Giant Cardinal, 1957. Print.

Walker, Nancy. *A Very Serious Thing: Women's Humor and American Culture*. Minneapolis: U of Minnesota P, 1988. Print.

——— and Zita Dresner. "Introduction to Redressing the Balance: American Women's Literary Humor from Colonial Times to the 1980s." 1988. Morris 131–39.

Weisstein, Nancy. "Why We Aren't Laughing . . . Any More." 1973. Morris 131–39.

7 "Listening to what she had almost said"

Containment and duality in Shirley Jackson's *We Have Always Lived in the Castle*

Ashleigh Hardin

Criticism of Shirley Jackson's work has frequently dealt with what is perceived as her "duality," citing the oppositions in Jackson's career, personal life, and legacy. She wrote for *Good Housekeeping*; she wrote for the *New Yorker*. She was a housewife and mother; she was a respected practitioner of her craft. She was nurturing and rather conventional; she was deeply interested in the occult and witchcraft. Although her short story "The Lottery" is one of the most anthologized in twentieth-century American fiction, her oeuvre otherwise has been largely ignored by scholars. Judy Oppenheimer, her biographer, returns frequently to the trope of Jackson's dual nature, claiming that it allowed her to write in multiple genres and create characters with multiple or fragmented personalities (Oppenheimer 139). The implication is that Jackson's novels are reflections of her complex psychology and consequently divorced from their contexts, and this thesis motivated much of the criticism of her fiction. Ahistorical readings of Jackson are still en vogue in the twenty-first century, as Jonathan Lethem claims in his 2006 introduction to *We Have Always Lived in the Castle* that Jackson had been practicing "splitting *her* aspects among several characters in the same story" (ix, my emphasis). Thus are two of the characters in that novel, the willful, volatile, and murderous Merricat Blackwood and her nurturing and acquiescing sister, Constance, seen as two halves of the same person, Shirley Jackson herself.

As scholars of the postwar era have pointed out, however, to have a dual or multiple personality was the status quo for the middle-class married woman. The title of Doris Fleischman's popular memoir posits that a wife was "many women" in the postwar period, especially those like Fleischman (and Jackson), who married and had children but retained their own names and independent careers. Duality was not simply the experience of individual women, rather, but the diagnosis of what was "wrong" with women in general. In *Modern Woman: The Lost Sex*, psychologists Ferdinand Lundberg and Marynia Farnham concluded that the titular figure, feeling pressure to find satisfaction outside the home, "finds herself facing her fundamental role as wife and mother with a divided mind," when in actuality she should be fulfilled by housekeeping and mothering, as "the domain [they] suggest for women broadly includes all of biology, psychology, sociology, medicine, pedagogy, philosophy, anthropology, and several other systematic disciplines" (241, 370). Full-page advertisements for the "Toastmaster" frying pan ran in *Good Housekeeping*, reminding women "You lead two lives," hostess and homemaker (McGraw-Edison 184). Within the pages of this magazine, Shirley Jackson published her "domestic" nonfiction, stories of raising her four children and dealing with her husband, literary critic Stanley Edgar Hyman. She appears as another case of a woman with a dual nature: both motherly memoirist and best-selling novelist whose fictional work dealt primarily with themes of psychological and physical horror. Regardless of whether individual women consciously cultivated multiple personae, duality was viable because it corresponded to cultural narratives of female agency. As the foregoing examples suggest, fragmenting a woman's identity into multiple discrete parts or roles allowed what Elaine Tyler May calls women's "increasing sexual and economic emancipation" to be "channel[ed]" into the family (105). Therefore, Jackson's duality should be understood not as an essential facet of her individual psychology but as a tenuous, historically situated arrangement that was as much a perception of her as an act of will on her part.

In terming Jackson a "proto-postmodernist," Darryl Hattenhauer attempts to account for the neglect of Jackson and provide a paradigm for examining her work that would account for its emphasis on multiple personality, including the narrative oddities of *Castle* and its unreliable narrator, Merricat. Unfortunately, Hattenhauer, like many critics of Jackson, does not move beyond a psychological understanding of her duality into a notion of duality as a historically constructed theme of her writing and her carefully cultivated public persona. Angela Hague, drawing on the words of Jackson's husband, argues for a reassessment of Jackson as providing "a faithful anatomy" of her historical moment specifically through her characters' "isolation, loneliness, and fragmenting identities, their simultaneous inability to relate to the world outside themselves or to function autonomously" (Hague 74). Hague points out that, even in her own time, Jackson was misunderstood as writing primarily about personal psychology rather than the symptoms of a culture of "repression, containment, and paranoia" (74). As Hague notes, attempts by feminist critic Lynette Carpenter to reevaluate Jackson's work produced some renewed interest, but did not, ultimately, persist (73). Neither have critics, other than Hague, considered Jackson's work in the context of the Cold War.

The consequences of this neglect of context for interpretations of *Castle* and its narrator are intriguing and somewhat troubling.[1] In an effort to redeem the memorable protagonist critics frequently aligned with the author herself, Merricat has been construed as a liberator rather than a murderer.[2] True to the "dual nature" paradigm, critics also have tended to view Constance as assisting with the murders to some degree. Hall claims she colludes with Merricat (116), and Rubenstein carries this further by suggesting that "the two women are 'two halves of the same person' – in fact, two aspects of Shirley Jackson herself" (143). Thus, the end of the novel, when Merricat and Constance are sequestered in the burned-out remains of the house, sleeping on the floor of the kitchen, is often read as a positive outcome.³ Though critics such as Hall, Egan, and Hattenhauer acknowledge the Gothic qualities of the ending and suggest that they trouble any optimistic interpretation, by reading Jackson psychologically rather than historically, none have been willing to suggest that Merricat's "triumph" discloses the dependency of cultural narratives of containment on a domestic ideology that stunted and silenced women.

The presumed complementarity of Merricat and Constance Blackwood needs to be re-examined. The title of the novel, with its emphasis on the plural first person, suggests readers may conclude that the "we" and "always" represent the harmonious and unchanging state of the sisters' relationship. The first sentence, however, shatters this illusion: the narrator announces, "My name is Mary Katherine Blackwood" and from then on introduces a number of idiosyncratic narrative devices that highlight the limitations of her perspective. Nonetheless, Merricat has a tendency to conflate the singular and the plural, declaring several times throughout the novel that "we" are, were, or are going to be "happy."⁴ In other words, Merricat consistently tries to contain Constance within the family home and within her totalizing "we," and she succeeds in the end when Constance forfeits any ideas about leaving the home and gasps, "Merricat, *I* am so happy" (145, my emphasis). Constance, for her part, attempts to contain Merricat by managing her sister's emotions and preventing her from facing the consequences for her actions, whether by sneaking her food upstairs when their father has sent her to bed without dinner or by taking the fall when Merricat poisons the family. Rather than being complementary, then, Merricat and Constance are constantly in tension, each trying to contain the energy of the other. These efforts at containment, particularly on the part of Merricat, are furthermore always in danger of spilling over, becoming excessive, erupting in violence, and it takes an explosion of violence to ensure, finally, that Constance will stay in the home as Merricat's caretaker.

Narratives of containment, like *Castle*'s, permeated Cold War culture. As Alan Nadel cogently argues, to view entities as containing binary oppositions, thus requiring greater external vigilance, is a feature of "containment culture," a series of narratives proliferating through multiple media in the postwar era to contain the spread of communism and the threatening energies of changing norms of sexuality, gender, and race (34). The "dual nature" of Shirley Jackson and the "we" of *We Have Always Lived in the Castle* mark the text as a Cold War novel by illustrating the dependence of containment on unstable narratives of domesticity. The end of the novel, which finds Constance and Merricat still contained within the family home but in greatly reduced circumstances, suggests the failure of containment to account fully for all the "disparate narratives upon which it relied" (Nadel 53). It is the failure of containment that Nadel argues produces American postmodernism, marked by its preoccupations with excesses, endings, and ontology. Considering the novel as a product of "containment culture" provides a rubric to interpret the assumed complementarity of Constance and Merricat and the formal aspects of *Castle* (especially those that Hattenhauer terms "proto-postmodernist").

Untangling Merricat's motives from Constance's shows the tremendous pressure necessary to contain oppositions and make duality appear "natural." Merricat's violence is not merely the opposite of Constance's timidity; it, not mutual affection, is the binding force of their relationship. In Merricat Blackwood, we are shown the logic of containment taken to its extreme, and her desire to prevent Constance from leaving the family home illustrates the dependence of all narratives of containment on the postwar ideology of domesticity. Evidence in the text of Constance's resistance suggests that, rather than being an enabler of or colluder with Merricat, Constance is actively trying to escape her. In fact, it is Constance's resistance to Merricat that drives the plot. In a 2009 review essay, Joyce Carol Oates suggests that Constance's apparent attraction to her mercenary cousin, Charles, can be read as "a measure of her desperation" for "a way into a possible new life" (Oates 12). This desire is evident from the very beginning of the novel, before Charles arrives on the scene. Merricat's narration begins on a day when Constance has ventured further than ever beyond the house's garden (Jackson 19). Merricat takes Constance's prediction that she'll go even further into the village as "teasing" but is disturbed when Constance continues to make allusions to it (Jackson 21, 24). In a calculated rage, she "content[s herself] with smashing the milk pitcher which waited on the table" and leaves the mess so "Constance would see [it]" (Jackson 27). The broken pitcher signals, if not a threat, at least Merricat's displeasure, and Constance reacts to this displeasure by becoming more reserved and cagey when she speaks of leaving. Instead of speaking of it as an inevitability, she tries to appeal to Merricat's self-interest by asking if *she* wouldn't like to leave some time. When Merricat responds hostilely, Constance's face is "very serious for a moment," before she smiles at Merricat and tells her not to worry, saying, "Nothing bad will happen" (Jackson 54). On subsequent occasions, Constance censors herself as she conspires with other people to leave the house. Merricat walks in on Constance talking with Mrs. Wright and Helen Clarke, presumably about leaving, since when Merricat enters, she drops the subject and offers Merricat a placating smile: "' – do with Mary Katherine?' Constance was saying, and then she turned and smiled at me in the doorway" (Jackson 28). Later, Constance stops herself midsentence, "'But I'll have to if I – ,'" when Merricat brings up the subject of moving Julian to a hospital. She then returns to cooking and asks Merricat about the applesauce she plans to make. Merricat certainly understands what Constance is planning as she tells the reader she "sat very quietly, listening to what she had almost said" (Jackson 84). The struggle between Constance and Merricat then is one that occurs largely beneath the surface of their interactions and the narration. However, as the foregoing examples illustrate, Constance is aware of Merricat's dangerous potential and at least contemplating a life without her.

Perhaps one of the reasons critics have tended to overlook Constance's resistance to Merricat is that the image of Constance that Merricat provides for the reader is one of extreme docility and subservience – it is an image of conventional postwar femininity. Merricat believes that Constance likes only "books about food," so this is what she brings her from the library[5] (Jackson 2). She thinks that

Constance is emotionally fragile, so she offers to turn away an unexpected visitor. Despite Constance's protests that she can handle the visitor, Merricat insists, "I won't *have* you frightened . . . I want to send them away" (Jackson 24). Conceiving of Constance as the soft, nurturing complement to Merricat reinforces readings of Jackson and the novel as having a dual nature, but the novel suggests that Merricat's interpretation of Constance is based in a specific kind of literary fantasy: the fairy tale. This is one of the two genres (the other being history) that Merricat specifically names as her preferred reading (Jackson 2). Merricat remembers,

> When I was small I thought Constance was a fairy princess. I used to try to draw her picture, with long golden hair and eyes as blue as the crayon could make them, and a bright pink spot on either cheek; the pictures always surprised me, because she *did* look like that.
>
> (Jackson 20)

Critics have similarly viewed Constance as a stereotypically docile and nurturing woman. John G. Parks terms her a "virtual handmaiden of nature, raising and canning fruits and vegetables, and tending flowers all over the estate" (Parks 26). In Rubenstein's article, Constance is "saintly," the good daughter (and eventually the mother figure) that survives the poisonings and the good half of Merricat that must be contained (319–20). Though she recognizes that Merricat has idealized Constance, when she comes to the question of Constance's motives, Rubenstein suggests that the idealization is not merely Merricat's but the novel's. In other words, Jackson's and Merricat's conceptions of Constance are coextensive. However, in addition to the evidence of Constance's resistance and the presence of characters like Charles and Helen Clarke,[6] who contradict Merricat's vision of Constance, Jackson peppers Merricat's narration with fantasies, games, and even hallucinations to remind the reader of the limitations of her perspective.

Merricat also places herself in a privileged position with regards to Constance, claiming to be able to see and understand her in ways others do not. She "sees" that Constance "detested having anyone near her but [Merricat]" (Jackson 26). Of course, Merricat's claims to this closeness are, like her image of Constance, mostly subjective and self-serving. At one point, Merricat ascribes discomfort to Constance despite Constance's claims to the contrary and without looking at her. The construction of the sentence showing Merricat's privileged insight invites skepticism: "Without turning I could hear from her voice that she was quiet" (Jackson 24). The sentence is both almost contradictory (hearing quietness) and unnecessarily descriptive of Merricat's position. The emphasis on "turning" suggests that Merricat cannot see Constance, making "quietness" something one can hear *and* see, rather than an absence of sound. Other episodes in the novel suggest that Merricat confuses seeing and hearing in some fundamental way, and the limitations of her perspective have been critiqued. Few critics have pointed out, though, how self-serving Merricat's claims to access to Constance as well as her constructed image of Constance as having a zest for the feminine mystique really are.[7] If, as I am suggesting, Merricat is trying to imprison Constance rather than free her from the "dangerous illusion" of "heterosexual romance" (Carpenter 36), it is not to make her an equal partner in a feminist utopia at novel's end but to promote Constance from older sister to "Mom."

Merricat's desperation to keep Constance at home aligns her with the ideology of containment, and she embodies the prejudices, paranoia, and violence necessary to sustain it. As Elaine Tyler May convincingly argues, the political strategy of containment depended on a corresponding ideology within the home. During the Cold War, people increasingly returned to the home, both physically and psychically, as the nuclear family seemed to offer both "a secure, private nest removed from the dangers of the outside world" and "a psychological fortress that would protect them against themselves" (May 1, 13). Cold War domesticity also had its own dark duality; it "ultimately fostered the very tendencies it was intended to diffuse: materialism, consumerism, and bureaucratic conformity" (May 13). In the case of *We Have Always Lived in the Castle*, although Merricat has rebelled against her parents by ending their lives, she nonetheless inherits their class prejudices. Her father fenced in the Blackwood property at her mother's request, because "The highway's built for common people . . . and [her] front door is private" (18). Merricat also cultivates a fetishistic attitude toward the family's wealth and material objects. Merricat buries her teeth and jewelry to protect the property. She also makes "offerings" of jewelry and dresses in her family's clothes on Thursday, her "most powerful day." Her identity and her sense of her family's identity are bound up in material objects: "we always had a solid foundation of stable possessions" (Jackson 1). To punish Constance, she breaks dishes, and when she discovers the villagers have broken one of her mother's Dresden figurines during the ransacking of the house, she wants to punish them too (Jackson 110). Perhaps the most highly symbolic item in Merricat's mystical arsenal is a small black notebook her father kept, which contains the names of "people who owed him money, and people who ought, he thought, to do favors for him" (Jackson 53). This book she keeps nailed to a tree on the property, and when Charles arrives shortly after it falls, she immediately connects his presence to the book's failure. Merricat's imbuing of the book with magical powers literalizes the economic power her father wields in the community and his extended family. After the elder Blackwoods die, Merricat repurposes the objects that served as symbols of their status to effect the same distance from the outside world. By the end of the novel, she has reenacted her father's enclosure of her mother within the family home by trapping Constance there and ensuring, through fear rather than physical barricades, that intruders will not return.

The contradictory and reciprocal nature of her paranoia regarding intruders further establishes Merricat's connection to containment. McCarthyism, writes Nadel, is "a term that describes generically the growing fear of subversion and the extreme measures to counter it" (71). This climate fosters and exploits paranoia, as constant vigilance is required not only to police one's neighbors but also to make sure one's own behavior is above suspicion. In *Castle*, Merricat repeatedly places herself in positions to observe "outsiders" (both the villagers and visitors to the Blackwood house) while carefully denying them the same access, often through silence or through scripted conversations she does not deviate from (from her formulaic conversations with Stella to her reliance on a grocery list for interactions at the store) and also through such rules as not eating in front of other people. What the villagers "know" about the Blackwoods, however, is not the truth; they seem to believe that Constance murdered the family and got away with it, perhaps because of her family's privilege. Their distrust of Constance is more threatening to Merricat than if they suspected the truth, for Merricat depends on Constance not only for food and care but also to legitimize her worldview. By not going outside, Constance confirms Merricat's position that "the world is full of terrible people" (Jackson 54). Merricat ardently strives to inculcate her own paranoia in Constance. Only at the end of the novel, when the villagers are convinced that the reclusive sisters can see and hear their "sins" and so begin bringing them food to beg forgiveness, has Merricat's paranoia manifested itself in the larger community. Intruders are now tolerated (if not welcomed) on the grounds near the house "turreted and open to the sky" (Jackson 120), because they behave with proper deference to Merricat in recognition of the "extreme measures" of which she is capable.

Significantly, Merricat's violence also is linked explicitly with the potentially destructive, unstable energies of the atomic age. Under stress, she repeatedly describes herself as "chilled" and "held tight" or otherwise bound.[8] Merricat's stress is invariably caused by the threat of Constance leaving the house. That her reaction to this threat ineluctably evokes containment and the "Cold" War underscores containment's reliance on the domestic and its inherent instability. Though chilled and contained, Merricat in this state feels as though she will "explode." She repeatedly attempts to channel her destructive energies through magic words and talismans and breaking dishes rather than combusting from the inside. While Merricat's use of "magic" has led some critics to classify Jackson as a writer of "weird" (i.e., genre) fiction,[9] Nadel's explication of the relationship between containment and American postmodernism provides a way to read Jackson as a "proto-postmodernist" (as Hattenhauer suggests) while reading *Castle* in its Cold War context. By reading the end of the novel through this lens, I argue that the conclusion is pessimistic not only about domesticity's ability to free itself from containment culture, but also about the continued viability of working women writers' so-called duality.

Merricat has two seemingly oppositional impulses when it comes to resolving her conflict with Charles: she wants to turn back time to before he appeared and make sure nothing ever changes, but she also wants to move forward, to escape to "the moon" with Constance and Jonas. Her primary goal when she starts destroying the bedroom where Charles is staying is to erase his presence by wiping his fingerprints off doorknobs and breaking a watch he has wound by winding it backwards. Nevertheless, she finds that she cannot return the watch or house back to an original state, so she chooses to "alter" her father's room, where Charles is staying. As a result, "Charles would be lost, shut off from what he recognized, and would have to concede that this was not the house he had come to visit and so would go away" (Jackson 87). After erasing his presence fails to disorient him,

Merricat knocks a lit pipe into a wastebasket full of newspapers. Though this is apparently a deliberate act, Merricat's narration serves to make it passive. She seems to deny the fire as she "wonders" about her eyes: "one of my eyes – the left – saw everything golden and yellow and orange, and the other eye saw shades of blue and grey and green; perhaps one eye was for daylight and the other was for night" (Jackson 99–100). Just as she appears to believe human vision can be contained within separate eyes (which, incidentally, denies the cognitive abilities necessary for sight), she believes that the fire can be contained to a single room of the house. Of course, Merricat's "magic" is no more effective here than it is elsewhere in the novel. It is significant that this failure of containment follows so quickly on Merricat's attempt to separate day and night in her two eyes. With vision as a metonym for her perspective, the novel offers apocalyptic consequences for Merricat's ideology. The energy Merricat hopes to control is too unstable to be contained. The fire burns the house Merricat wanted to protect and serves as a reason for the villagers to intrude and further destroy it. She is capable of containing Constance within the house, but that act of containment too requires Merricat's own unstable energy and exacts a price from both sisters.

The kitchen is the only room left to the sisters when they return to the house. Materially, this signifies the foreclosure of Constance's desires to leave the site. Because Merricat set the destruction of the house in motion in order to prevent Constance from leaving, this reduced sphere of movement can be interpreted as the consequence of attempting to escape. Nonetheless, like many Cold War–era housewives, Constance had prepared for such an event by stocking her cellar with canned goods. These canned goods and Constance's unshakeable middle-class fear of shabbiness (she is shocked by the suggestion that they allow the windows of the burned-out remains of the home to become dirty and insists they use cups with handles so that they may take their meals "like ladies"; Jackson 121) allow the Blackwood sisters to establish a new pattern for their days.

Moreover, the home has also been converted to "the moon," a location that Merricat mentions no fewer than thirteen times over the course of the short novel. When Constance wakes up in the forest after the fire, Merricat tells her, "We are on the moon at last" (Jackson 112). When Constance finally agrees that she too is very happy, Merricat reminds her, "I told you that you would like it on the moon" (Jackson 145). Lape suggests that the moon for Merricat is a symbol of female power, "the eternal great mother, the eternal feminine" (Lape 159). No critic of the novel has yet considered that Merricat's moon mythology might be more contemporary than ancient. It was during the time Jackson was writing *Castle* that exploration of the moon started to seem inevitable, so much so that Carl Sagan was able to posit in 1960 that "the extensive deposition of both hard- and soft-landing packages on the lunar surface seems to be imminent" (396). As with the debates over the use of nuclear power, late 1950s and early 1960s discussions of the moon were influenced by containment narratives. In particular, the national and international science communities were concerned (as Sagan exemplifies) with possible contamination of the moon by biological agents from earth. The threat of an unseen microbe infecting an entire planet mirrored the fears of the power of the infinitesimal atom to destroy the earth. The International Congress of Scientific Unions formed a committee on Contamination by Extraterrestrial Exploration in 1958. Concern about the moon's "virginity" infiltrated mainstream culture, as articles in *Reader's Digest*, *Newsweek*, and *Time* during that same year attest. Despite the invocation of this ancient metaphor, the moon was losing its status as mythological object and becoming real. An explosion of articles between 1957 and 1961 in mainstream periodicals focused on the moon's physical characteristics (its surface, atmosphere, orbit, and temperature), suggesting that the average American's knowledge of the moon was increasingly empirical and scientific. A 1958 *Good Housekeeping* article even prophesized the "end of moon myths" in the age of space exploration when "we'll know, finally and for sure, what's up there," debunking "all those strange and wonderful things that someone, somewhere, has always believed about the moon" ("Coming" 152). The moon, as both celestial body and symbol, is in danger of being contaminated by human intervention.

Merricat's musings about the moon endow the place with the fantastic elements humanity could once believe existed there: from the exotic "scarlet fish in the rivers" (Jackson 15) to the opulent "feathers in our hair, and rubies on our hands ... golden spoons" (60), the mythological "cat-furred plants and horses dancing with their wings" (75), and the familiar "rose petals" (58) and "our mother's pearls" (75). Most importantly, the moon is a place of security ("Everything's safe on the moon"; 44) and abundance ("On the moon we have everything"; 75). Furthermore, the moon cannot be contaminated by the villagers, Charles, or even the lingering effects of Merricat's own actions: "on the moon Uncle Julian would be well" (75). The moon as the frontier exists in Merricat's imagination as a place she can keep creating, adding to, and making the consummation of her desires. When Merricat terms the burned-out house "the moon," she has removed it from its mythological status and made "the moon" the charred building and ash-covered land created by her inability to contain her rage. Merricat's fantasies may remain for her at novel's end, but Constance does not share in them.

Beyond the "final frontier," the material conditions of the Blackwood sisters, particularly Constance, have not improved. It is telling that Constance is now literally confined to the kitchen, her routines reduced to caring for Merricat and preventing further decay. Constance certainly does not behave as one liberated from patriarchy. Hiding in the dark while the villagers ransack the house, Constance finally asks Merricat if she was the one who poisoned the family. Merricat tells us that they had never spoken of it before. Perhaps Constance speaks only out of utter shock, as in the ensuing pages, she's described as pale and still: "Constance, who was always dancing, seemed now unwilling to move" (117). Later, she apologizes to Merricat, saying she was "wicked" to "have reminded you of why they all died" (130). Constance has been silenced, having been made aware once again of what Merricat is capable. To make sure she is not a victim of Merricat's rage, Constance will "never talk about it again" (130), and she consents to take care of the "poor baby" Merricat (112).

Even if Merricat's fantasies remain, her ability to communicate them to the outside world has been changed. In the new order she has created, the outside world infiltrates through the gifts the villagers bring, but all attempts to make sense of what has happened in narrative break down. Merricat finds herself in a state of confusion: "we had somehow lost ourselves and come back through the wrong gap in time, or the wrong door, or the wrong fairy tale" (114). She narrates eating her breakfast after sifting through the rubble in the destroyed kitchen but notes, "I do not know when I found three chairs and when I ate buttered bread, whether I had found the chairs and then eaten bread, or whether I had eaten first, or even done both at once" (Jackson 116). Even though the destruction of the home is the direct result of events that Merricat set in motion, she cannot conceive of herself as responsible, and thus finds both past and present untethered from a comprehensible series of causes and effects.

Significantly, this is a new order into which Julian is not permitted. Julian, the novel's housebound, wounded writer, spends his postpoisoning life obsessed with the "unsolved" case. In this, he embodies modernist poetics described by Brian McHale as dominated by epistemological concerns (McHale 9). Julian worries he will not be able to account for every detail: he tells Constance, "I have a thousand details to remember and note down, and not a minute to waste. I would hate to lose any small thing from their last day; my book must be complete" (Jackson 50). He relishes the possibility of talking to Cousin Charles in order to be filled in on "details" during the trial he could not have observed himself; he also worries that additional details, crucial though they may be to his sense of "completion," will further hinder his progress (62). Information and time are inversely related to each other. Julian sees himself on an epistemological quest to account for an infinite number of details within a finite number of pages and within a finite number of years. Perhaps, as a result of the poisoning, the ontological uncertainty that McHale finds to be the distinguishing characteristic of postmodernism is introduced into Julian's project. Julian begins to ask if "it" really did happen (Jackson 32, 66). He is reluctant "to invent, to fictionalize, to imagine" (66), but he feels that he will be forced to. He names Constance as his literary heir, hoping she will be a "worthy cynic" (43). Constance assures him that the poisonings really happened and agrees to accept his papers, thereby suggesting the possibility that the "housewife" might become the writer, with the blessing of her predecessors to tell stories "not too concerned with the truth" (43). Julian seems to allude to the inevitability of the breakdown of containment narratives and to suggest that a previously silenced voice, Constance's, might be allowed to speak.

In one sense, Constance does act as Julian's heir: after the majority of her clothes burned in the fire, she wears, as Merricat puts it, "the skins of Uncle Julian" (137). By placing his papers in a box and promising never to speak of the poisonings again, however, Constance demonstrates that her association with Julian the writer is only "skin" deep. Instead, the "writer" that emerges is the narrator, Merricat, telling her story to an interlocutor who seems as uncurious about the poisonings as she is. The story Merricat tells, then, is of the time that Constance almost escaped and the lengths to which Merricat went in order to contain her within the home. Merricat's power, her narrative, and the very title of the book rely on the presence of Constance, the "fairy princess" trapped in her kitchen, unaware of the time of day or even how old she is, silenced forever and subsumed within Merricat's "we," but of course, as Merricat tells us, "very happy."

Notes

1 Critics have viewed Merricat as "bold" (Oppenheimer 165), "creative, imaginative" (Carpenter 202), "compulsively appealing" (Downey 189), the "most complex and satisfying of Jackson's creations" (Lape 25), and the only truly happy character in all of Jackson's fiction (Murphy 20). Carpenter finds that Constance "empowered" Merricat to poison the family (202); Egan terms her an accomplice after the fact (23). Hattenhauer suggests that Constance is actually the mastermind of the pair, "a passive-aggressive enabler who unconsciously uses her cloying sweetness to get the dark Merricat to do her dirty work. She is the one who taught Merricat about poisons. And Merricat administered it by slipping it into the sugar that Constance put on the table" (Hattenhauer 177).
2 Merricat's actions are characterized as a rebellion against the patriarchy (Carpenter 202), to free her helpless sister Constance (Lape 173) from oppression and perhaps even sexual abuse (Hall 111) by murdering their mother, father, aunt, and younger brother.
3 The ending is called a "triumph" (Oppenheimer 165), a "woman-centered life" (Lape 25), a matriarchal new order held together by "the sisters' mutual affection" (Carpenter 202), free of "domestic expectation, free of schedules, deadlines, and responsibility to others" (Lape 180).
4 See pages 61, 125, 136, 145, and 146 of *Castle*.
5 Merricat perhaps hints that the reason she brings Constance books from the library is not really to fulfill Constance's desire to read cookbooks, but because Julian likes the "look" of a woman reading: "Although Uncle Julian never took up a book, he liked to see Constance reading in the evenings while he worked at his papers, and sometimes he turned his head to look at her and nod. 'What are you reading, my dear? A pretty sight, a lady with a book'" (Jackson 2).
6 Though Charles is clearly mercenary and critics have tended to read him as a threatening male figure, he disrupts Merricat's conventional image of Constance. Charles calls her "Connie," rather than "Constance," the diminutive signaling not only familiar affection but also a reluctance to dwell on the past and foreclose change, impulses which both Merricat and Julian entertain. He is the only member of the Blackwood family who is content to eat whatever Constance cooks instead of "ordering" food each morning (Jackson 64). He reminds Merricat that Constance "works like a slave" (81). Merricat even notes that he makes his own bed and assumes that "his mother must have taught him" (76).
7 In an interesting take on the novel, Marilyn Boyer argues that Merricat exploits Uncle Julian's disability to ensure her own survival (i.e., Constance's continued presence in the house). See "Disability as a Survival Mechanism in the Works of Shirley Jackson" in *Studies in Weird Fiction 25* (2003): 12–21. Print.
8 For references to Merricat being chilled, see pages 19, 21, 27, 39, 50, 55, 90, 92, and 130. For references to her being bound or held tight, see pages 27, 57, 61, 84, and 92.
9 See Egan, James. "Sanctuary: Shirley Jackson's Domestic and Fantastic Parables." *Studies in Weird Fiction*. No. 6 (Fall 1989): 15–24, and Joshi, S.T. "Shirley Jackson: Domestic Horror." *Studies in Weird Fiction*. No. 14 (Winter 1994): 9–28. Also, in Paul N. Reinsch's *A Critical Bibliography of Shirley Jackson, American Writer (1919–1965): Reviews, Criticism, Adaptations*, he notes that "the view of Jackson as an, admittedly exceptional, author of occult horror literature still dominates critical discussion" (Reinsch 1).

Works cited

Carpenter, Lynette. "The Establishment and Preservation of Female Power in Shirley Jackson's *We Have Always Lived in the Castle*." *Frontiers: A Journal of Women Studies* 8:1 (1984): 32–8. Web. JSTOR. 5 Feb. 2010.

"Coming: The End of the Moon Myths?" *Good Housekeeping* 147 (September 1958): 152. Print.

Downey, Dara. "'Reading Her Difficult Riddle': Shirley Jackson and Late 1950s' Anthropology." *It Came from the 1950s!: Popular Culture, Popular Anxieties*. Eds. Darryl Jones, Elizabeth McCarthy, and Bernice M. Murphy. New York: Palgrave Macmillan, 2001. 176–97. Print.

Hague, Angela. "'A Faithful Anatomy of Our Times': Reassessing Shirley Jackson." *Frontiers* 26:2 (2005): 73–96. Web. ProjectMuse. 30 Apr. 2010.

Hall, Karen J. "Sisters in Collusion: Safety and Revolt in Shirley Jackson's *We Have Always Lived in the Castle*." *The Significance of Sibling Relationships in Literature*. Eds. JoAnna Stephens Mink and Janet Doubler Ward. Bowling Green, OH: Bowling Green State UP, 1993. 110–18.

Hattenhauer, Darryl. *Shirley Jackson's American Gothic*. Albany: State U of New York P, 2003. E-book.

Jackson, Shirley. *We Have Always Lived in the Castle*. New York: Penguin, 1962, 2006. Print.

Lape, Sue Veregge. "The Lottery's Hostage: The Life and Feminist Fiction of Shirley Jackson." Unpublished dissertation. Ohio State U, 1992. ProQuest.

Lundberg, Ferdinand and Marynia F. Farnham. *Modern Woman: The Lost Sex*. New York: Harper & Brothers, 1947. Print.

McGraw-Edison Company, Toastmaster Appliances. Advertisement. *Good Housekeeping* (Dec 1960): 184. Print.

McHale, Brian. *Postmodernist Fiction*. London and New York: Routledge, 1987. Print.

May, Elaine Tyler. *Homeward Bound: American Families in the Cold War Era (Fully Revised and Updated 20th Anniversary Edition, with a New Post 9/11 Epilogue)*. New York: Basic Books, 1988, 1999, 2008. Print.

Murphy, Bernice M. "Introduction." *Shirley Jackson: Essays on the Literary Legacy*. Ed. Bernice M. Murphy. Jefferson, NC: McFarland and Company, 2005. 1–21. Print.

Nadel, Alan. *Containment Culture: American Narratives, Postmodernism, and the Atomic Age*. Durham: Duke UP, 1995. Print.

Oates, Joyce Carol. "The Witchcraft of Shirley Jackson." *New York Review of Books* 56:15 (8 October 2009): 11–13. Print.

Oppenheimer, Judy. *Private Demons: The Life of Shirley Jackson*. New York: G. P. Putnam's Sons, 1988. Print.

Parks, John G. "Chambers of Yearning: Shirley Jackson's Use of the Gothic." *Twentieth-Century Literature* 30:1 (Spring 1984): 15–29. Web. JSTOR. 5 Feb. 2010.

Reinsch, Paul N. *A Critical Bibliography of Shirley Jackson, American Writer (1919–1965): Reviews, Criticism, Adaptations*. Lewiston, NY: E. Mellen P, 2001. Print.

Rubenstein, Roberta. "House Mothers and Haunted Daughters: Shirley Jackson and Female Gothic." *Tulsa Studies in Women's Literature* 15:2 (Autumn 1996): 309–31. Web. JSTOR. 5 Feb. 2010.

Sagan, Carl. "Biological Contamination of the Moon." *Proceedings of the National Academy of Sciences of the United States of America* 46:4 (1960): 396–402. Web. JSTOR. 8 Jul. 2011.

8 Knowing and narration
Shirley Jackson and the campus novel

James E. Dobson

In *The College Novel in America*, John O. Lyons's 1962 survey of the American college novel, Lyons argues that the novel of academic life is one in which education itself, rather than the social lives of students, is taken seriously as the text's main subject. It must, he adds, also feature students or professors as the major characters. Lyons's survey was the first to consider the possibilities of the American college experience as material for producing what he considered a "serious" national novel. He relies upon conventional understandings of the novel during the midcentury, including Lionel Trilling's now well-known oppositional pairing of the romance and the novel. Lyons proceeds to examine a large set of contenders for the serious novel of university life, from Nathaniel Hawthorne's *Fanshawe* (1828) to Mary McCarthy's *The Groves of Academe* (1951), in making his compelling case that the American campus novel could fit into his contemporary criteria for a serious novel. His criteria for selection leans, as one might expect, toward the rather male and middle-class. When he turns to consider the female variant of the academic novel, he names Shirley Jackson's odd representation of Natalie Waite's troubling first-year college experience in *Hangsaman* (1951) "the most impressive novel about an undergraduate's experience at a women's college" and devotes the majority of this slim chapter to a reading of this text.[1]

Despite this important positioning, Jackson's novel has, for the most part, disappeared from considerations of the American campus novel. Once the novel went out of print, it gradually ceased to be an object of discussion. Even the feminist critique of Lyons's early canon of college books ignores Jackson's place in this literary tradition. What seems most interesting about Lyons's assessment of *Hangsaman* within the bounds of the genre as he defines it is the degree to which higher education is not taken seriously at all by the novel or the characters. Jackson's novel is one of the more critical and ambivalent accounts of American college life. *Hangsaman* reveals a deeply alienating culture that both enables and complicates the possibility of the transformative experience that has been assumed as the goal of undergraduate education, since at least John Henry Newman's classic *The Idea of a University* (1852). Within the American context, campus novels, including Jackson's, also address the degree to which another kind of promised transformation associated with higher learning, economic and class, may have become increasingly difficult during the twentieth century. The recent republication of Jackson's novel by Penguin in 2013 provides an opportunity to reconsider her novel and its representation of college life and the undergraduate experience. Indeed, it is only through the recovery of *Hangsaman*'s place within this tradition that we can uncover the roots of a disturbing countercurrent within the modern American campus novel and, at the same time, make Jackson's novel a little less strange.

The campus novel is a novel set primarily at a college or university and, despite Lyons's protestations, concerns both the academic and the social lives of students. This genre takes advantage of the similarity in confusion and naiveté between the student protagonist and the reader to introduce the new and frequently self-contained world through which the student will undergo some transformation. In a recent critical essay, Jeffrey Williams notes the division between the academic and the campus novel and the growing interest in the former category at the present time. Williams produces the distinction as such:

> "campus novels" . . . tend to revolve around campus life and present young adult comedies or dramas, most frequently coming-of-age narratives [while] "academic novels" . . . feature those who work as academics, although the action is rarely confined to a campus, and they portray adult predicaments in marriage and home as well as the workplace, most familiarly yielding mid-life crisis plots.
>
> (562)

Williams's key characteristic for the campus novel, the transitional "coming-of-age narrative," has been at the center of discussions about many campus novels, and the degree to which this narrative structures Jackson's *Hangsaman* has framed most of the existing critical work on the novel. The challenges to the coming-of-age plot within the college or university setting have certainly been the subject of the campus novel since its early forms, from Owen Johnson's *Stover at Yale* (1912) to F. Scott Fitzgerald's *This Side of Paradise* (1920), through May Sarton's *The Small Room* (1961) to Tom Wolfe's *I Am Charlotte Simmons* (2004), and Jeffrey Eugenides's recent take on the genre in *The Marriage Plot* (2011). Jackson's *Hangsaman* adds an important corrective to the college novel's coming-of-age plot through its depiction of the complications encountered by a female college student in adapting herself to a fundamentally alienating narrative structure with a predetermined ending. Jackson shows how this restrictive environment is fundamentally at odds with the promise of American universities and colleges to enable numerous class, social, and personal transformations.

Within critical takes on the idea of the university, the concept of self-transformation has also remained an ideal. Andrew Delbanco's recent argument for the retention of liberal education within the American university, *College: What It Was, Is, and Should Be* (2013), places itself directly in conversation with the topics concerning the authors listed earlier. Fictional representations of campus life are among his key sources for examining the idea of the university within the American cultural imaginary. And why not? As a professor of English,

Delbanco well knows the power of representational forms such as the novel to materialize and test the highest ideas and ideals of a culture. He cites a response from John "Dink" Stover, the protagonist of Johnson's *Stover at Yale*, to his question of the purpose of college: "I'm going to do the best thing a fellow can do at our age, I'm going to loaf!" Defending the ideal of contemplation and the possibility of transformative experience that depends upon the wide-ranging liberal study forming the conditions of possibility for contemplation, Delbanco's *College* explicitly engages with the coming-of-age narrative within the discourse of the campus novel.

While Lyons's *The College Novel in America* (1962) set the tone for the discussion of the campus novel for years to come, recent surveys such as Shirley Marchalonis's *College Girls: A Century in Fiction* (1995) and Elaine Showalter's *Faculty Towers: The Academic Novel and Its Discontents* (2005) provide updated accounts. Marchalonis explicitly responds to Lyons's thesis by noting the marginalization of accounts featuring women's colleges or the experiences of women in coeducational institutions. She selects works written by authors attending college during the period from 1890 to 1910 and thus is unable to contend with Lyons's assertion that Jackson's novel is a crucial text in the understanding of fictional representations of a women's college. In addition, Marchalonis argues that her selected texts struggle with a double-bind to simultaneously represent going to college as a novel experience while demonstrating that college women were no different than the others. This results in the idealization of the women's college that Jackson's novel seeks to undermine:

> The early writing presents a women's space that nourished community – a space, called the green world in this book, with its own rules; it offered women more room to define themselves than they could find anywhere else. This women's space is the core of all good in the early fiction.
>
> (4)

Showalter's *Faculty Towers* takes a different tack through her shifting of emphasis from novels of student life to those featuring professors – the subgenre that both she and Williams refer to as the academic rather than campus novel. Showalter's list of novels charts out a deeply satirical subgenre that questions the idealistic assumptions held by many novels focusing on student life.

If the campus novel generally concerns the process of self-definition and the representation of the liberal ideal of a transformative experience for the undergraduate student, it also has a tendency to invoke what might be called the flip side of this romance plot. Mirroring the description of an internal transformation, we also find Gothic college tales that show the degree to which the spires and towers of academe have frequently concealed a darker story of class stratification and conflict, sexual assault, binge drinking, and drug use. In this narrative social concerns and student life issues overwhelm and interfere with what Lyons would consider the serious plot of education. We find examples throughout the literary representation of the university, from the radicals attempting to end secret societies and social privilege in *Stover at Yale* and *This Side of Paradise* to the depiction of overworked and abandoned students, like May Sarton's Jane Seaman in *The Small Room*. In our present moment, student life issues have become pressing; with the Department of Education's recent use of Title IX to investigate the preponderance of sexual violence and discrimination on college campuses, discussions of previously unreported and underreported activities and crimes are finally being taken seriously. For authors like Shirley Jackson and certainly for far too many students, Marchalonis's "green world" was artificially maintained.

My aim in this essay is not to reveal a submerged network of reference and citation within and directed toward *Hangsaman* – although one could certainly do this – but to ask what Jackson's novel can teach us about the promises and failures of the mid-twentieth-century American college. I will begin by locating *Hangsaman* in relation to Shirley Jackson's larger depiction of college students, faculty, and campus life and in relation to her specific representation of Bennington College. I then position Jackson at the origins of a Bennington-centric literary tradition of critical campus fiction. Finally, I'll offer my own reading of *Hangsaman* that brings together the numerous topics, figures, and, most importantly, critiques that collectively haunt this tradition.

In the spring of 1945 Shirley Jackson moved to rural North Bennington, Vermont, with her husband, Stanley Edgar Hyman, from Greenwich Village in New York City. Hyman was to teach at Bennington College at the invitation of Kenneth Burke. At the time, Jackson was already well known within literary circles for several short stories that she had published in the *New Yorker*. In 1948, she published her first novel, *The Road Through the Wall*, and in June of the same year, her infamous "The Lottery" appeared in the *New Yorker*. This was also the year in which Hyman published his assault on contemporary literary criticism, *The Armed Vision: A Study in the Methods of Modern Literary Criticism* (1948). In dedicating his volume of criticism to Shirley, "A critic of critics of critics," he draws attention to the importance of Jackson's critical faculties by naming her a metacritic. In 1949 Jackson, Hyman, and their three children moved from Bennington to Westport, Connecticut; they returned to North Bennington in 1952, and Hyman once again took up teaching at Bennington College.

Hangsaman was Jackson's second novel. It was published by Farrar, Straus & Young in 1951 during the Hymans' three-year absence from North Bennington. The novel describes the first-semester experiences of Natalie Waite at an unnamed and recently founded women's college that has more than some resemblance to Bennington College. It opens during Natalie's last few weeks at home with her family, and the early section turns around a Sunday afternoon cocktail party at her family's home prior to her departure. During the party, and under the cover of darkness, Natalie is led into the woods by a friend of her father's and sexually assaulted. With no notice taken of her state by her family, she denies and quickly represses any memory of this event and prepares to leave for college. Natalie arrives on campus, enrolls in a slate of dull introductory courses, and encounters a cast of collegiate archetypes: Rosalind, a conspiratorial friend who later turns against her; Arthur Langdon, her English professor, who mirrors her own father and for a short while serves as the object of her affections; Arthur's disenchanted and alcoholic young wife, Elizabeth, only a few years older than Natalie; two older students, Anne and Vicki, who are engaged in a romantic tryst with Arthur; and Tony, a mysterious acquaintance who appears to be called into being by Natalie's imagination. Feeling alienated by everyone else, Natalie and Tony ultimately decide to reject college life and leave the campus. Arriving in a wooded space at the end of town, Tony's suddenly strange behavior frightens Natalie, and she decides to make a break with Tony. Tony disappears into the woods, and Natalie solicits a ride back to town from a passing vehicle, briefly considers suicide, and then returns to the campus.

A major plot element of Jackson's novel, Natalie's or possibly even Tony's departure from college for the woods, closely resembles the real-life disappearance of a twenty-one-year-old Bennington student, Paula Jean Welden. Welden hitchhiked from Bennington on December 1, 1949, to take an evening hike on an extended trail network known as the "Long Trail." Welden was never found, and her sudden disappearance continued to haunt Jackson's imagination. A later story, uncollected until the publication of *Just an Ordinary Day* (1996), evidences the long-term impact of Welden's disappearance on Jackson. "The Missing Girl" appeared in *Fantasy and Science Fiction* in December of 1957. The story concerns the disappearance of a camper by the name of Martha Alexander from a girl's summer camp, the "Phillips Educational Camp for Girls Twelve to Sixteen." Despite switching the setting from Bennington College to a summer camp, Jackson continues her exploration of the logic that allows a figure within an institution to disappear without a trace. After several weeks of searching for Martha, the search ends. The camp director, "Old Jane," and the local police chief, Hook, scrub their respective official records clean of any presence of Martha. In order to make life easier for themselves, her roommate, Betsy, and Martha's extended family deny Martha's existence. The body is eventually found and buried without much notice. Jackson's story shows how much easier and more acceptable it is to erase Martha from existence than to acknowledge the social failures of the camp to look after its own campers.

Jackson's experiences with college resembled those had by more than one of her fictional characters. She first attended the University of Rochester in Rochester, New York, in 1934. She left in the spring semester of 1936 reportedly because of poor academic performance. After a year of sustained, daily writing back at home, Jackson applied to and was accepted by Syracuse University, where she studied English and communication. She was active in several student publications as a contributor and editor. Jackson earned her BA in English in June of 1940, alongside her then-boyfriend and future husband, Stanley Edgar Hyman.[2] Her first story, "Janice," was published in 1938 in the Syracuse literary annual, *The Threshold*. "Janice" is shorter than most Jackson stories but the origins of her art can be found in this, her first publication. "Janice" is just over one page of a narration of an afternoon and evening in the life of a student who has attempted suicide earlier in the day in response to the news that her parents can no longer afford to send her to college. An unnamed friend narrates "Janice" and listens as

Jan compulsively tells her friends about how she started a car in the family garage but was interrupted by a neighbor cutting the grass. The narrator listens to the story, first over the phone and then in a social setting with others, and each time asks for minor details about the event. The story ends on the start of Jan's third repetition of what has become her refrain: "nearly killed myself this afternoon" (566). The narrator and Jan's friends demonstrate a complete lack of compassion; other than curiosity about the near-death experience, these friends seem uninterested in Jan. From "Janice" we can draw two major threads that we find repeated in Jackson's other works of college fiction, including *Hangsaman*: the existence of an institutionally and socially alienated student and difficulty in self-narration that leads to narrative reproduction rather than transformation and re-creation.

Jackson's college students seek escape from institutions and the limiting narrative structures in which they are frequently embedded. An unnamed college student frequents a small bookstore to take furtive glances at a copy of William Empson's *Seven Types of Ambiguity* in a story that takes its title from Empson's monograph. Unable to afford this text, the student returns to the store again and again to read it in segments. His habit is broken only by the purchase of this text, in the student's absence, by a man who the student assisted in locating well-known and canonical books of interest. In "The Man in the Woods," a story first brought into print in April of 2014 by the *New Yorker*, a young male protagonist named Christopher rather spontaneously leaves his college only to find a cottage in the woods and the site of his own possible murder. Christopher describes his departure from school as such: "One day I was there, in college, like everyone else, and then the next day I just left, without any reason except that I did" (180). Like "The Missing Girl," this story enables Jackson to work through the possible reasons for Paula Welden's sudden disappearance from Bennington. Christopher is like most of Jackson's student protagonists; they seldom seem at home on campus and are in a restless search for alternatives and escapes. In so doing, students also animate animosities between faculty wives and faculty members and upend the supposedly safe campus for certain groups of people. From *Just an Ordinary Day*, "The Very Hot Sun in Bermuda" concerns a young undergraduate by the name of Katie Collins, who, like many other female students in Jackson's work, engages in a quasi-secret romantic tryst with her professor, Peter. Throughout the story, Collins refers to Peter's wife as a "hag" while pressuring Peter to leave with her for a vacation to Bermuda.[3] *Hangsaman* examines a variation on this theme through the flirtations between Arthur Langdon and Anne and Vicki, two of his students.

Whereas the wives are neglected and humiliated, the faculty husbands are inept and in possession of a stereotypically inflated sense of self-importance. Jackson almost routinely represents her academics as idiosyncratic, arrogant, and incompetent. *The Haunting of Hill House*'s Dr. John Montague is an example of such an academic. Dr. Montague is an anthropologist who, in apparent opposition to his more rationally minded peers, studies supernatural manifestations. He brings a group of strangers together to live in Hill House as an experiment for his research into the supernatural. Jackson describes the conclusion of his experiment as an utter failure: "Dr. Montague finally retired from active scholarly pursuits after the cool, almost contemptuous reception of his preliminary article analyzing the psychic phenomena of Hill House" (417). James Harris, one of Jackson's frequently used figures within her shorter fiction, takes the role of an academic in a story titled "Of Course." This Mr. Harris is an oppressive patriarchal figure, much like the other academics found in Jackson's work and perhaps resembling academics most familiar to Jackson, in particular her husband, Stanley Hyman. Harris is a controlling scholar who "writes monographs" for a profession and disapproves of almost all popular culture, from board games, the radio, movies, to newspapers, the latter of which he refers to as "a mass degradation of taste" (182). Harris's high-culture disapproval of popular entertainment alienates his wife and son from all society, including the family's new neighbors, the friendly and disruptively modern Taylor family.

Perhaps Jackson's best-known representation of college life can be found in a satirical essay describing her experiences as what she terms a "faculty wife" in an essay for *Mademoiselle* in December of 1956, five years after the publication of *Hangsaman*. In this essay, Jackson creates a persona that allows her the distance needed to produce a critique of the social relations that appear in a different form in *Hangsaman*. She writes of herself, as she does in some of her other work, as a housewife and thus removes any relation between her as the authorial subject of this fictionalized autobiography and her occupation as a writer. Jackson's Bennington is an antagonistic environment in which she feels devalued and constantly compared to the faculty, the other wives, and the students. When responding to a student's question about her own prior attendance at college and "how come you just ended up doing housework and stuff," Jackson responds, "I have a job. I cook and sew and clean and shop and make beds and drive people places and – ." Cut off and ignored by this student, Jackson concludes her essay with a humorous threat: "I think that maybe I will invite a few of my husband's students over for tea one of these days and drop them down the well."

Her feeling of displacement as a faculty wife, to be sure, an overdetermined role in a small college town, also appears in her autobiographical memoir of domestic and family life that was published shortly after *Hangsaman*, *Life Among the Savages* (1953). In this text, which was produced from several of her successful magazine pieces, Jackson describes anxiously arriving at a hospital for the birth of her third child and her encounter with a skeptical nurse:

"Age?" she asked. "Sex? Occupation?"
"Writer," I said.
"Housewife," she said.
"Writer," I said.
"I'll just put down housewife," she said.
(68)

Not having a distinct and visible role within the community, it seems that Jackson cannot claim the professional role as author. This dialogue also exhibits potential anxieties resulting from turning everyday domestic situations into the material for her professional work as a writer. If telling the story of being a housewife enabled her to sustain herself as a writer – and, we should note, her writing sustained the entire family, as Stanley's income was quite small compared to the money that Jackson was able to command for her magazine publications – then she would be forced to reenact a version of this scene between herself and the nurse with her reader.

Having made North Bennington her home after her initial departure, the small New England town and its liberal arts college continued to animate Jackson's imagination until her untimely death. Although still a very young institution – founded in 1932, Bennington College was hardly a decade old when Jackson and Hyman arrived – she saw a Bennington that had quickly become like every other institution despite its initial radical conception. "Anything which begins new and fresh," she writes in the early pages of *Hangsaman*, "will finally become old and silly" (47). Her fictionalized depictions of Bennington are frequently negative; *Hangsaman* critiques what she sees as the great distance between the ideals and the lived reality of the college. Her narrator describes the aims of the institution as such:

> The college to which Arnold Waite, after much discussion, had decided to send his only daughter was one of those intensely distressing organizations which had been formed on precisely the same lofty and advanced principles as hoarier seats of learning, but which applied them with slight differences in detail; education, the youthful founders of the college had told the world blandly, was more a matter of attitude than of learning.
>
> (47)

The proper attitude, as *Hangsaman* explains, means being open to what it calls "experience," and it is experience that this fictionalized institution seeks to impart. Yet the institution is not prepared to handle or render teachable the actual experiences of its students. According to her narrator, the college was caught between two states of being that prevented it from functioning as an idealized academic community:

> Thus the college was, in brief, a place modern, authentic, progressive, realistic, honest, and humane, with decent concessions to the fact that it was supposed to be, and had to be a strictly budget-balanced proposition, a factory in which the intake must necessarily match the outgo.
>
> (50)

We find, then, in Jackson's novel a depiction of an institution that has made a whole series of "concessions" between two positions that work to shift the focus from academics to socializing and led to the employment of an undertrained and incompetent faculty.

The Bennington College that Jackson was intimately familiar with, however, was a little different. Faculty and visitors were involved in the production of many important works of literature and literary criticism. Bennington left a lasting impact on numerous writers and critics who had a relationship with the institution, including, but hardly limited to, Ralph Ellison, Mary Oliver, Howard Nemerov, and Anne Waldman. Many of these figures were guests of Hyman and Jackson, and after visiting Bennington, several authors, including Ellison and Nemerov, exchanged numerous letters and manuscripts with Jackson. Shirley Jackson's work and her critique of college life have produced a profound influence on a generation of former Bennington College students, including Jonathan Lethem, Donna Tartt, and Bret Easton Ellis. This group, all of whom attended Bennington in the early 1980s, shared a common set of concerns and criticisms centered on the fundamental problems of social inclusivity and the impediments to economic and social transformations found within Bennington's privileged and increasingly wealthy student body. Having become coeducational in 1969, the Bennington these students found was certainly much different from the single-sex institution encountered by Jackson. In 1982 when Jonathan Lethem arrived at Bennington and took up residence in North Bennington, he felt that the town was still marked by the presence of Shirley Jackson. He remarks on this presence in an introductory essay to *We Have Always Lived in the Castle* that was reprinted under the title "Outcastle" in a recently published collection of his nonfiction essays: "Jackson is one of American fiction's impossible presences, too material to be called a phantom in literature's house, too in print to be 'rediscovered'" (373). Not only was Jackson still present, but so too were some of those who had inspired her: "some of the local figures Jackson had contended with twenty years before were still hanging around the town square where the legendary lottery took place" (375). The difficulties for outsiders, especially those from less privileged families, that Jackson found at this insular and small liberal arts college remained a fertile source for the literary imagination.

Donna Tartt and Bret Easton Ellis followed Jackson in writing campus novels set at Bennington. The local history and aura of this town and college informed their cynical and Gothic take on the campus novel. Donna Tartt had first entered the University of Mississippi before she transferred to Bennington in 1982. *The Secret History* (1992) was her first book and was written while she was a student at Bennington. Like many campus novels, *The Secret History* narrates the experiences of an outsider figure attempting to navigate an inclusive institution and social scene. Like herself, Tartt's protagonist Richard Papen transfers from an institution quite different from a small New England liberal arts college. Tartt set *The Secret History* at "Hampden College," a lightly fictionalized Bennington, and the novel details two murders committed by a small group of exclusive and wealthy classics majors. One section of the novel concerns the believed disappearance, following his murder, of a student named "Bunny" in the dark woods surrounding Hampden. Tartt's use of this trope participates in the same referential gesture to Paula Welden's disappearance as Jackson's *Hangsaman*. When Bunny vanishes from the campus, we see little notice or concern on the part of the other students. In keeping the secret of both murders, Richard is able to successfully transform himself into an insider and gain acceptance from the other classics majors.

Bret Easton Ellis was at Bennington at the same time as Tartt and published his first novel, *Less Than Zero* (1985), while still a student. His second novel, *The Rules of Attraction* (1987), is set at a small New England college named "Camden College" that has more than some resemblance to Bennington. Opening with a student recalling her rape by several students, Ellis's dark campus novel details the sexual and social lives of the disenchanted and suicidal students of the mid-1980s. The majority of the chapters in *The Rules of Attraction* are first-person narrations of the experiences of an interconnected yet isolated student body during a single academic year. The novel formally depicts the indeterminacy of several events by narrating each from multiple perspectives with very different understandings of the content and meaning of these events. Experience, in Ellis's novel, trumps education as his highly experimental students switch friends, drugs, and sexual partners. Ellis revitalizes the campus novel by restoring the private lives of students and imagining a whole new set of behaviors and practices that he understands to be operating within what Andrew Delbanco has termed the modern college's "playground of unregulated freedom" (19). Ellis's novel suggests that this playground is only for the privileged, as his fictionalized campus has no characters like Tartt's Richard Papen, who desire to transform their socioeconomic class.

Christopher Findeisen has recently argued that the American campus novel has a special concern with examining the class-leveling promise of higher education. Findeisen identifies an alternative tradition within the genre that demonstrates that the promise of higher education to "address society's economic inequalities" (292) was never a real possibility. He opens his essay with a reading of *The Rules of Attraction* in order to propose that this novel is an exception to the norms of the genre: "*The Rules of Attraction* – a campus novel that denies the transformative power of education – is thus at odds with the dominant cultural narratives surrounding the social uses of universities in neoliberal America" (292). To make this argument, Findeisen turns to Tartt's *The Secret History* and her depiction of Richard Papen as an outsider who successfully converts himself into an insider through an inclusive institution of higher education. While the event that makes Papen's social transformation possible is the shared secret of the murders and not the result of any institutional practice or the outcome of any pedagogical practice, Findeisen is correct about the greater economic diversity found in Tartt's depiction of Bennington. Yet this does not enable any sort of fundamental transformation of the students; Papen achieves social acceptance through his wealthy sociopaths, not economic transformation or the promise of future monetary success – the novel, after all, ends with Richard in a doctoral program in English. While *The Secret History* and *The Rules of Attraction* share a set of references and make gestures toward each other's novels – the result of writing together in undergraduate workshops at Bennington – neither contains explicit references to Jackson's *Hangsaman*. Rather, it is their shared interest in examining the hostility of insular and privileged students to the outsider figure wherein we find a useful representational relay.

The unofficial "motto" of Natalie's unnamed women's college reads "theory is nothing, experience is all" (49). Throughout *Hangsaman*, Jackson relentlessly mocks this institution for insufficient academic rigor, loose requirements, unrestrained sexual relations between students and faculty, and lack of collegiality between students, yet she too believes in the power of experience. But the experience that Jackson values is not to be found through association with faculty – that results only in a repetition of familiar and familial relations – rather, she has in mind private experience, a category of events that Jackson's novel withholds through narrative elision and oblique reference. Narratively indeterminate events produce epistemological uncertainty within the novel and only increase in occurrence during Natalie's first year at college. It is only through her developing ability to become the author and interpreter of her experience that Natalie survives the process of institutionalization.

There are two main methodological frames that have been the most successful in the interpretation of Natalie and in understanding what takes place in *Hangsaman*: the psychological and the psychoanalytic. To these we might add trauma theory and an account of PTSD, or post-traumatic stress disorder. While these readings reveal important aspects of the novel, Natalie's struggle to exercise control over her own narrative signals its participation in the logic of the coming-of-age story that characterizes the campus novel. This is not to say that the novel is uninterested in an exploration of Natalie's psychological state, but that Jackson represents Natalie's interiority, her sense of self, as a developing set of narratives that are under constant threat by others. Natalie is foremost a writer and the extent to which she has control over her own narratives is crucial to Jackson's representation of her development. Everyone in the novel demands that Natalie produce narratives. We find a demand for writing or confession in three major locations: her daily diary entries that her father requests and reads, the academic writing required by her professors, and the confessions demanded by other students.

The novel opens with a depiction of Natalie producing several major narratives at the same time. These are threaded throughout the first chapters and include her private fantasy detective story, the repressed event of her sexual assault in the woods, and the written narratives produced by Natalie that her father reads back to her. Once Natalie leaves home for college, several of these narratives are replaced with her dialogues with her friend Tony, but her discourses with her father continue, now via letters exchanged through the mail. Natalie then produces academic papers and creative stories for her English professor, Arthur Langdon. These writings differ from the others since they are not the same sort of confessional stories or character sketches demanded by her father. As Natalie develops, she gradually rejects or restructures the importance of these demands for narratives throughout the novel by withholding and reworking her private experience.

Jackson first introduces the idea that coming-of-age for Natalie means control against narrative multiplicity through a scene in which Natalie reflects on the world and herself in the one space at her home in which she feels the most free and in the most possession of her personality, the garden. Lying on the grass, Natalie looks out over the fields and the mountains in the distance and absorbs this fanciful vision as the material for her private imagination:

> she was not able to leave the fields and mountains alone where she found them, but required herself to take them in and use them, a carrier of something simultaneously real and unreal to set up against the defiantly real-and-unreal batterings of her family.
>
> (23)

This is a scene of awakening: Natalie realizes "her capacity for creation," and it is this creative and defensive act that awakens something in her that will, by the end of the novel, render her a "solitary functioning individual." But at this point she contains multitudes and remains subject to the "real-and-unreal" of family and institutional life.

We had already seen elements of the real and unreal in the most striking of *Hangsaman*'s narratives, the private fantasy unfolding within Natalie's head of her interrogation by a private detective. In this story, which Jackson's narration forces into a confusing overlay with the action of *Hangsaman*, a detective follows Natalie as she conducts the everyday tasks necessary to prepare and execute a Sunday afternoon cocktail party. Believing Natalie to have committed a murder, the "secret voice" of the detective probes and inquires. The narrator makes it clear that this dialogue is secret and the detective imaginary by signaling the reader that Natalie speaks "back to him in her mind" (5). Likewise, another private and highly creative narrative enables Natalie to remove herself from the too real realities of the domestic scene: "Natalie, because her mother and father were bickering, transplanted herself to an archeological expedition some thousand years from now" (21). The archeological fantasy space is distinct from the detective story, but it does share several features; in both narratives Natalie imagines herself as the primary subject of analysis and producer of self-knowledge.

In a daily ritual, Natalie meets her father, Arnold, in his study after breakfast with her mother and brother to review her notebooks. In addition to giving her writing assignments to complete, Arnold demands access to Natalie's writing. He reads these, "savoring" the contents, and critiques her writing. On the morning of the cocktail party, Arnold reads while Natalie imagines the study transformed into a murder scene, soaked with blood. Arnold has given her an assignment to describe him, and he reacts strongly to the critical image she creates of him. Informing Natalie that it is natural that she feels some "filial resentment" because of the "basic sex antagonism" that separates them, he explains that it will be difficult for them to be honest with each other and thus he will continue to "assign" character descriptions like the one she just completed. Giving Natalie's notebook back to her, he tells her, "I shall learn from you" (15). Arnold desires these descriptions not because he believes that practice will improve Natalie's facility with language and help her become a writer but because he thinks writing reveals something that Natalie can repress or hide in her speech.

Like the controlling Mr. Harris, Arnold Waite wants to maintain order within his family. He exercises this control most obviously during his cocktail party. While he flirts with a young woman only a little older than his own daughter, he symbolically offers his daughter to a strange friend of his, who leads Natalie off into the woods. Jackson represses what happens next between paragraphs, but it is unambiguously a traumatic assault. Natalie's last thought before this event and the end of her evening concludes the paragraph: "Oh my dear God sweet Christ, Natalie thought, so sickened she nearly said it aloud, is he going to *touch* me?" (43). She speaks only upon waking in her bedroom the day after: "No, please no." This is a delayed speech act that answers the action by the unnamed man during the night before with a clear denial of consent that crosses the narrative lacuna that encloses the unnarrated event of her sexual assault. Once she speaks the word "no," a constant stream of denial flows from Natalie: "nothing happened, nothing happened, nothing happened, nothing happened" (43). Jackson depicts Natalie's repression of this event as a response to its status as a real event, unlike those "real-and-unreal" events within her everyday life at home.

While the cocktail party was not a going-away party for Natalie – her departure still twenty-one days away – her assault at the hands of her father's friend marks the end of her time at home. A section break follows, and the next page opens with a description of Natalie's college. Jackson represents Natalie, like many college students, as imagining that by leaving home and attending college she will encounter the possibility of a "new start" (50). The novel depicts her home as an oppressive environment: her father's authority, her mother's depression and alcoholism, and the site of her sexual assault. College, however, fails to be such a fresh start because it too closely replicates this environment. Certain figures are doubles of her family: Elizabeth Langdon doubles her mother, Arthur Langdon her father, and other students resemble her younger brother, Bud. Natalie's symbolic ties to her family structure are reproduced simultaneously with the cruel actions of her fellow students and a continued exchange of written text with her father.

Shortly after arriving at college, Natalie is forced to undergo a hazing ritual or what her fellow students refer to as freshman initiation. Wearing masks, the older students quickly wake up all first-year students at 3:00 a.m. Physically and verbally harassing the students while calling them what Natalie refers to as the "movie word," frosh (57), these older students herd the nervous first-year students into a large circle on the floor of a large bathroom on the second floor of her dormitory. A single chair is placed in the center of the circle, and the students attempt to force their randomly selected victims into the center and onto the chair. Jackson's initiation scene repeats earlier depictions of Natalie as undergoing interrogation; throughout the novel she is constantly asked to take on the role of a storyteller and to rehearse a narrative. Like all scenes of initiation, this ritual works to sort the students into an organizing hierarchy; Natalie "needed abruptly to establish her own position" and the ritual was understood as providing an institutionally sanctioned forum for her to become a member of the community (61). Yet in asking for the sexual status ("virgin?") of the first-year students, the older students force Natalie to re-encounter her recent traumatic assault. Natalie refuses to answer the question and then is asked to tell a dirty joke. This too she refuses because she "was more afraid of being found not to know dirty jokes than of being found to have a rich supply" (62). This request for her to produce a narrative would by necessity be linked to her knowledge of sexual activity and thus her own assault. Her refusal results in the students collectively rejecting Natalie from the community and the game: "Bad sport, rotten sport, not fair." Natalie exits to return to her own room, where she takes up her pen and begins the production of yet another narrative, this time in the form of a letter to her father.

Arnold Waite's letters to Natalie preserve his authority over her interiority while providing a space for him to compete, on several fronts, with his double, Arthur Langdon. He competes, for example, with Langdon over the judgment and assessment of grammatical and stylistic errors in her writing: "I sent you to college to enjoy yourself, not to get an education, but, my dear, please hereafter *do* try not to split infinitives" (96). In another letter, he remonstrates with Natalie for the style she used in her last letter home. He quotes a paragraph of her letter and proceeds to suggest modifications and corrections. In one letter he asks if Arthur Langdon has seen his last essay for the *Passionate Review* and says that she "may use its argument as your own . . . and confound him" if he has not (105). Arnold Waite writes in a letter to Natalie to be "extremely cautious" in her dealings with Langdon; he warns her: "do not under any circumstances allow Arthur Langdon to convert you to any philosophical viewpoint until you have first consulted me" (118). Understanding himself as also in competition with Langdon for Natalie's affections, he warns her against listening to Langdon's advice. Arthur Langdon is, after all, a younger version of Arnold Waite. Their names combined together produce the name of a single individual, Arthur Waite, the creator of the Rider-Waite tarot card system and an important reference in this book that makes several explicit references to the "Hanging Man" tarot card.

Natalie also writes letters to herself. These are, of course, her diary entries, but because of the focalization of narrative through the third-person narrator, they are the only way that we get direct access to Natalie's consciousness. One diary entry comes directly after she reads a letter from her father (105). In this entry, Natalie adopts a clinical gaze and examines herself as if from the outside. She writes, "I suppose you have even noticed – Natalie seems so strange lately, she seems so withdrawn and distant and quiet, I wonder if Natalie is coming along all right, or if there is something troubling her" (105). Lenemaja Friedman argues that the diary entries and Natalie's distancing perspective in these letters evidence "schizophrenic tendencies" (92), but rather than resorting to a psychological accounting for this self-division, we might understand Jackson as seeking to represent transformation in the absence of another person. What this passage suggests is Natalie's attempt to measure and assess her own progress, to examine whether she is "coming along all right." Perhaps we could understand this not so much as a manifestation of some deeply rooted psychological problem, as Friedman would have us do, but as the registration of Natalie's complicated participation in the coming-of-age narrative. Her diary entry continues:

> Well, that's why I'm writing this now. I could tell, my darling, that you were worried about me. I could feel you being apprehensive, and I knew that what you were always thinking about was you and me. And I even knew that you thought I was worried about that terrible thing, but of course – I promise you this, I really do – I don't think about it at all, ever, because both of us know that it never happened, did it?
>
> (106)

The "terrible thing" that she references in this diary entry is her repressed sexual assault. This event functions to complicate her reconciliation of narratives by refusing to be brought into representation. It is an event that she cannot mention.

Natalie has no privacy. Her letters to her father are intercepted by two older students who tell Elizabeth Langdon, Arthur's wife, about the content of these letters: "We're all afraid of Nat anyway; do you know that she writes the most *wicked* descriptions of all of us to her father? I positively *dream* sometimes of what Nat is telling Daddy about me" (125). The students, who have admitted to entering Natalie's room by using their key, which happens to open the rooms above their own, attempt to use the existence of these narratives to end a developing friendship between Elizabeth and Natalie. They do so because they are pursuing a relationship with Arthur Langdon. Langdon, like her father, conducts conferences with Natalie to discuss her written work. During one of these conferences, she says to Langdon, "My father discusses my work with me very much as you do" (102). Despite Natalie's hesitations about the act of literary creation and what she sees as its pointlessness, Langdon encourages her to write and to become a writer. He dismisses her serious questions by calling them "metaphysical nonsense" before inquiring about her ideas regarding death.

Faced with continual demands for her to produce narrative, she turns to her private diary to confess her own views about the work of confession. Imagining what it would be like to talk to a psychoanalyst and finally fulfill the ongoing demand for the entirety of her internal life, she writes,

> I think if I could tell someone everything, every single thing, inside my head, then *I* would be gone, and not existing any more, and I would sink away into that lovely nothing-space where you don't have to worry any more and no one hears you or cares and you can say anything but of course you wouldn't *be* any more at all and you couldn't really *do* anything so it wouldn't *matter* what you did.
>
> (107)

Natalie links herself, her "I," to a capability to produce new narratives. The possibility of running out of stories to tell, much like her fear during the hazing scene, frightens her. At the same time, she realizes that in order to be she must withhold some part of her self.

Instead of undergoing analysis, Natalie finds or invents a friend that she believes can understand her without the compulsive need to produce dialogue, a friend with whom she can engage in friendship without demands. She and Tony play a series of games, sleep together, shower together, and read erotica together. In short, they have a brief romance. It is only when Tony begins to push Natalie, when she begins to make demands and control her, that Natalie rejects Tony. Tony desires to be an authoritative figure, another version of Natalie's father or Arthur Langdon. A turning point occurs when they have run away from the campus and are in the woods together. Tony says to Natalie, "later I might let you go back" (213). Deciding to leave Tony and the mystery of the woods behind, Natalie reflects on Tony's demands and says to herself, "everything is waiting for me to act without someone else" (214).

Natalie seeks to have the capacity to be alone, but she can do so only once she has resisted the Other's desire for access to her interiority. Natalie's insight is what prevents her suicide and enables her to return to her campus. On the boundary between the campus and the town, while standing on the bridge that marks this division, she contemplates jumping, only to realize that her death would only increase the interest in her narrative:

> More people were nearby on the bridge, but she was not embarrassed to turn away from the parapet and walk quietly toward the college; it occurred to her that unless she actually jumped over the parapet into the river she was of small interest to them.
>
> (218)

She climbs down, and these students walk "quietly along without interest" in her. She returns to her dormitory: "[a]s she had never been before, she was now alone, and grown-up, and powerful, and not at all afraid" (218). Darryl Hattenhauer claims that we cannot trust the narrator and that any suggestion of a conclusion of Natalie's initiation into adulthood is both a "sop" to the reader's desire for a happy ending and an ironic start of another plot. Yet it is likely that Jackson has created a campus novel that seems unfamiliar because the novel rejects a feminized version of the coming-of-age plot that requires Natalie to undergo her transformation within the space of the institution. Instead, Jackson's heroine makes a series of decisions that include giving up her infatuation with Arthur Langdon, rejecting Tony, choosing not to jump from the bridge, and returning to the campus. These decisions demonstrate Natalie's attainment, in spite of her college, of the ability to interpret her own experience and to act independently, once again, as a "solitary functioning individual."

We find a contrary experience in another piece of Jackson's college fiction that shares some similar elements with *Hangsaman*. "Family Treasures" opens during the first days of Anne Waite's sophomore year. At the end of the previous academic year Anne's mother had died. Her father already deceased, Anne has become an orphan and her university has become her only home. Initially, following her mother's death, her fellow students offered her sympathy and friendship, but now, in the fall semester, they all slowly returned to their previously cool treatment and Anne into "anonymity": "Anne faded back into the colorless girl on the third floor who lived alone, had no friends, and rarely spoke" (121). She begins to steal from the other girls in the dormitory; she takes only a few small items, in the process reading diaries and letters as she "penetrated the secrets buried in handkerchief boxes, under beds, in the darkest corners of closets" (130). Once others become aware of the thefts, the housemother, Miss McBride, launches an exhaustive search of the entire dormitory with the assistance of a small group of students. This search results in a scene of complete exposure and the breakdown of sociality:

> No one cared to speak; each one knew the secrets of all the others; no one was inviolate any longer. It would be a long and painful process to build new privacies, secure them safely against intrusion, learn to trust one another again; there was a great destruction that went on in the house that night, of ruined treasure being burned, torn, cut with nail scissors.
>
> (132)

Rather than developing a rich sense of internal life that might enable her to function independently within her now indifferent campus community, Anne Waite secretly packs up her stolen items into her overnight bag and leaves the university: "she slipped quickly out the front door and down the street, carrying the overnight bag; mighty, armed" (133). While Anne needs to destroy all sense of privacy before she leaves, Natalie can return to her college only after she gains some control over her private narrative.

Hangsaman depicts a college student learning to narrate her discontinuous experience through what I have argued was a deeply alienating culture. Jackson finds midcentury Bennington College an inhospitable site for women, and this inhospitality produces the strangeness in Jackson's depiction of the college. John Lyons notes that Jackson's pessimism links her to other authors of college fiction who seek to address the experience of women within colleges and universities: "All of the novels about women's colleges, and especially those about Vassar, are not only violently critical but bad. All of them tend to be a potpourri of anecdotes and bitter reminiscences" (62). While we should reject Lyons's aesthetic judgments, he is right about the degree to which the strong institutional critique frequently is accompanied by the lack of a linear plot. While Lyons blames the institutions for failing to impress upon students the mission of the women's college, to "make themselves clear" to students, it seems more likely that the "potpourri of anecdotes" are deeply related to the narrative difficulties inherent in attempting to yoke together a story of self-transformation to an alienating encounter with an inhospitable environment. Symptomatic of the inability to tell a story of progressive change and transformation, these discontinuous narratives gesture toward the fragility of the promise of American higher education to improve the lives of students.

Jackson's fiction has had a measurable impact on the campus novel and the tight-knit group of Bennington College authors who followed her in writing accounts of college life. The indeterminate and discontinuous narrative of *Hangsaman* forces us to recognize that the campus novel's "master narrative" of the coming-of-age transformative experience is a mere fiction. In a later moment Donna Tartt and Bret Easton Ellis both offer depictions of disenchanted students, much like Jackson's Natalie Waite, attempting to survive the process of institutionalization. Whereas Ellis and Tartt make use of postmodern literary aesthetics to construct multiperspectival critiques of Bennington College, Jackson, as I have argued, produces a division within Natalie's self that contains a private component that resists the Other's desire to know. Thus we can understand *Hangsaman* as a fundamentally anti-institutional narrative that imagines the possibility of being in an institution but not of it.

Notes

1 I would like to thank Mira Rogulski for introducing me to the magic of Shirley Jackson during a seminar on Jackson that she conducted at Dartmouth College in 2013. Thank you to Barbara Will, associate dean of the humanities, and Donald E. Pease for organizing the seminar. I owe much to Louis A. Renza for many stimulating discussions about the campus novel and for helping me to think through a few of Jackson's stories. Thank you also to Rena J. Mosteirin for carrying on years of arguments about college culture and for coming back, the hard way. Most importantly, I need to acknowledge the students at Dartmouth who took my "Campus Life" course during the 2013–2014 academic year. In particular, I would like to thank Allison G. Wishner, Maya Poddar, Ryan Schiller, and Abena Frempong for their invaluable and insightful contributions to my understanding of the campus novel, campus life, and Jackson's *Hangsaman*.
2 As of 2015, there is only one biography of Jackson's life, Judy Oppenheimer's *Private Demons: The Life of Shirley Jackson*. I have relied upon this for much of the biographical information presented in this essay.
3 The recently published "Still Life with Teapot and Students" also concerns the presence of student-professor relationships on campus. In this story Louise Harlowe, the wife of a professor, invites two of her husband's students over for tea and warns them to stop "making passes at my husband" (17).

Works cited

Delbanco, Andrew. *College: What It Was, Is, and Should Be*. Princeton: Princeton UP, 2013. Print.
Ellis, Bret Easton. *The Rules of Attraction*. New York: Vintage, 1998. Print.
Findeisen, Christopher. "Injuries of Class: Mass Education and the American Campus Novel." *PMLA* 130.2 (2015): 284–98. Print.
Fitzgerald, F. Scott. *This Side of Paradise*. New York: Oxford UP, 2009. Print.
Friedman, Lenemaja. *Shirley Jackson*. Boston: Twayne Publishers, 1974. Print.
Hattenhauer, Darryl. *Shirley Jackson's American Gothic*. Albany: State U of New York P, 2003. Print.
Jackson, Shirley. "Family Treasures." *Let Me Tell You: New Stories, Essays, and Other Writings*. Eds. Laurence Jackson Hyman and Sarah Hyman DeWitt. New York: Random House, 2015. 119–33. Print.

———. *Hangsaman.* New York: Penguin, 2013. Print.
———. *Haunting of Hill House.* New York: Penguin, 2006. Print.
———. "Janice." *Novels and Stories.* Ed. Joyce Carol Oates. New York: Library of America, 2010. 565–66. Print.
———. *Life Among the Savages.* New York: Penguin, 1997. Print.
———. "The Man in the Woods." *Let Me Tell You: New Stories, Essays, and Other Writings.* Eds. Laurence Jackson Hyman and Sarah Hyman DeWitt. New York: Random House, 2015. 173–87. Print.
———. "The Missing Girl." *Just an Ordinary Day: The Uncollected Stories of Shirley Jackson.* New York: Bantam, 1997. 339–49. Print.
———. "Of Course." *Novels and Stories.* Ed. Joyce Carol Oates. New York: Library of America, 2010. 179–83. Print.
———. "On Being a Faculty Wife." *Mademoiselle* 44.2 (1956): 116–17, 135–36. Print.
———. "Still Life with Teapot and Students." *Let Me Tell You: New Stories, Essays, and Other Writings.* Eds. Laurence Jackson Hyman and Sarah Hyman DeWitt. New York: Random House, 2015. 15–20. Print.
———. "The Very Hot Sun in Bermuda." *Just an Ordinary Day: The Uncollected Stories of Shirley Jackson.* New York: Bantam, 1997. 32–36. Print.
Joshi, S. T. "Shirley Jackson: Domestic Horror." *Studies in Weird Fiction* 14 (1994): 9–28. Print.
Lethem, Jonathan. *The Ecstasy of Influence.* New York: Doubleday, 2011. Print.
Lyons, John O. *The College Novel in America.* Carbondale: Southern Illinois UP, 1962. Print.
Marchalonis, Shirley. *College Girls: A Century in Fiction.* New Brunswick: Rutgers UP, 1995. Print.
Oppenheimer, Judy. *Private Demons: The Life of Shirley Jackson.* New York: G. P. Putnam's Sons, 1988. Print.
Showalter, Elaine. *Faculty Towers: The Academic Novel and Its Discontents.* Philadelphia: U of Pennsylvania P, 2009. Print.
Tartt, Donna. *The Secret History.* New York: Alfred A. Knopf, 1992. Print.
Williams, Jeffrey. "The Rise of the Academic Novel." *American Literary History* 24.3 (2012): 561–89. Web.

ID # 9 The haunting of *Fun Home*

Shirley Jackson and Alison Bechdel's queer Gothic neodomesticity

Jill E. Anderson

Near the end of Shirley Jackson's 1959 novel *The Haunting of Hill House*, Mrs. Montague, a medium and the wife of the man who has gathered three volunteers – Eleanor, Theodora, and Luke – at the Victorian-era mansion called Hill House to experience its supernatural occurrences, arrives at the mansion. Her goal is to communicate with Hill House's spirits, and she sets about doing so in a no-nonsense, practical manner. Before settling in for her first night, Mrs. Montague expresses her self-righteous optimism in attempting to draw out the spirits: "It is such a blessing . . . to know that the beings in this house are only waiting for an opportunity to tell their stories and free themselves from the burden of their sorrow" (144). But, shortly after retiring to their respective beds for the night, the mansion's inhabitants experience another supernatural cacophony of knocking and pounding in the hallways. "Could we have exhausted the repertoire of Hill House?" Theodora nonchalantly quips, while the panicked and psychologically fragile Eleanor silently considers, "We are in the eye of the storm; there is not much more time. . . . I am disappearing inch by inch into this house, I am going apart a little bit at a time because all this noise is breaking me" (147, 148–49). Each woman is experiencing the mansion's "noise" differently and in ways that reflect their overall states of mind. But Mrs. Montague's comment is a metafictional moment that encodes Eleanor's concerns as the "burden" of never being able to be free. Eleanor lacks a story and a home, so she experiences Hill House's noises and hauntings, particularly the voice that calls out to her, "ELEANOR COME HOME," as a frightening yet ultimately appealing trap. In one way, Hill House seems to be calling her home, into the strange bosom of the mansion's interior; in another, the demanding voice that requests Eleanor "come home" is a comfort to her rejected sense of being. In other words, for Eleanor, arriving at, inhabiting, and encountering the spirits of Hill House become the markers of the beginning of *her* story, her opportunity to realize a sense of belonging, however fraught and frightening, after years of caring for her demanding, unappreciative, invalid mother.

Alison Bechdel, in her 2006 graphic memoir entitled *Fun Home*, also utilizes the intersections of belonging, home space, and storytelling in order to unravel Bechdel's relationship with her father, Bruce, who died by an apparent suicide after his homosexuality and his many affairs with younger men were exposed.

Bechdel[1] opens the memoir with a chapter called, "Old Father, Old Artificer," in which she ruminates on her father's relationship to the family's Victorian-era home in their small Pennsylvania town (purchased in 1962, not long after the events of *Hill House*). She portrays her father as a meticulous renovator and decorator,

> an alchemist of appearance, a savant of surface, a Daedalus of design ... that skillful artificer, that mad scientist who built the wings for his son and designed the famous labyrinth and who answered not to the laws of society, but to those of his craft.
>
> (6–7)

Bruce practices this craft at the cost of his own family's well-being, and Alison sets her own aesthetic in opposition to her father's: "Spartan to my father's Athenian. Modern to his Victorian. Butch to his nelly. Utilitarian to his aesthete" (15). The attention to detail also figures into Bruce's occupation as an undertaker in the family-owned funeral home (the "fun home" of the title). The care Bruce takes to create this home environment is, according to Bechdel, a manifestation of his identity. Alison's own sense of belonging is bound up in his identity, so oppositional yet identical to her own. The story of her father's coming-out is also the story of Alison finding a place in the world and within her own home.

Because huge, old, possibly haunted Victorian homes figure prominently in Jackson's classic novel of Gothic horror and Bechdel's acclaimed graphic memoir, I find it impossible to ignore how characters' attempts at storytelling figure into their encounters with their domestic environments. Relationships to history – public and personal – are an extension of how Eleanor and Alison incorporate themselves into a home environment as well as how they challenge the conventions that bear heavily on those environments. The embodiment of domestic practices in both texts uncovers not just essential acts of storytelling but also how storytelling leads to empowerment. Both Eleanor and Alison tell stories from within their respective homes to create and voice personal histories tied to domestic practices that disrupt normative life trajectories. This disruption of normativity produces, as J. Jack Halberstam explains, "alternative temporalities by allowing their participants to believe that their futures can be imagined according to logics that lie outside of those paradigmatic markers of life experience – namely, birth, marriage, reproduction, and death" (2). But these practices go beyond developments toward Alison's burgeoning lesbian identity and Eleanor's presumed, suppressed lesbianism into the realm of "queer time," "a term for those specific models of temporality that emerge within postmodernism once one leaves the temporal frames of bourgeois reproduction and family, longevity, risk/safety, and inheritance" (Halberstam 3). Essential to their narratives of futurity is the dismay each feels at the possible life trajectories placed before them. Situated within the Gothic mansions, Alison and Eleanor inhabit and enliven a queer time and space, which allows them to voice narratives of alternative futures and to upset the productivity of family life that conventional domesticity lauds.

Because I posit that both novels are works of domestic fiction, Kristin Jacobson's phrase "neodomestic fiction" is pertinent here. Jacobson argues that neodomestic fiction "map[s] a revised generic conception of domesticity that self-consciously addresses the ways in which various Americans have been (dis) enfranchised" (29). Because nineteenth-century domestic fiction emphasizes the struggles of straight, white, Protestant, usually middle-class women, neodomestic fiction articulates the stories of others. It also, like earlier domestic fiction, "feature[s] a self-consciousness about the home's physical space and the project of homemaking," but unlike it, "neodomestic fiction advances a politics of domestic instability, particularly emphasized through its distinctive domestic spaces and conclusions" (3). This instability, Jacobson explains, is manifest in the fiction through three interconnected practices:

> (1) "mobility," bell hooks's notion that home is not one place but locations; (2) "relational space," an understanding that the domestic sphere depends on 'outside' or 'foreign' relations and vice versa; and (3) "renovation" or "redesign," the active construction and (re)design of the (conventional) domestic sphere and its concomitant effects on community and the self.
>
> (29)

Although Jacobson's work focuses exclusively on novels written after 1980, her emphasis on instability and the need for a general troubling of categories is central to my reading Jackson and Bechdel's work as neodomestic fiction. To varying degrees, *Hill House* and *Fun Home* renovate accepted, conventional domestic practices, inside and outside the home, in relational spaces. Eleanor and Alison also enact attempts at mobility or mapping other communities and homespaces in order to alleviate alienation from their own biological families and to destabilize accepted "chronobiopolitics." This is Elizabeth Freeman's term for the concept of "having a life" that is "event-centered, goal-oriented, intentional, and culminating in epiphanies or major transformations. The logic of time-as-productive thereby becomes one of serial cause and effect: the past seems useless unless it predicts and becomes material for a future" (5). While the manner in which Eleanor and Alison "have" lives within their domestic environments and construct their narratives seems oriented toward transformation, a closer look at these specific events confirms they are productive in creating other paths.

In particular, these domestic practices include acts of revisionist history-making, reading, writing, and storytelling that subvert normative histories and engage with what could be labeled queer possibilities.[2] I like Diana Fuss's argument that "[h]omosexual production emerges ... as a kind of ghost-writing, a writing which is at once a recognition and a refusal of the cultural representation of 'the homosexual' as phantom Other" (4). Fuss sees the need for ghostwriting as stemming from "a certain preoccupation with the homosexual as specter and phantom, as spirit and revenant, as abject and undead" (3). This invocation of ghostliness not only connects the practice of queer production to the Gothic tradition, which I discuss later in this essay, but also emphasizes the wider possibilities of crafting one's history in opposition to accepted conventions.

Jackson's best-selling volumes of domestic sketches, 1953's *Life Among the Savages* and 1957's *Raising Demons*, preceded the publication of *Hill House*. The two volumes collected the writings Jackson had previously published in women's magazines, work she did to earn income to support herself and her family. To my mind, the sketches provide an important model for Jackson's attitude toward domestic life, an attitude that is amplified in such works as *Hill House*, her short stories, and other novels, like *We Have Always Lived in the Castle* (1962) and *The Sundial* (1958). As the collections' titles would suggest, Jackson's tone fluctuates between bemused frustration and humored distraction as she (or the narrator, who is never named but is most assuredly based closely on Jackson herself) recalls the exploits of her four children and her daily domestic struggles. In the second sketch in *Life Among the Savages*, Jackson opines, "all women, but especially housewives, tend to think in lists" (77). After finding multiple scraps of paper in her coat pocket with random reminders written on them, Jackson

> realized how thoroughly the housekeeping mind falls into the list pattern, how basically the idea of a series of items, following one another docilely, forms the only possible reasonable approach to life if you have to live it with a home and a husband and children, none of whom would dream of following one another docilely.
>
> (77)

She highlights the routineness of her domestic practices, and while she never openly expresses dissatisfaction with this life, she is always working from the sense that domestic life is, after all, disappointing and restrictive at its best. *Raising Demons* actually includes an epigraph that excerpts the *Grimoire of Honorius*, a textbook of black magic attributed to Pope Honorius III during the twelfth century. It is the book's conjuration, which requests the demons to arrive in "comely human form when you are called" and to "make [no] attempt upon the body, soul, or spirit of the reader, nor inflict any harm on those who may accompany him." "Raising demons," then, refers to not only bringing up her children but also the conjuring of the demonic spirits writing and reading such a book would confer.

As the demonic conjuration in *Raising Demons* would suggest, Jackson is interested in elements of darkness and possible evil of the Gothic tradition. The most obvious aspects that connect Jackson to this long-standing genre is her reliance on elements of fear and thrill-seeking, her characters' relationship to an old home that harbors secrets, the use of plot devices such as mystery, darkness, madness, and doubling, and a reliance on the supernatural. While the purpose of this essay is not to rehash other critics' legitimate arguments in this vein, there are some elements of Gothic literature that are pertinent to my argument about the queer domestic practices in both Jackson and Bechdel. Generally, Gothic literature features the prospect that "[w]hen the domestic realm itself figures as a site of terror, however, domestic ideology is undercut. Misery, unhappiness, and crime not only pervade households, they arrive from within them" (Wagner 110). The home cannot be a site of idealized family life and clear-cut domestic responsibilities. Instead of underscoring the clockwork-like nature of the daily activities of maintaining a household, Gothic literature emphasizes the temporality of survival, whether physical or psychological. The familial home, rather than providing a space of safety and security from the outer world, actually replicates the dangers and anxieties experienced in public spaces.

As Dr. Montague explains in *Hill House*, the mansion is specifically planned to be "off." "[E]very angle is slightly wrong" in Hill House (105). The physical and psychic discomfort experienced by the inhabitants is deliberate. Hugh Crain, the mansion's first owner and the architect of its strangeness, disrupts expectations about "right" angles: "Angles which you assume are the right angles you are accustomed to, and have every right to expect are true, are actually a fraction of a degree off in one direction or another" (105). The inhabitants experience this off-ness through darkness, claustrophobia (Hill House feels to Eleanor like "a very tight belt"), and drifting, often losing large amounts of time merely trying to navigate the mansion to find the dining room, for example. This feeling of off-ness and drifting begins to take its toll on Eleanor's sense of well-being and disrupts the way she imagines her time at the mansion. Hill House appears "somehow to have formed itself, flying together into its own powerful pattern under the hands of its builders, fitting itself into its own construction of lines and angles," colliding with the idea that its inhabitants are what make a home a home (25).[3]

Because much of *Hill House* takes place during what we might call the "leisure" time of the inhabitants, Jackson underscores the domestic practices that effectively queer notions of accepted, idealized housework. Even though Eleanor declares herself "on vacation," she is actually an active participant in Dr. Montague's supernatural experiment. Her "work" there consists of being receptive to the possibility of ghostly encounters, and in turn recording her observations of the strange occurrences around Hill House. Her work is to *be*, to exist and observe. But stripped of regular domestic tasks – cooking, cleaning, and caretaking – Theodora and Eleanor develop a fondness for playfully listing activities aloud to each other and mocking household duties in the manner of upper-class ladies-at-leisure. Activities such as tending grapes, searching for gravestones around the estate, and holding picnic lunches by the brook are named but ultimately remain unperformed by the end of the novel. Naming these activities, I would argue, is the women's way of acting as inhabitants of a cohesive household. This verbal play is one way they "have a life" during their time in Hill House. Indeed, the women share many things throughout the novel – clothing, a bed, secrets, plans for their futures – and develop a bond that has been read by many critics as essentially a lesbian relationship, which would certainly upset the conventional life trajectory for women in the midcentury.[4]

In a world in which a young woman's options are fairly limited, the painfully shy Eleanor cannot ultimately reconcile herself to a life that might include, after meeting Theodora, a same-sex companion. While some critics label Theodora explicitly lesbian, the doubling that occurs with Eleanor marks her as a queer presence in the novel as well. Eleanor has a mantra – "Journeys end in lovers meeting" – and it serves to remind her that not only does her excursion to Hill House hold the possibility of a new future for her but also the journey will presumably end in some manner. Besides, "lovers" is general enough to cover multiple possibilities. At one point, Eleanor seemingly weds herself to Hill House, thinking she will never leave, marking the house itself as a lover. Colin Haines, in *Frightened by a Word: Shirley Jackson and the Lesbian Gothic*, notes that "lesbian apparationality" – that is, lesbianism as it exists through ghostly presences – is reversed in *Hill House* because the mansion itself "emulate[s] heterosexual coitus" (63). Haines notes that much of the haunting that occurs in the novel is through Hill House's "attempt to make them identify with its normative vision but also its attempt to dissuade them from identifying in any other way" (63). Perhaps the idea that the house reinforces heteronormativity and reprotime, with Hugh Crain's patriarchal figurehead still looming over the inhabitants, is what makes Theodora and Eleanor's homemaking practices so poignant. The acts of homemaking that occur between these two signal domestic practices that *cannot* exist in real time. They are fantasy, essentially, and in a realm where keeping time and having a life seem to be valued, unrealizable fantasies are finally useless. Eleanor's earlier fantasy about wandering into a "fairyland, protected poisonously from the eyes of people passing" proves unrealizable (20). In this fantasy fairyland, she plays the prodigal princess, for whom "the queen waits, weeping, waiting for the princess to return. She will drop her embroidery when she sees me . . . And we shall live happily ever after" (20). The most obvious way to read the queen-princess relationship would be as a mother-daughter one; given hints of Eleanor's proclivities, though, the fantasy could underscore Eleanor's same-sex desires.

The foil to Theodora and Eleanor's playful taskmistresses and Eleanor's fantastical fairyland is the mansion's caretaker, Mrs. Dudley. She has an obsessive timing of her own domestic duties which stands in sharp contrast to Eleanor and Theodora's easygoing leisure time:

> I set dinner on the dining-room sideboard at six sharp. You can serve yourselves. I clear up in the morning. I have breakfast ready for you at nine. That's the way I agreed to do. I can't keep the rooms up the way you'd like, but there's no one else you could get that would help me. I don't wait on people. What I agreed to, it doesn't mean I wait on people.
>
> (27)

In Mrs. Dudley, we see domestic practices as methodical and necessary to the functioning of the household. Since Mrs. Dudley lives off-site, she is able to leave, unlike Eleanor, and can remove herself from the strange activities of the others. Despite her role as "house-keeper," she is not actually a part of the household.

Dara Downey, however, recognizes Mrs. Dudley as essential to the functioning of Hill House as a "polluted space":

> With Mrs. Dudley as its agent, everything in Hill House remains in its appointed place, and nowhere else, leaving little or no room for alteration or addition. As a result of this, its malevolence resides . . . in the negative effect that it has on those who themselves pollute it by violating its boundaries – in other words, by adding something that is not *proper* to it.
>
> (187)

So, as Mrs. Dudley maintains the "proper" orderliness of the home objects and timing, Theodora and Eleanor disturb it with their unconventional domestic practices. Using Downey's reasoning would mean that Hill House's malice does not come in the form of the vengeful and tormented ghosts that others imagine reside there; instead the darkness resides within Eleanor and her queered sense of being.

But the fantasy also reveals just how precarious and liminal Eleanor's life is. Significantly, an initial fantasy occurs while Eleanor is en route to Hill House from her sister's home, in which she occupies a small room. The fantasies cause Eleanor, in imagining this "new time," to dream up other domestic activities that would go along with her leisure time. Driving past a large, old home in the town outside Hill House, she spots stone lions flanking the steps, and thinks, "in these few seconds I have lived a lifetime in a house with two lions in front" (12). What follows is a detailed description, imagined in the past tense, of the meticulous care she would take of the stone lions and the life she would live out in the home. Her ability to fast-forward to "having a life" so quickly and to imaging the small, domestic responsibilities she would have on her own reveal what Bernice M. Murphy sees as "a very real link between Jackson's obvious preoccupation with houses and living spaces and the enormous and rapid changes in American living and domestic patterns which took place the time at which she wrote" (18). While Hill House is decidedly not suburban, isolated on a hill outside of the tiny town of Hillsdale, it is important to note Murphy's insistence that the "liminal status" of the suburbs, "neither one thing, nor another, but something in-between – is part of what helps make American suburbia the perfect breeding ground for fictional expressions of anxiety and unease. Fear breeds in cracks" (20). For Eleanor, Hill House is simultaneously a relational, transitional space, between her old life with her mother and sister to her new life, on her own or with Theodora, and a permanent resting place. When Eleanor, finally at the peak of her instability and madness, realizes she is home at Hill House, that hominess is accompanied by a strange set of practices – she declares that she has flown "in and out the windows" and has danced with Hugh Crain's statue. She climbs to the tower on her way to the library at night and continues to goad Theodora about her future plans. She occupies another liminal space during this time between a hopeful, almost drunk, joyousness and the terror of knowing that she is becoming even more unstable. These two states of mind coexist in Eleanor, eventually making her unable to stay at Hill House but ultimately homeless, incapable of being anywhere at all. Eleanor is haunted by her in-between-ness, and it eventually proves deadly.

Real ghosts also appear to haunt Eleanor. For one, her mother speaks to her from the grave, attempting to beckon her back to the home from which Eleanor always felt alienated. As the caretaker to her now-dead mother, Eleanor is so accustomed to her mother's demands and their domestic rhythms that they invade Eleanor's sleep. Tricia Lootens sees this "intimacy, which is simultaneously familial and erotic" as the most terrifying aspect of the hauntings:

> What happens in Hill House is a process, not merely a "sighting"; a haunting, not merely a ghost. At its source is the house's growing knowledge of its inhabitants' illusions and of their deadly needs. Hill House's ghosts are what Jackson called the "statement and resolution" of its inhabitants' apparently insoluble problems; the haunting is personally designed for the haunted. What Hill House reveals to its guests is a brutal, inexorable version of the "absolute reality" of nuclear families that kill where they are supposed to nurture.
> (151)

Further, Lootens sees *Hill House* as a novel in which "women are destroyed by the nuclear family, sexual repression, and romantic notions of feminine self-sacrifice," and she argues that the ultimate source of terror in the novel is the "disintegration of a woman's personality" (152, 151). It is the separation from her familial home and nuclear family that allows Eleanor to escape, while simultaneously destroying her in the end. If Hill House, at least in the beginning, signifies freedom, Eleanor is able to form her own family unit: Dr. Montague and company "were a family, greeting one another with easy informality and going to the chairs they had used last night at dinner, their own places at the table" (71). I would even argue that Dr. Montague and company's reading of the Crain family documents is a generative act of family formation. Dr. Montague relates the family's history to the others as a father would to his children.

But the ghostly mother is deeply ingrained in Eleanor's psyche, and she attempts to draw Eleanor back into a world of loneliness and containment from which she narrowly escapes (only after stealing the car she partially owns with her sister, who has forbidden it to her). The ghost mother is the embodiment of the past as well as a personification of Eleanor's attempts to reconcile herself to her previous imprisonment within her mother's home. Despite her desire to write her own story and to establish a set of domestic practices on her own terms, she is not just haunted by the ghost mother. Ensconced in Hill House, she is only replicating her imprisonment, but it seems like imprisonment on her own terms. When Theodora asks Eleanor to tell her about her home, Eleanor crafts an elaborate lie about living alone in an apartment where "[e]verything has to be exactly the way I want it, because there's only me to use it" (64). But it is a poorly crafted lie, and it does not hold up under scrutiny. Eleanor's lie further emphasizes her innate aloneness.

Again, Eleanor's storytelling is instructive of her hopes for future happiness along a route of living that cannot ultimately suit her. In *The Promise of*

Happiness, Sara Ahmed explains, "[t]he biography of a person is intimately bound up with objects. We could say that our biographies are biographies of likes and dislikes" (27). "The promising nature of happiness," Ahmed further clarifies, "suggests happiness lies ahead of us, at least if we do the right thing" (29). Orientation toward the "right" kinds of objects, ones that can be considered as "social goods," puts one "in line" with a particular affect or community based on that affect. One goes "out of line with an affective community," Ahmed argues, when one does "not experience pleasure from proximity to objects that are attributed as social goods" (41). Eleanor constructs a fantasy of her wanted life, centering on things like the stone lions mentioned earlier, and white curtains in an apartment of her own. These objects, to her mind, are "in line" for a young woman. Eleanor attaches to such fantasies because, as Jackson explains early in the novel, she

> could not remember ever being truly happy in her adult life; her years with her mother had been built up devotedly around small guilts and small reproaches, constant weariness, and unending despair. Without ever wanting to become reserved and shy, she had spent so long alone, with no one to love, that it was difficult for her to talk, even casually, to another person without self-consciousness and an awkward inability to find words.
>
> (3)

Much of *Hill House*, then, is about Eleanor's pursuit of happiness, and "Eleanor, in short, would have gone anywhere" to find it (4). Just as she is setting out for Hill House, Eleanor admonishes herself for having "let more time go by," wondering, "what had been done with all those wasted summer days; how could she have spent them so wantonly?" (10). She comes to consider time and her orientation toward the future and possible happiness in the "miles and hours" of her "lovely journey" since "[t]ime is beginning in June, she assured herself, but it is a time that is strangely new and of itself" (11, 12).

Surprisingly, after the first prolonged haunting incident, Eleanor awakes, thinking,

> I am unbelievably happy. Journeys end in lovers meeting; I have spent an all but sleepless night, I have told lies and made a fool of myself, and the very air tastes like wine. I have been frightened half out of my wits, but I have somehow earned this joy; I have been waiting for it for so long.
>
> (100)

It is debatable, however, whether Eleanor's pursuit of happiness is successful. On the one hand, she feels for a time the unbelievable joy of belonging to a place and a family of her choosing, but on the other, she deliberately steers her car into a tree when she is forced to leave the mansion for her own "good." Eleanor, despite her imaginative efforts to engage in domestic practices that help her to craft a narrative from which she can draw a sense of belonging, finally fails. Her failure, I would argue, occurs for two reasons: through no fault of her own, having been born in a world that offers women limited options outside of the normative trajectory, the queer, ungrounded Eleanor "must" die; and secondly, because she insists on the redemptive power of Hill House, an "insane," horror-inducing place, she absorbs and is absorbed by its off-ness.

The Gothic revival home in *Fun Home* is not haunted or horrific in the same way as Hill House. It is not insane or at odd angles. Instead, the anxieties and horrors of Bechdel's work of Gothicism emerge from reflections of the domestic practices that occur there. Here, I reference the Oxford English Dictionary's definition of *horror* as a way to invoke elements of Gothic horror fiction pertinent to my argument about domestic practices: "A painful emotion compounded of loathing and fear; a shuddering with terror and repugnance; strong aversion mingled with dread; the feeling excited by something shocking or frightful." Perhaps it is overstating the matter to say that *Fun Home* is full of loathing, repugnance, and strong aversions (although these are emotions that Eleanor clearly feels for her own mother in *Hill House*). In fact, Stephen King explains, "The purpose of horror fiction is not only to explore taboo lands but to confirm our own good feelings about the status quo by showing us extravagant visions of what the alternative might be" (298). Like *Hill House*, *Fun Home* provides its narrator with a collection of domestic practices that challenges the status quo, both inside and outside the familial home. To a lesser extent, then, the painful emotions and shock that Alison feels at her father's secret life and his eventual suicide reveal the kinds of domestic practices in which she engages in order to "have a life."

Part of this challenge to status quo and stability comes through the hauntings that occur throughout Bechdel's memoir. The text is haunted by the likeness of her father as well as the redrawn ephemera of her family life. Some critics also argue that the multilayered representations of Bechdel's literary influences are a pointed attempt at raising the "low" status of the graphic narrative. While all of these elements are essential in reading Bechdel's work as both autobiography and graphic narrative (or "autographic," to invoke Gillian Whitlock's term, to define the convergence of the visual-verbal techniques used in works of graphic autobiography), my focus on hauntings here borrows from the idea that

> the sense of the past that pervades Gothic literature does not encourage the writer to explain origins in clear relation to end-points in a seamless linear narrative. Nor does the writer seize on history as a coherent field that is subject to authorial control.... Instead, history controls and determines the writer. Gothic texts return obsessively to the personal, the familial, and the national pasts to complicate rather than to clarify them, but mainly to implicate the individual in a deep morass of American desires and deeds that allow no final escape from or transcendence of them.
>
> (Savoy 169)

For Bechdel, the act of writing about her past and the way that past continuously haunts Alison's life is never an orderly, stabilizing task. Crafting a story of her personal past follows a nonlinear trajectory of its own, and at times she aligns it with pivotal moments of national history, like the Stonewall Riot and the Bicentennial, as a way of illustrating Alison's tenuous but very real connection to past events. Along these same lines, Hilary Chute argues,

> Bechdel's redrawn archive, then, says more about comics as a *procedure of what I am calling embodiment*, and the instantiation of handwriting as a gripping index of a material, subjective, situated body, than it does about the state of the archive as a stable register of truth.
>
> (193)

Altogether, this instability contains a marked concern with how one fits in the narrative of normativity.

Bechdel's formulation of both a personal, family archive and a queer, public history handily challenges the public/private split. As Alison travels with her family to New York City just a few weeks after the Stonewall Riots, she witnesses the interplay of "bourgeois vs. aristocratic, homo vs. hetero, city vs. country, eros vs. art" (102). Unlike Eleanor, Alison is in tune with political events and their parallels with her own life. She describes the "many heavy-handed plot devices to befall" her family during the summer of Nixon's impeachment as a means of connecting shared, public moments with her own family's turmoil (155). Alison's reference to Randy Shilts's *And the Band Played On* and its opening lines connect the beginning of the AIDS epidemic to the Bicentennial celebrations in New York City: "Or maybe I'm trying to render my senseless personal loss meaningful by linking it, however posthumously, to a more coherent narrative. A narrative of injustice, of sexual shame and fear, of life considered expendable" (196). So in this way, Alison's narrative is not just haunted by her personal ghosts but also full of the specters of others who have suffered at the hands of homophobia and ignorance.

Normativity and homophobia are concerns for Bechdel in other bodies of work. As an early archivist and activist for the lesbian community, Bechdel ran her groundbreaking comic strip *Dykes to Watch Out For* for over two decades. In the cartoonist's introduction to the 2008 collection *The Essential Dykes to Watch Out For*, Bechdel briefly sketches her trajectory from a child who doodled to college student whose coming-out was facilitated by writers such as Adrienne Rich and magazines like *Common Lives, Lesbian Lives*. As Bechdel portrays herself in the various panels, sifting through old film reels in a huge library full of filing cabinets, trying to locate files of her old work, she directly addresses the reader:

> I had set to name the unnamed, to depict the undepicted, to make lesbians visible, and I had done it! ... You can't pin things down without *changing* them, somehow. Good lord. How many young women have told me these were *the first lesbians they ever met*? That my cartoon characters were – oh, I can hardly say the words – *choke* – role models!
>
> (xvii, emphases in original)

She further worries: "Have I churned out episodes of this comic strip every two weeks for *decades* merely to prove that *we're the same as everyone else*?!" (xviii). Indeed, Bechdel's concern raises some of the same issues of the various branches of the LGBTQ movements, the idea that the push for rights associated with heteronormative life – marriage, childrearing, benefits, and so forth – merely replicates that same heteronormative life to which many in the LGBTQ community stand openly or implicitly opposed. I include this bit from Bechdel's comic collection because it signals a general concern about where lesbians and gays fit into the structured, established chronobiopolitics, to invoke Freeman's phrase. In turn, *Fun Home* seeks the domestic practices that mark normative family life, with a family headed by two biological parents who "make" a home to at least facilitate the façade of normative living. But, as Bechdel points out over and over, Alison's family has very little to do with "everyone else." Unlike Eleanor in *Hill House*, who seeks to *make* a family from the people assembled in the mansion, Alison illustrates that the very presence of a nuclear family does not actually signal a normative life.

When Alison describes her familial home as "an artists' colony," she is highlighting both their familiarity and division: "We ate together, but otherwise were absorbed in our separate pursuits" (134). This description accompanies a panel depicting the home's exterior and bubbles with the shadows of each member of the household engaged in their own practices – brothers playing guitar or building airplane models, mother at her piano, father at his renovation work, and Alison drawing at her desk. This view as an outsider looking in disrupts the narrative of the family's artistic pursuits and reminds the reader that they are not, just as Alison is not at times, part of the domestic practices that make this home a home and this family a family. But as Bechdel hands us the possibility that Alison desires to run from her familial home, as Eleanor does in *Hill House*, she argues that that home and those artistic practices Alison inherits and learns from her family are essential in the formation of Alison's narrative:

> It's tempting to suggest, in retrospect, that our family was a sham. That our house was not a real home at all but a simulacrum of one, a museum. Yet we really were a family, and we really did live in those period rooms.
>
> (17)

But Alison's "way of life," with her readymade family and fairly comfortable, carefully curated home, is just as fragile as Eleanor's life as she moves from her mother's home to her sister's and finally to Hill House. The desire to flee seems to be a logical conclusion for these women who feel imprisoned in their familial environments. As they enact their domestic practices, though, the need to get away, to "have a life," and to write one's own history is legible only through the familial bonds.

Alison's preservation of certain domestic practices highlights the complex, oppositional practices she performs in order to set herself apart from her family dynamic. Alison explains, "I grew to resent the way my father treated his furniture like children and his children like furniture," after several frames in which Bechdel illustrates the meticulous and passionate care Bruce takes of his household goods (14). By opening the narrative with an explanation of Bruce's obsessive care and focus on the antique, overly adorned, and florid goods, Bechdel is highlighting Alison's disdain for and distrust of an overemphasis on home interiors. Part of this distrust stems from how "[t]he visual realm is thus experienced by young Alison as a patriarchal sphere of control – a sphere with which she must negotiate to claim her own vision and gender identity" (Lyndenburg 107). For Alison, seeing and witnessing the curation of her father's household goods are another way of experiencing his hold over her personal history. This idea of home as a patriarchal sphere of control carries another connection to Jackson's novel. Hill House, as I mentioned earlier, is "off" and at odd angles, designed and constructed by Hugh Crain, the long dead but still very present patriarch. The discovery of a huge marble statue in the conservatory, with Crain as a mythological figure attended by his two nymph daughters, is a "symbol of protection of the house," "carefully, and at great expense, constructed to offset the uncertainty of the floor on which it stands" (Jackson 79, 80). The statue is a symbol of Crain's control, much in the same way Bruce's drapes and ornate lamps control the way Alison experiences her home life.

But *Fun Home* is an important "statement of liberation, in that it suggests that the lesbian – in constructing her family narrative as well as her own subjectivity – is free to reverse roles, shatter spatiotemporal limitations, and give birth to herself through a narrative act of reproduction" (Mitchell). Alison repeatedly queers her relationship to her familial home and the seemingly stable nuclear family within it. The prolonged lie perpetuated by her father as well as her mother's silences and powerlessness cements her opposition to marriage. "'[T]he unspoken compact" that she would avoid marriage so that "I would carry on to live the artist's life they had each abdicated," occurs only after Alison witnesses the animosity and tension within her parents' marriage (73). As a result, Alison sets up a binary between people who lead a life driven by artistic pursuits and people who choose family and domesticity.

Reading and writing take a central position in Alison's domestic agenda as a way of bonding with her father. Alison describes her artistic pursuits as obsessive-compulsive and autographic, and importantly, the first words in her diary are in her father's hand: "Dad is reading." This simple sentence, placed within Alison's diary and written in her father's hand, is a symbolic and literal ascription dedicated to their shared literacy. Like in the artist's colony frames, "That Old Catastrophe" closes with a panel that is from outside the home, looking in. Alison and Bruce are each framed by library windows, lighted from within and outlined by the home's ornate shutters and curtains – the careful work of Bruce. Alison is in the act of writing a check to herself and her father is reading a biography of Zelda Fitzgerald. The "last, tenuous bond" that closes the chapter is Alison's hope and insistence that her father's death had something to do with her, despite her suspicion that he had timed it to coincide with F. Scott Fitzgerald's. Reading and authorship are, for Alison and Bruce, one way of establishing and sanctioning a familial bond. This emerges not just from the act of Bechdel penning her memoir but also from the creation and reproduction of a specific archive in *Fun Home*.[5] Bechdel's archive deserves attention since, according to Ann Cvetkovich, "it provides such a compelling challenge to celebratory queer histories that threaten to erase more disturbing and unassimilable inheritances" (126). Further, part of Cvetkovich's project is to "queer perspectives on trauma that challenge the relation between the catastrophic and the everyday and that make public space for lives whose very ordinariness makes them historically meaningful" (112).

Because she can live in between and has transferable skills (i.e., multiple literacies), Alison thrives, unlike Eleanor. Eleanor's experiences with literacy are limited to reading romance novels to her bedridden mother and crafting her own stilted stories. When she arrives at Hill House, she remains suspicious of reading, particularly as she avoids the library. Eleanor does not see the library as the intellectual center of the home but rather as a repository for the materials of her fear, suspicion, and captivity. Her suspicion of the library is compounded by the discovery of Hugh Crain's book. He wrote and illustrated a series of frightening and grotesque instructions for his daughters, based on biblical excerpts:

> Honor thy father and thy mother, Daughter, authors of thy being, upon whom a heavy charge has been laid, that they lead their child in innocence and righteousness along the fearful narrow path to everlasting bliss, and render her up at last to her God a pious and virtuous soul.
>
> (Jackson 124)

Crain's book only reinforces the patriarchal control he still holds over Hill House, even in death, but the books Alison is surrounded by in her father's library actually perform her independence. So even while Bruce's library in *Fun Home* is carefully curated to contain *his* idea of great intellectual material and Alison eventually rejects that version of the canon, it starts her on her own literary discoveries. Bruce does not explicitly attempt to rein in Alison with her choice of reading material. Literacy is autonomy in their family, not the act through which a mother controls a daughter's mobility. Consequently, Alison does not have the same association with libraries that Eleanor has. While Hill House's library is haunted by stories Eleanor ties to her mother's abuse, the library in Alison's home becomes a space for the cultivation of her own liberation and literacy.

Alison's literacy is a transferrable skill, which allows her to move from the domestic sphere to public places. Pointedly, the reading practices that Alison cultivates outside her familial home are the practices that allow her to craft her sexual narrative in order to assimilate it with her domestic self. As so many lesbian authors before her have explained, the recognition of Alison's lesbianism takes linguistic form first, as a prominent word in her dictionary. What follows, through reproductions of literary, biographical, and scientific texts, is Alison's own reading practice becoming solidified in her own life as well as the narrative. For example, Radclyffe Hall's *The Well of Loneliness*, a decisive work of the lesbian canon, is marked as pivotal not just for Alison. Alison's alternative canon links her oppositional reading practices and her burgeoning identification as a lesbian, socially, academically, and physically. In a clear attempt to meld theory with practice, Bechdel illustrates Alison's semester spent in bed reading with her lover – inspired by Alison having overheard someone explain, "Feminism is the theory. Lesbianism is the practice" (80). Bechdel clearly represents the connection between Alison's reading of certain canonical works – *The World of Pooh*, for example, and the dictionary – as an oppositional practice set alongside her sexual practices. It is essential that her canon is oppositional to her father's and starts to take shape outside of her familial homespace. After she discovers her father's sexuality and infidelity, she notes, "Home, as I had known it, was gone. Some crucial structure seemed to be missing, like in dreams I would have later where termites had eaten through all the floor joists" (215–16). Unlike the artists' colony Alison imagines before, a family working together yet separately, the home is fractured, a "tinderbox," according to her mother. This fracturing impels Alison to abscond to the local library as another way to reinforce her reading practices – this time picking up Kate Millet's *Flying* and examining Millet's participation in the lesbian community.

Alison experiences this fracturing again in reconstructing her father's library – not just the physical space but the objects themselves – in *Fun Home*. Bruce's elaborate play between fact and fiction is pointedly encoded in the space of the library. The library becomes a site of fantasies that tie Bruce's sexual identity and machinations to his pretense to great literacies. Bechdel points out the indicators of the library's affectation and falseness – statues of Mephistopheles and Don Quixote, gilded valances, and flocked wallpaper – and then Bechdel illustrates Bruce as a "Fitzgerald character." Bechdel also shows Bruce with copies of *This Side of Paradise* and *The Great Gatsby*, and later Alison aligns her father's suicide with Wallace Stevens's "Sunday Morning," "because its juxtaposition of catastrophe with a plush domestic interior is life with my father in a nutshell" (83). Bruce's canon is illustrative of the long-established white, hetero, masculinist tradition to which Alison sees herself as heir and rebel. Hilary Chute sees this "narrative conceit of telling and showing a private story through 'great books'" as another kind of haunting: "of replication – of generation, of reproduction, of repetition-only-maybe-with-a-difference" (183). Generating a space in the narrative for Bruce's library and reading practices allows Bechdel to explore other, creative types of reproduction.

Map drawing is another pivotal reproduction in *Fun Home*. Maps destabilize ideas of public space and private space, because they inscribe Alison's personal history and life through outdoor, public spaces. Alison shows the map in her *Wind in the Willows* coloring book next to a map of where her hometown is situated near the Allegheny Mountains. She finds that "the best thing about the *Wind in the Willows* map was its mystical bridging of the symbolic and the real, of the label and the thing itself. It was a chart, but also a vivid, almost animated picture" (147). This closing of the gap between signified and signifier is for Alison another important way of recognizing the multivalent possibilities of storytelling. When she maps the trajectory of her father's existence, she does so because she is telling *his* story as well as repeating the link between domestic practice and the outside world. The map includes his places of birth, childhood, death, and his gravesite all within a narrow mile and a half diameter. Alison notes, "This narrow compass suggests a provincialism on my father's part that is both misleading and accurate" (30). Later, Bechdel presents the map again, ascribed with Bruce's trajectory – BORN, LIVED, DIED, BURIED – and the admission that "my father's life was a solipsistic circle of self, from autodidact to autocrat to autocide" (140). She connects this to her own tendency toward autobiography, but with a difference, of course. Because she is not interested in the seeming smallness of her life, she chooses to illustrate her own narrative as one both deeply preoccupied with the domestic life of her family and in considerable resistance to it. Put another way, the drawing and reading of maps allow the reader to see the creation of the physical space that aids in the telling of the story. Simultaneously, Alison's narration of the maps calls attention to the fact that the reader cannot inhabit that same world themselves – Alison's or Bruce's. This recognition is another critical move to destabilize expectations and categories. Again, it is a creative and generative involution of a specific domestic sphere that reiterates Alison's project of identity formation and family history.

The domestic spheres represented in *Hill House* and *Fun Home* are radically different, but the depictions of big, haunted, Gothic homes which began this project led me to question how storytelling and history-making are invoked as a domestic practice. Nina Baym, who most likely coined the term "domestic fiction" in 1978 as a descriptor of women's writing during the nineteenth century, explains,

> Their fiction is mostly about social relations, generally set in homes and other social spaces that are fully described. The detailed descriptions are sometimes idealized, but more often simply "realistic." And, in accordance with the needs of plot, home life is presented, overwhelmingly, as unhappy. There are very few intact families in this literature, and those that are intact are unstable or locked in routines of misery. Domestic tasks are arduous and monotonous; family members oppress and abuse each other; social interchanges are alternately insipid or malicious. Domestic setting and description, then, do not by any means imply domestic idyll.
>
> (26–27)

Both *Hill House* and *Fun Home* demonstrate the interpenetrability of domestic life and public influence, with Hill House becoming the stage for a woman's social anxieties made manifest in private hauntings and Bechdel's home the site of another young woman seeking stability through the various acts of reading and writing her family's history. Besides forming narratives of identity and history, both authors show the power, however fraught, queering conventions can hold. Ultimately, even though Eleanor dies when she drives her car into a tree and Alison survives to illustrate more of her life, each woman serves as a marker for the power of the practice of storytelling and alternative ways of having a life.

Notes

1 From here, I will refer to the author of *Fun Home* as Bechdel, and the character who appears within the text as Bechdel's alter ego as Alison. Because I do not have the space here to consider the nuances between the genres of fiction and memoir, I argue from the position that Bechdel's text is a work of fiction – based on her life, of course – rather than a memoir. This generic elision does not significantly alter my reading of Bechdel's work in any way.
2 This is not to suggest that other women have not historically engaged in subversive domestic practices or rewritten histories from the domestic sphere in order to imagine alternative acts and communities, or that other feminist authors have not charted the tensions between domestic practices and their writing career. In fact, in "Experience and Fiction," Jackson's much-cited essay about the craft of fiction writing, she explains the link between her writing career and her domestic life. After her daughter suggests that Jackson open a stuck refrigerator door with magic, Jackson "left the refrigerator where it was and went in to my typewriter and wrote a story about not being able to open the refrigerator door and getting the children to open it with magic. When a magazine bought the story, I bought a new refrigerator" (219). Experiences within the home not only provide Jackson with the material of her work but also convert those experiences into capital with which to fund that work and household.
3 The genesis of *Hill House* came from Jackson's reading of a book of psychic researchers who experiment with living in a haunted house during the nineteenth century, much like Dr. Montague and his crew. Jackson claims the group "thought they were being terribly scientific" with their methodology and reporting of the goings-on ("Experience and Fiction" 225). The book, however, turned out not to be an account of the haunted house but "the story of several earnest, I believed misguided, certainly determined people, with their differing motivations and backgrounds" (225). Jackson rightly points out that the stories of houses are actually the stories of those who inhabit them.
4 One such critic is Holly Blackford, who argues that Mrs. Dudley is actually Eleanor's double, in the same way that Mrs. Danvers doubles Rebecca in du Maurier's *Rebecca*. Blackford notes, "the house is a site of desire for young protagonists because it displaces their awakening sexual desires and makes female desire both productive and palatable" (234). Blackford argues that Eleanor's inability to be alone, her desire to be intimate with Theo, stems from "the mental effects of the ethics of care" and the time she has spent taking care of her mother (250). For another, more explicit exploration of lesbianism in *Hill House*, see Chapter 7 in Haggerty, George. *Queer Gothic*. Urbana-Champaign: U of Illinois P, 2006. Print.
5 For another take on Bechdel's archive, see: Rohy, Valerie. "In a Queer Archive: *Fun Home*." *GLQ: A Journal of Gay and Lesbian Studies* 16.3 (2010): 340–61. *Project Muse*. Web. 21 April 2014.

Works cited

Ahmed, Sara. *The Promise of Happiness*. Durham, NC: Duke UP, 2010. Print.
Baym, Nina. *Woman's Fiction: A Guide to Novels by and about Women in America, 1820–1870*. Ithaca, NY: Cornell UP, 1978. Print.
Bechdel, Alison. *The Essential Dykes to Watch Out For*. Boston: Houghton Mifflin, 2008. Print.
———. *Fun Home*. Boston: Houghton Mifflin, 2006. Print.
Blackford, Holly. "Haunted Housekeeping: Fatal Attractions of Servant and Mistress in Twentieth-Century Female Gothic Literature." *Literature Interpretation Theory* 16 (2005): 233–61. Print.

Chute, Hillary L. "Animating an Archive: Repetition and Regeneration in Alison Bechdel's *Fun Home*." *Graphic Women: Life Narrative & Contemporary Comics*. New York: Columbia UP, 2010. 175–217. Print.

Cvetkovich, Ann. "Drawing the Archive in Alison Bechdel's *Fun Home*." *Women's Studies Quarterly* 36.1–2 (2008): 111–28. Print.

Downey, Dara. "'Reading Her Difficult Riddle': Shirley Jackson and Late 1950s' Anthropology." *It Came from the 1950s!: Popular Culture, Popular Anxieties*. Eds. Darryl Jones, Elizabeth McCarthy, and Bernice M. Murphy. New York: Palgrave MacMillan, 2011. 176–97. Print.

Freeman, Elizabeth. *Time Binds: Queer Temporalities, Queer Histories*. Durham, NC: Duke UP, 2010. Print.

Fuss, Diana. "Introduction: Inside/Out." *Inside/Out: Lesbian Theories, Gay Theories*. Ed. Diana Fuss. New York: Routledge, 1991. 1–12. Print.

Haines, Colin. *Frightened by a Word: Shirley Jackson and the Lesbian Gothic*. Uppsala, SE: Uppsala U Library, 2007. Print.

Halberstam, Judith. *In a Queer Time and Place: Transgender Bodies, Subcultural Live*. New York: New York UP, 2005. Print.

Jackson, Shirley. "Experience and Fiction." *Come Along with Me: Classic Short Stories and an Unfinished Novel*. 1968. Ed. Stanley Edgar Hyman. New York: Penguin, 2012. 219–30. Print.

———. *The Haunting of Hill House*. 1959. New York: Penguin, 2006. Print.

———. *Life Among the Savages; Raising Demons*. New York: Quality Paperback Book Club, 1998. Print.

Jacobson, Kristin. *Neodomestic American Fiction*. Columbus: Ohio State UP, 2010. Print.

King, Stephen. *Danse Macabre*. 1981. New York: Gallery Books, 2010. Print.

Lootens, Tricia. "'Whose Hand Was I Holding?': Familial and Sexual Politics in Shirley Jackson's *The Haunting of Hill House*." *Shirley Jackson: Essays on the Literary Legacy*. Ed. Bernice M. Murphy. Jefferson, NC: McFarland and Company, 2005. 150–68. Print.

Lydenberg, Robin. "Under Construction: Alison Bechdel's *Fun Home: A Family Tragicomic*." *European Journal of English Studies* 16.1 (2012): 57–68. Print.

Mitchell, Adrielle. "Spectral Memory, Sexuality, and Inversion: An Arthrological Study of Alison Bechdel's *Fun Home: A Family Tragicomedy*." *ImageTexT* 4.3 (2009): n. pag. Web. 24 Apr. 2014.

Murphy, Bernice M. *The Suburban Gothic in American Popular Culture*. New York: Palgrave MacMillan, 2009. Print.

Savoy, Eric. "The Rise of American Gothic." *The Cambridge Companion to Gothic Fiction*. Ed. Jerrold E. Hogle. New York: Cambridge UP, 2002. 167–88. Print.

Wagner, Tamara. "Gothic and the Victorian Home." *The Gothic World*. Eds. Glennis Byron and Dale Townshend. New York: Routledge, 2014. 110–20. Print.

Whitlock, Gillian. "Autographics: The Seeing 'I' of the Comics." *Modern Fiction Studies* 52.4 (2006): 965–79. *EBSCOHost*. Web. 29 May 2014.

10 The tower or the nursery?
Paternal and maternal re-visions of Hill House on film

Shari Hodges Holt

Film historian Barry Curtis asserts that "[t]he idea of the ghostly has accompanied cinema from its earliest manifestations." Like other communication technologies, such as the telegraph, telephone, and radio, "the cinema created 'phantasms' – replicas of human beings that had a life of their own" (150–51). Film's uncanny ability to preserve and reanimate the dead, its simultaneous existence in the past and the present, gives it the power to manifest our cultural past while addressing the cultural present, bridging the gaps of time and space to present us with preternatural doubles of our own experience. Curtis notes that "[t]he metaphor of 'haunting' has been deployed to explain the ways in which films can be possessed by the milieu in which they are produced," acting as "a sensitive barometer of mood and cultural dispositions" (164). Film adaptations, in particular, have acted as such cultural barometers by providing us with new ways of reanimating past texts for current and future audiences by adapting them to new cultural concerns. Shirley Jackson's *The Haunting of Hill House* has inspired two film adaptations that envision the novel's themes from drastically different perspectives determined by the cultural climate of each film's production. Both films deal with the fraught nature of female subjectivity addressed in the novel, but each film's construction of the haunted house and its attendant ghosts manifests the gender anxieties that haunted American culture at two different periods in the history of feminism. Robert Wise's 1963 film *The Haunting* depicts patriarchal power as the haunting force of Hill House, while Jan De Bont's identically titled 1999 production depicts maternal forces as equally powerful (and ultimately triumphant). Influenced by the respective ideologies of second- and third-wave feminism, these cinematic manifestations of Jackson's narrative thus reanimate and transfigure the novel's complicated gender dynamics to meet varying sociopolitical needs.

An overview of the scholarly debate about what haunts Jackson's famous edifice may provide an effective introduction to the contrasting perspectives of these films. Melanie Anderson summarizes one significant critical approach to the novel, describing Jackson's haunted house "as a symbol of patriarchal domination" that finally turns the protagonist, Eleanor Vance, into the ghost she has been all along because of her social marginalization in a male-dominated culture (200). Distinguished by a phallic tower rising from the family library, Hill House is a patriarchal structure, a reflection of the distorted mind of the paterfamilias Hugh Crain, who constructed the house as domicile and eventual prison for his wife and two daughters. The house then develops a history of subsuming and destroying every woman associated with it (including Eleanor), thus dramatizing, according to Anderson, the spectralization of women in a patriarchal culture that denies them agency (204).

However, several scholars have likewise noted the maternal significance of Hill House,[1] which, despite its phallic motifs, is described as "all so motherly," "so soft," "so padded," with "[g]reat embracing chairs and sofas which turn out to be hard and unwelcoming when you sit down, and reject you at once" (Jackson 154). From this perspective, the house embodies the desire for maternal love and the reality of maternal rejection haunting the recently orphaned Eleanor. The novel begins with Eleanor leaving behind her life as subservient daughter to a dead, hated mother only to end with her inability to escape from a home that haunts her with guilt over her mother's death and her own corresponding need for maternal affection. The house's construction in concentric circles (Parks 134) centering on the womb-like nursery and the ghostly manifestations in which the house seems to bleed associate it with the reproductive functions of the female body. Responding to the spectral message, "Help Eleanor Come Home," written on the walls in what appears to be menstrual blood, Eleanor finally regresses into a childlike state during her last night in the house and chases a voice she assumes is her mother's throughout the labyrinthine domicile. As Judie Newman asserts, Eleanor's final union with the house is a "reabsorption by the mother" that she both resents and desires (qtd. in Hattenhauer, *American Gothic* 161), thus dramatizing her fraught relationship with maternity and her own female sexuality.

The house is also an emblem of family, which, according to Linda Metcalf, "is the most powerful institution of all" in Jackson's fiction (154). In a narrative filled with dysfunctional families, the distorted house embodies the twisted nature of family dynamics, the guilt, codependence, and self-sacrifice too often clothed in the illusion of domestic happiness. Tricia Lootens asserts that the novel is about "the ways in which people, especially women, are destroyed by the nuclear family, sexual repression, and romantic notions of feminine self-sacrifice" (168). The novel's terror therefore lies in its depiction of women as "tied to mother or children, ruled by father or husband, bound by family law and family romance, [. . .] by the stultifying narrowness of home and the imaginative failure to construe alternative modes of living" (Metcalf 156). One of the most nightmarish hauntings Eleanor and Theo experience at Hill House occurs when, wandering in the estate gardens, they are suddenly compelled down a blackening path where at "its destined end" they see an uncanny vision of a happy family picnic, a beaming mother and father at its center, a vision that sends them racing to the garden walls, "scratching wildly," "screaming . . . and begging to be let out" (Jackson 130). Eleanor's longing for home and family and her converse terror at this vision of the domestic idyll express women's complex, conflicted relationship with the domestic realm as both sanctuary and prison, source of fulfillment and site of oppression.

All of these interpretations suggest that the house acts as a nexus of the complexities of female identity. Eleanor's death dramatizes her inability to escape not only patriarchal domination but also female biological and maternal imperatives, her failure to balance the need for individual independence with the drive for family and communal connection, and her ultimate inability to reconcile the complex, often incompatible demands of female subjectivity. Woman's problematic rapport with masculine and feminine models is embodied in the paradoxical image of the house as phallic mother, a threatening combination of male power and maternal indulgence represented in the romantic allure and repellent terror of both the tower and the nursery.

While the novel posits the haunted house as an emblem of tortured female identity resulting from both paternal and maternal family dynamics, Robert Wise's 1963 film adaptation *The Haunting* highlights the novel's critique of male-dominated culture by re-envisioning Hill House as an icon of distinctly patriarchal dominance. Wise's Hill House is an edifice of phallic spires, staircases, and towers in which even the womb-like nursery is transformed into a patriarchal prison where Hugh Crain infantilizes and incarcerates his daughter, a fate that will be replicated for Eleanor (Julie Harris) as the house's final female victim.

Throughout the film, low-angle shots of the mansion contrasted with high-angle photography of its inhabitants visualize the house's dominance (see Figures 10.1 and 10.2).[2] Steven Jay Schneider notes that Wise's camerawork endows the domicile with "a kind of proto-consciousness," creating "a virtual dialogue" between the house and Eleanor in particular by "alternating between medium shots of Eleanor and location shots of the house itself" (171) (see Figure 10.3).

One scene frighteningly suggestive of a paranormal sexual assault illustrates the visual dynamic the film establishes between Eleanor and Hill House. As she stands outside at the base of the phallic tower, Eleanor's eye is slowly attracted upwards (Figure 10.4).

Fig. 10.1 The low-angle perspective of exterior shots of Hill House emphasizes the structure's power over its occupants. *The Haunting*, 1963, Warner Home Video.

Fig. 10.2 Robert Wise typically photographs the inhabitants of Hill House from a high angle. Dr. Markway, Luke, Theo, and Eleanor (from left to right) climb the main staircase, one of the house's many phallic structures. *The Haunting*, 1963, Warner Home Video.

Fig. 10.3 A striking dissolve transition foreshadows Eleanor's eventual spectralization and assimilation by the haunted house. *The Haunting*, 1963, Warner Home Video.

Fig. 10.4 The phallic tower of Hill House attracts Eleanor's gaze just prior to a ghostly sexual assault. *The Haunting*, 1963, Warner Home Video.

A sudden bird's-eye-view subjective shot from atop the tower presents the house's perspective of Eleanor. The camera then violently swoops down upon her, throwing her back into the arms of a waiting male as if the house were forcibly claiming her as lover. The camerawork and composition of interior scenes similarly evoke the house's sense of menace toward its tenants. Interior long shots emphasizing the size of the edifice in comparison to the occupants are contrasted with tightly framed shots of claustrophobic rooms, while the cluttered *mise-en-scène* evokes a repressive Victorian domesticity filled with motifs of female imprisonment, including women immobilized as statues, minimalized by interminable corridors and turrets, or trapped as reflections in distorted mirrors (see Figure 10.5).

In addition, the film makes several alterations to Jackson's narrative to focus on destructive patriarchy. The house's maternal ghostly manifestations, such as the bleeding walls, are eliminated to emphasize instead the house's patriarchal history. Most notable is the addition of a prologue (narrated by the male voice of Dr. Markway – the film's substitute for Dr. Montague from the novel) visualizing Hugh Crain's domination of his wives and daughter. The sequence includes an extended depiction of each wife's death, the first in a carriage accident that will be visually echoed in Eleanor's death at the end of the film, and the second in a tumble down a phallic staircase (her housekeeping keys landing conspicuously on the floor beside her) that will be paralleled in Eleanor's ascent up the tower staircase just prior to her death. The prologue likewise interpolates a scene of the patriarch imprisoning his daughter, Abigail. A sinister low-angle shot of Crain reading scripture to Abigail over the body of her dead mother is followed by shots of Abigail in the nursery, where her dolls have been removed and replaced by her father's massive Bible. The womblike nursery set design, featuring curved ceiling beams on which Crain has

Fig. 10.5 The *mise-en-scène* of interior scenes frequently parallels Eleanor with images of female immobility and imprisonment. *The Haunting*, 1963, Warner Home Video.

inscribed an ominously truncated version of Christ's words, "Suffer the Little Children," visualizes the usurpation of feminine space for a patriarchal agenda. Abigail evidently remains incarcerated in the nursery for the rest of her life, as is implied by a series of tightly framed superimpositions of her aging face against the blank background of the nursery pillow, depicting the progression of time while Abigail remains forever infantilized. In a final foreshadowing of Eleanor's fate, the prologue concludes with the suicide of the now elderly Abigail's young female caregiver (who parallels Eleanor's own caregiver relationship with her invalid mother). The caregiver's suicide is prompted in the novel by female squabbling over ownership of the house, but transformed in the film into the caregiver's act of guilt for her failure to respond to the dying Abigail's calls for help because she succumbed instead to the seductions of a male visitor. The caregiver hangs herself, significantly, from the staircase in the phallic tower.

Destructive male intervention between females is likewise emphasized in the scene in which Eleanor first asserts her right to leave her family and begin the journey to Hill House. Having received the doctor's invitation to join the ghost-hunting experiment shortly after her mother's death, Eleanor demands to take the family car, which she co-owns with her sister. The novel portrays this as a conflict between the sisters indicating continuing maternal control, as Eleanor's sister Carrie refuses the demand, asserting that she is "doing what Mother would have thought best. Mother had confidence in me and would certainly never have approved my letting you run wild" (Jackson 7). In the film, however, the majority of the dialogue takes place between Eleanor and her brother-in-law, who, as the primary objector and obstacle to Eleanor's independence, is placed between the sisters as a divisive figure in the center of the frame's composition, while sister Carrie remains a model of domestic submission, quietly sewing to one side. Therefore, Eleanor's defiance in this scene becomes a rebellion against patriarchal rather than matriarchal control.

Although Eleanor finally takes the car in a symbolic act of agency and self-assertion, the sense of female agency is illusory since her journey to Hill House is controlled by the male doctor, who instructs her through the authority of the written word, as she refers repeatedly to his letter for directions. But the "round and rosy and bearded" Dr. Montague who invites her to the house in the novel (Jackson 43) becomes the decidedly younger, more dashing Dr. Markway (Richard Johnson) in the film, fulfilling Eleanor's repeated refrain from the novel, "Journeys end in lovers meeting" in a more literal manner. Whereas in the novel Eleanor's hope for affectionate connection with the group at Hill House represents her need for family, a complex of desire embodied in the paternal figure of the doctor, the male lover (Luke), and the sister/female lover (Theo), this relational dynamic is simplified in the film to a romantic attraction between Eleanor and Dr. Markway. As Steven Jay Schneider notes, Markway's replacement of Luke as a more viable romantic interest for Eleanor allows the doctor to assume a hierarchical relationship with her on multiple levels: "not only as scientist-subject, teacher-pupil, and doctor-patient, but as potential lovers" (170).

Consequently, the potential lesbian relationship between Eleanor and Theo implicit in the novel is accentuated in the film to act as a threat to the normative heterosexual relationships valued by patriarchy. As Schneider points out, despite strong indications of her lesbianism, Theo's sister/lover attraction to Eleanor is ambiguous at best in the novel, and her growing affinity for Luke as she distances herself from Eleanor may even suggest her bisexuality. By contrast, in the film Theo (Claire Bloom) makes deliberate sexual advances to Eleanor while evincing a sometimes violent antipathy to the flirtations of Luke (Russ Tamblyn). She expresses anger toward Eleanor only as the product of jealousy toward Eleanor's growing intimacy with Markway. Eleanor, while exhibiting a consistent affection and growing longing for Theo in the novel, viciously rejects her in the film in a homophobic diatribe, calling her "unnatural" and "one of nature's mistakes," which is evidently interpolated into the script to connect Eleanor more strongly to the heterosexual patriarchal figure of Markway (*The Haunting* 1963). Normand Lareau notes how the film expresses this character dynamic through the composition of photography of the two women. Julie Harris, who plays Eleanor, is filmed in a series of lingering, luminous close-ups as the object of the cinematic (inherently male) gaze, while Claire Bloom as Theo is often placed in the background or to the side of the composition (Lareau 46–47), sometimes appearing as the disruptive third element in intimate two-shots of the romantic couple.

The transformation of the doctor into a romantic interest in the film necessitates the transformation of his wife into a romantic rival of Eleanor. In the novel, the doctor's wife is a spiritualist, an overbearing motherly figure, who arrives unexpectedly at the house to disrupt her husband's ostensibly scientific investigations with séances to comfort the house's suffering spirits by letting them know "that we are thinking of them lovingly" (Jackson 135). In comparison, the film portrays Markway's wife (Lois Maxwell) as a skeptic, a usurper of "masculine" rationalism determined to disprove her husband's investigations. The film's depiction of her arrival is dominated by visually unstable three-shots of Markway, his wife, and Eleanor that often place Markway between the two women as if they are competing for him. In the novel, the ineffectual feminine and masculine paradigms that plague Eleanor are parodied in the motherly Mrs. Montague and her hypermacho partner in paranormal investigation, Arthur, as they conduct bumbling experiments that comically misinterpret the house's sinister intentions toward Eleanor. In the film, however, Mrs. Markway plays a much more critical role in the house's apparent attempts to claim Eleanor. Upon her arrival, the overly assertive Mrs. Markway is promptly relegated to the nursery, where she disappears, apparently kidnapped by the presiding spirit of the house in a ploy not only to punish the presumptive woman but also to arouse the jealousy of Eleanor, who has been resisting the house's ghostly attentions. The romantic rivalry is then transposed into a rivalry for possession of the house, or rather to be possessed by the house. Eleanor resents Mrs. Markway as a rival not only for Markway's affection but also for the attention of the house, thinking Mrs. Markway has supplanted her as the object of the house's desire. The playing of Eleanor and Mrs. Markway against each other in the final sequences of the film suggests that women have no agency of their own but are the pawns of patriarchal power, competing for male attention.

Her sense that Mrs. Markway has superseded her in the house's affections catalyzes Eleanor's climactic final trip to the library's phallic tower in the film. The library has both patriarchal and matriarchal associations in the novel. Its role as the repository of culture, by definition patriarchal, is emphasized by the discovery there of a book composed by Hugh Crain of scraps from innumerable canonical texts orchestrated to teach his daughter proper submission to her father, "the author of thy being," and signed in his own blood as a "vital fluid with which I bind you" (Jackson 126). Yet Eleanor's final visit to the library evinces the binding power of the mother as well as the father. Repelled from the library on her first visit by a smell of mold and decay that she associates with her mother, she is drawn back on the night before her own death by a voice that she assumes is her mother's, which leads her first to the nursery, then past the exterior of the tower, and back inside to the library. Arriving at the tower staircase, in a moment of penetration (pun intended), she thinks, "I have broken the spell of Hill House and somehow come inside. . . . I am home," she thought, "now to climb." Throughout her "intoxicating" climb up the dangerous staircase, feminine and masculine images of the house unite as Eleanor imagines it nestled in "soft green grass" and "rolling hills" with its "tower . . . rising triumphantly between the trees" (Jackson 171–72). The consummation of her union with the house as symbol of both father and mother, however, is interrupted by the arrival of the other ghost hunters.

The film eliminates the guiding voice of Eleanor's mother in this scene and instead depicts Eleanor's trip to the library solely as a union with a demon lover, sparked by Eleanor's jealousy of her romantic rival, Mrs. Markway.[3] Her ascent up the dangerous spiral staircase becomes an attempt to reclaim the affections of Markway (who makes valiant efforts to rescue her, unlike Luke's reluctant effort in the novel), as well as an attempt to reclaim the affections of the house, which leads her upward to the climax through a series of subjective camera shots that, according to film critic Normand Lareau, "romanticize the ascent for her" (45). At the top, Eleanor is united with Markway for a brief romantic moment; but in this case, the climactic union is prevented by the sudden appearance of the rival Mrs. Markway through an attic trapdoor at the top of the staircase, almost as if the house had thrown her in Eleanor's way.

Eleanor's near destruction prompts the ghost hunters to end their investigations and send Eleanor away from Hill House against her will, leading to her death when she drives her car into a tree. The novel depicts Eleanor's death ambiguously. As she drives away from the "family" that has rejected her, she deliberately aims her car at the tree, thinking, "I am really doing it, I am doing this all by myself, now, at last," only to reconsider in the final moments before impact, "*Why* am I doing this? . . . Why don't they stop me?" (Jackson 182). Her ambivalence reflects the inner division that has plagued her throughout the novel between conventional gender paradigms of masculine assertion and feminine passivity, independence and communal connection. She is a victim of her own inability to reconcile the conflicting needs of her nature. The film's revision of Eleanor's suicide into a more explicit possession by the masculine spirit of the house (which is depicted dominating the frame behind her as she drives away into the night) is perhaps its most significant change in specifying Eleanor as a victim of external patriarchal control. In another suggestion of the destructive way in which patriarchy sets women in competition with each other, the film depicts Eleanor's death as a direct result of a second encounter with her rival for Markway's and the house's affections. As Eleanor drives away, the house blocks her exit by again seeming to throw Mrs. Markway in her path. Dressed in spectral white (recalling Eleanor's own spectral appearance as she flitted around the house in her nightgown in earlier scenes), Mrs. Markway appears out of nowhere and runs in front of the car, thereby directing it toward the same phallic tree that killed Hugh Crain's wife in the carriage accident at the beginning of the film. When Eleanor swerves to avoid her, the steering wheel suddenly assumes a life of its own and sends the car careening into the tree while Eleanor screams out her protests. Thus, Eleanor's competition for male affection contributes to the house's ability to wrest control of her own destiny from her, allowing the house to kill and finally subsume her. In a concluding visual parallel that brings the pattern of male domination full circle, the tire of Eleanor's overturned car recalls the broken wheel of Mrs. Crain's wrecked carriage from the film's prologue. The patriarch has claimed another victim.

The film's focus on patriarchal power as the haunting force of Hill House and its consequent suppression of the novel's maternal references may result from the film's cultural context within the nascence of second-wave feminism. The adaptation's simplification of the gender dynamics of Jackson's novel particularly reflects attempts by the Women's Liberation movement to locate the blame for problems with female subjectivity within the patriarchy and the consequent rejection by many feminists of biological reproduction and the family as the tools of patriarchal oppression (Birke 2–3). But second-wave feminism's equation of female agency with a repudiation of maternity and family would leave women fraught with conflicting desires. Eleanor's own conflicting needs for independence and domesticity as she is haunted by both the power of the tower and the comfort of the nursery seem to forecast the fact that, as historian Charlotte Brunsdon notes, second-wave feminism would continue to be haunted by "a ghost of past femininities" (40). This sense that something vital had been lost to women in the rejection of feminine cultural paradigms would lead to a reassessment of conventional femininity in the postfeminist movement.

While Wise's Hill House embodies the radical feminist concept of the home as an inescapable patriarchal prison, Jan De Bont's depiction of the haunted house in the 1999 film adaptation of Jackson's novel is informed by the postfeminist attempt to reclaim domesticity and femininity, not as mechanisms of female subordination but as foundations of female empowerment. Although De Bont's production is cinematically far inferior to Wise's, sacrificing suspense for the overblown spectacle of elaborate CGI effects, the film is culturally intriguing in its postfeminist approach to Jackson's narrative. Several striking revisions to Jackson's story transform Eleanor from mousy victim to heroic mother figure.

Dispossessed of her home by the death of her mother, Eleanor (Lili Taylor) is summoned to Hill House not by the paternal figure of Dr. Montague but by the spirit of Hugh Crain's second wife, who – in a significant alteration from the novel – is revealed to be Eleanor's great-great-grandmother. There Eleanor regains her lost maternal heritage by uniting with her grandmother's ghost to rescue the spirits of murdered child laborers, who had been incarcerated and killed in the house as past victims of Hugh Crain's industrial ambitions. The home becomes the battleground of warring paternal and maternal spirits, as the maternal force attempts to repossess the domestic sphere from patriarchal exploitation through Eleanor's mediation. To exorcise the abusive paterfamilias, Eleanor conflates conventional gender paradigms by assuming the traditionally "masculine" role of detective for a maternal purpose. She investigates and exposes Crain's patriarchal crimes, finally banishing his spirit from the house in a triumphant assertion of maternal power that recovers the home as a site for mothering.[4]

The film's opening sequence places Eleanor in a much different relationship to domesticity than in the novel. The novel opens with Eleanor living with her sister and brother-in-law following the death of her domineering invalid mother, to whom she devoted eleven grueling years of caregiving. She sees the Hill House experiment as the first significant event of her life and gateway to a new existence, an escape from a domestic situation she hates and resents. Conversely, De Bont's film begins with Eleanor fighting not to escape but to keep the apartment she shared with her mother, from which her brother-in-law, who "is not even real family," in Eleanor's words, is attempting to evict her (*The Haunting* 1999). Throughout the scene, her resentment is projected not toward the dead mother, whom she obviously misses, but toward the uncaring family members who have exploited her domestic service while denying its worth. The brother-in-law appreciates the apartment only for its "market value" without recognizing it as the home that Eleanor has established through long and difficult labor. In a significant change from the novel, Eleanor's sister offers her the dead mother's car in exchange for the apartment in an attempt to entice her out of the home. In response, Eleanor furiously berates her sister for "taking away my home and giving me a twenty-year-old car" (*The Haunting* 1999). In the novel, Eleanor is forced to steal the car she co-owns with her sister as an assertion of independence. But in De Bont's adaptation, Eleanor recognizes the car as a symbol of false emancipation, an attempt to separate her from the home she loves. By the time this film adaptation was made, the feminist movement had offered women escape from the domestic sphere and provided them with over twenty years of the kind of freedoms that the car represents, but Eleanor's situation dramatizes the kind of loss emancipation entailed for many third-wave feminists, who experienced freedom at the cost of family and domestic stability.

In a last attempt to remove Eleanor from the apartment, her sister invites Eleanor to live with them and care for their atrociously spoiled son, Richie, because with their "busy" lives, they "could use someone to do the cooking and the cleaning" (*The Haunting* 1999). The insulting implication of this offer is that homemaking, "woman's work," does not carry the importance of work in the public sphere. "Come live with us, Nell," her sister pleads. "You have no idea how hard it is out there." "You have no idea how hard it was in here," Eleanor replies, ordering her unappreciative relatives to "get out of my home" (*The Haunting* 1999). In Jackson's novel, Eleanor fantasizes about having a home of her own, but the Eleanor of the 1999 film already has a home from which the uncomprehending forces of both patriarchy and feminism (voiced respectively by her brother-in-law and sister) would drive her.

Eleanor's hard domestic labor is confirmed rather than belied by the immaculate nature of her mother's apartment, which she has obviously preserved with much pride. The *mise-en-scène* throughout the apartment sequence emphasizes Eleanor's positive relationship to domesticity despite the strenuous work it has entailed. The rooms are pristine without being antiseptic, adorned by small mementos and graced by warm lighting. When she enters her dead mother's bedroom, enticed by a gently billowing curtain that she seems briefly to mistake for her mother's returning ghost, the affection she holds for her mother becomes even more apparent in the décor. Implements suggesting the hardships of invalid care – the bedpan, hospital screen, and IV stand – are counterbalanced by soft, inviting furnishings decorated with gentle pastels and floral prints. An embroidered sampler, "A Place for Everything, and Everything in Its Place," hangs above the headboard of the bed from which an antique locket, clearly a feminine family heirloom, is suspended. As Eleanor picks up the locket (later disclosed as the property of Eleanor's great-great-grandmother, Caroline Crain) composer Jerry Goldsmith's musical score uses a soft flute solo to create a nostalgic leitmotif (titled "A Place for Everything" on the film soundtrack) that will recur throughout the film as an indicator of Eleanor's domestic affections. As the flute plays, Eleanor assumes the maternal identity by placing the locket around her neck while examining herself in the mirror with a wall plaque announcing, "Home Is Where You Hang Your Heart," conspicuously visible beside her. At that moment, an unexpected telephone call (which the film later reveals came from Eleanor's dead great-great-grandmother) invites her to look at the newspaper ad for the "psychological study" to be conducted at Hill House. Eleanor is about to be evicted from the home she has worked hard to create, but she will establish a new home at Hill House through this maternal invitation.

While Eleanor represents the strong domestic woman whose achievements are undervalued, Theo (Catherine Zeta-Jones) embodies the liberated woman whose emancipation is overrated. Arriving at Hill House in her black Prada boots and leather miniskirt with a mound of luggage in tow, she flaunts a contrived material girl persona and flippant attitudes toward sex, family, and her own career as an artist. When Theo tells Eleanor that she has joined the experiment at Hill House to escape romantic problems, Eleanor cuts immediately through Theo's brash charm, declaring, "You mean you have trouble with commitment." Theo replies, "Well, my boyfriend thinks so; my girlfriend doesn't. We could all live together, but they hate each other." Theo's ambiguous sexuality in the novel is a marker of her greater independence in comparison to the neurotically romantic Eleanor.

But the character's overt bisexuality in De Bont's film indicates a casual attitude toward human relationships that is independent to the point of utter carelessness, evidently preventing her from establishing any stable human connections. "It's hard when you're the only one at the party," she tells Eleanor (*The Haunting* 1999). Thus, whereas Eleanor embodies the loneliness of the homemaker whose sacrifices go unappreciated, Theo exposes the illusion of the completely liberated woman, so emancipated from all commitments that she lacks substance and stability. Projecting her own lack of definition onto Eleanor, Theo describes Eleanor as a "blank canvas" (*The Haunting* 1999), expressing a conventional feminist stance toward the homemaker, assuming that because she has spent her life in domestic service, she lacks autonomy.

Psychologist Dr. Marrow (Liam Neeson), the film's substitute for occult investigator Dr. Montague, evinces a similarly conventional (in this case patriarchal) response to Eleanor's domestic service by branding her with a "classic dependent personality disorder" when he reads of her years as a caregiver in her psychological profile. He likewise misapplies the traditional patriarchal label of madness when Eleanor begins to experience ghostly visitations from the spirits of her great-great-grandmother and the abused children who haunt Hill House. Unlike Dr. Montague in the novel, Dr. Marrow has no belief in the supernatural; Hill House is merely a suitable environment where he can conduct an experiment in "group fear and hysteria" under the unethical guise of an insomnia study. Evincing a brutally clinical attitude toward his subjects (at one point, he refers to them as rats in a maze), he mistakes Eleanor's strong empathy for neurosis and attributes her paranormal visions to the "self-delusion and emotional instability" of a "sensitive woman" (*The Haunting* 1999).

But contrary to her neurotic behavior in the novel and the 1963 film, Eleanor in De Bont's adaptation displays the greatest composure, stability, and sincerity of all the characters involved in the Hill House experiment, and she possesses the clearest understanding of the house's haunted nature. The other characters variously admit to suffering from not only insomnia but also narcissism, panic attacks, and alcohol and drug addiction, none of which plagues Eleanor as she is depicted in the film. Instead she embodies the domestic woman who has been misrepresented by both patriarchy and radical feminism as unstable, weak, dependent, and enslaved.

A significant scene interpolated in the 1999 film tellingly expresses how Eleanor has felt trapped by a culture that repeatedly depreciates the domestic sphere. Upon their arrival at Hill House, Eleanor and Theo examine the massive doors to the main parlor, which are carved in imitation of Rodin's sculpture "The Gates of Hell." Eleanor notes that in contrast to the Rodin piece, the Hill House sculpture depicts the trapped souls of children (representing Hugh Crain's child victims), who are "reaching for heaven." When Theo, surprised, asks Eleanor if she has studied art (an obvious reference to Eleanor's supposed exclusion from male-dominated Western culture), Eleanor replies, "No, I studied purgatory. I was there once for eleven years. It's when your soul is caught between the living and the dead" (*The Haunting* 1999). She has existed in purgatory throughout her domestic service, trapped between heaven and hell, life and death, by ideologies that have failed to give home and family their due importance while demanding of her arduous service for a home that is eventually usurped from her. To transcend this limbo, she must rescue herself and the children of past domestic abuse. Therefore, rather than the house claiming her, as it does in the novel and the 1963 film, the postfeminist narrative of the 1999 film depicts Eleanor actively and successfully investigating the house's secrets to purge it of the oppressive forces that haunt it and reclaim it as a home. She works throughout the film to repossess the domestic sphere from a centuries-long purgatory of cultural and societal misinterpretation. Consequently, she is not the woman who lacks agency because of her domestic commitment, but rather she is the woman who has been gravely misperceived as such.

Through her paranormal investigations, Eleanor discovers the house's history of domestic exploitation, which features the spectralization of the women and children of the home by the patriarch. Building the home for his beautiful first wife with the profits of his textile mills, Hugh Crain "wanted more than anything . . . a house filled with the laughter of children" (*The Haunting* 1999). When each of his wife's children dies at birth, he takes child laborers from his factories, incarcerates them in the home, and eventually kills them in a homicidal mania that finally drives his wife to suicide. His second wife, Caroline (Eleanor's great-great-grandmother), is able to produce a child, but when she discovers her husband's atrocities, she flees the home, taking her child with her. Her ghost is the motivating force that draws Eleanor to Hill House to expose and punish its twisted crimes.

This demented ghost story reminds us that the family is the primary "organizing structure of the Gothic" and that the "Gothic romance is family romance," "pervasively organized around anxieties about boundaries (and boundary transgressions)" (Williams 22, 16). The story of Hill House in the 1999 film reflects the central terror that, according to Ann McGuire and David Buchbinder, informs popular Gothic narratives of film and television at the turn of the millennium, the idea that the family is "haunted by a fear of dissolution, of intrusion and invasion, of ceasing, finally, to be recognizable as a family" (300). The film's focus on Hugh Crain's industrial ambitions as the invading and corrupting force of the home deconstructs the convenient patriarchal binaries of private and public spheres in a manner typical of the Gothic "interpenetration" of perceived opposites – material and supernatural, past and present, feminine and masculine, human and technological (McGuire and Buchbinder 302). In fact, the Crain family story as recounted in the 1999 adaptation is rooted in the origins of the Gothic genre, which, as Kate Ferguson Ellis points out, coincided with the rise of domestic ideology, "as the middle-class home, distanced in ideology and increasingly in fact from the place where money was made, became a 'separate sphere' from the 'fallen' world of work" (ix). Gothic narratives expose the contradictions inherent in this "separate spheres" philosophy by providing women in particular with "a resistance to an ideology that imprisons them even as it posits a sphere of safety for them" (Ellis x).

De Bont's film visualizes the home as a Gothic environment where apparently stable boundaries have collapsed through the dynamically antithetical *mise-en-scène* of the Hill House interior, which is dominated by wild Byzantine mosaics on floors and walls, distorted funhouse mirrors, and motorized rooms that twist and turn, thereby suggesting how industrialist Crain has mechanized the home. The combating paternal and maternal forces of the home are externalized in statues of powerful guardian griffins and lions (which frequently burst violently into life) contrasted with sculptures of crying children trapped in the walls and doors, straining against imprisonment. Whereas the frozen statues that dominate the *mise-en-scène* of Wise's 1963 film visualize Eleanor's entrapment in the domestic sphere, the animated sculptures, portraits, and photographs of women and children with which Eleanor interacts in the 1999 construction of Hill House dramatize Eleanor's dynamic agency against the stultifying forces that have turned the home into a prison. The other characters quickly become terrified of this supernaturally animated environment, but Eleanor declares,

> All my life I've been waiting for an adventure, and I thought it would never happen to me. Adventures are for soldiers or for the women the bullfighters fall in love with. And here I am, paintings are calling out to me, strange noises in the night.
>
> (*The Haunting* 1999)

When she responds to the uncanny voices of the marginalized and abused and joins forces with her great-great-grandmother to lay to rest Hugh Crain's ghost and free the spirits of the children he exploited, she discovers that finally, the domestic sphere can be the locus of self-fulfilling adventure and heroic action. She tells the ever-skeptical Dr. Marrow that "it doesn't matter" if someone is concocting the paranormal phenomena to disturb her. "I can be a victim or I can be a volunteer," she declares. "I'm gonna be a volunteer."

This revision of Eleanor's character into an assertive psychic detective, who exposes the truth of the haunted house through her empathy with the dispossessed, places Jackson's narrative within an intriguing nexus of historical, literary, and cinematic movements that have expressed women's concerns. The film exposes the novel's intertextual connections to female Gothic and detective fiction, millennial developments in horror and haunted house cinema, and even the history of the spiritualist movement in American culture. First, the film's conflation of the novel's occult investigators – the pseudoscientist Dr. Montague and his wife, the paranormal medium – into a psychic detective heroine coincides with a revolution in the detective genre in the 1980s and 1990s. At this time, there was a "mini-explosion of women detectives" in fiction and film (Klein 231) that rewrote "the archetypal male detective from a female perspective" (Irons xi–xii), finally allowing the genre to "address the problems which women face in modern society" (Irons xii). As Eleanor searches out clues in old family stories, photo albums, and journals, the film places her in the amateur detective tradition of "nosy British spinsters," such as Agatha Christie's Miss Marple, who were allowed to function in a predominately male genre "so long as they employed the more stereotypically feminine talents of gossip and intuition" (Klein 3). But Eleanor's relative youth and historical position in the film likewise identify her with the "thirty-to-forty-year old women" who, in the wake of the feminist movement, could no longer "make the connection with 'grandmotherly' Jane Marple" and began at the turn of the millennium to create professional and amateur fictional female detectives from a wide variety of backgrounds (Dilley 126–27).

In particular, this revisionist version of Eleanor shares characteristics with post-feminist amateur female sleuths who "operate within the confines of 'femininity' and its implications of home, marriage, and children" (Dilley 96), but who work "to revise the definition" of femininity and endow it "with renewed strength and meaning" (Dilley xiii). Just as the amateur women sleuths of the 1990s used detection to strengthen and "reshape their families" (Dilley 116), often extending the family to include those with whom they may not have biological ties, Eleanor assumes the role of mother (in one scene she actually sees a pregnant reflection of herself in one of Hill House's many mirrors), adopting the spirits of the child laborers that her great-great-grandfather murdered. In her maternal advocacy of the abused, she exemplifies another critical difference in the women detectives of her time, who, unlike the stereotypical male detective, tend to identify more with crime victims than the criminals they are trying to catch, choosing "to avenge a victim by caring about the victim," rather than "becoming like a killer" (Klein 232–33). With their focus on "community . . . connection and responsibility," the female detectives of this period work for the restoration of order generic to detective fiction, not through restoring the patriarchy but through "strengthening the ties between members of the community or, where necessary, creating a more equitable community where one did not exist" (Dilley 150).

The depiction of Eleanor as an investigator of family crimes in a haunted mansion also underscores the narrative's connections to the eighteenth-century female Gothic novel in which the heroine becomes a "female detective who must cope with madness and imprisonment to solve her own personal mystery of identity," often through investigating a male villain's crimes against female family members (Nollen 40). The De Bont adaptation particularly evokes the typical female Gothic plot that Kate Ferguson Ellis has identified as an empowerment fantasy for female readers that subverted domestic ideology. Such plots hinged on the heroine's successful struggle "to purge the home of license and lust and to establish it as a type of heaven on earth" (xii), a narrative pattern replicated in the 1999 film adaptation.

These features of both contemporary female detective narratives and early female Gothic stories are reflected in the film's climactic showdown between Eleanor and Hugh Crain's ghost. When her investigations lead her to a portrait of her great-great-grandmother, who wears the same locket Eleanor has inherited from her mother, she decides to assert her maternal heritage in the entry hall of Hill House, where she fearlessly summons the ghost of Hugh Crain, declaring, "I'm not afraid of you. The children need me, and I'm going to set them free" (see Figure 10.6).

Emerging from his larger-than-life portrait atop a phallic staircase, Crain's ghost swoops down to confront Eleanor before the massive parlor doors sculpted

Hill House on film 175

Fig. 10.6 In Jan De Bont's adaptation, an empowered Eleanor prepares for her confrontation with Hugh Crain atop the phallic staircase. *The Haunting*, 1999, Warner Home Video.

to represent the gates of purgatory. When he tries to attack Dr. Marrow and Theo, Eleanor throws herself in the ghost's path, telling him, "It's not about them. It's about family. It's always been about family. Think about Caroline and the children from the mill; you can hear their voices. They're my family, Grandpa, and I've come home." As Eleanor backs to the parlor doors, the purgatory carvings spring to life and draw her and Crain into the animated bas-relief. After declaring that "purgatory's over" and exorcising Crain's ghost to hell, Eleanor is left hanging from the gates in a crucifixion pose as Crain's ghost is led away by attendant demons. The imprisoned spirits of Crain's child victims then emerge from the purgatory bas-relief to ascend to heaven, as Eleanor's body is gently lowered from the gates in an image evocative of the Deposition of Christ (Figure 10.7).

Fig. 10.7 Christian iconography transforms Eleanor into a female messiah who sacrifices herself to defeat the patriarch. *The Haunting*, 1999, Warner Home Video.

The scene ends with Eleanor undergoing transfiguration and ascending to join her new family, thus concluding Eleanor's remarkable metamorphosis from patriarchal victim to female messiah (*The Haunting* 1999).

This revisionist ending also connects Jackson's narrative to the subgenre of occult detective fiction in new ways more appropriate to postfeminist discourse, particularly in its evocation of the "Christ-like implications" that psychic investigators assumed in many occult detective narratives of the late nineteenth and early twentieth centuries (Tibbetts 345). The film follows the narrative pattern typical to many stories of paranormal detection in which "the psychic investigator learns that in his hands rests not just the fate of a case, but that of a soul," a realization that often prompts the detective into a paranormal showdown in which he is "transfigured, as a savior" as he exorcises the threatening supernatural forces from the household (Tibbetts 345). But while the psychic detectives of these narratives were exclusively male (e.g., Sheridan Le Fanu's Dr. Hesselius, Algernon Blackwood's John Silence, E. and H. Herron's Flaxman Low, and William Hope Hodgson's John Carnacki), frequently purging haunted homes in order to restore the male-dominated status quo, Eleanor as female psychic detective meets the third-wave feminist need for a savior who can reclaim the powers of femininity for a feminist agenda.

The film's conflation of Eleanor's character with the spiritualist medium Mrs. Montague from the novel likewise highlights the novel's connections with the history of spiritualism, the nineteenth-century movement to prove the existence of life after death through communication with the dead. Jackson's study of spiritualist investigations provided part of the inspiration for her description of the Hill House experiment (Metcalf 149), and the movement bears important connections to the women's issues the novel addresses. As transpired in many spiritualist investigations, the psychic experiment in De Bont's film becomes as much a criminal investigation as an attempt at occult communication. Maurizio Ascari notes that "the link between crime and the supernatural" in the popular consciousness was fostered by the spiritualist movement, which originated in New York in 1848 when two sisters, Kate and Margaret Fox, claimed to receive communications from the spirit of a man who had been murdered in their home (57). Spiritualism's rapidly developing transatlantic popularity led to the assimilation of elements of criminal detection and supernaturalism into novels of the sensation, Gothic, and detective genres throughout the latter half of the century (Ascari 58), paving the way for such twentieth-century haunted fictions as Jackson's novel. The movement also embodied "the fractured and contradictory nature of feminine subjectivity" (Owen 206) that Jackson's narrative interrogates. Most séances and spiritualist experiments consisted of attempts to contact dead relatives and therefore were conducted in the home (the sphere of female influence, according to contemporary domestic ideology). Likewise, the majority of spiritualist mediums were female because of the close connection of mediumship to cultural constructs of femininity (Braude 23), particularly "two allegedly feminine traits: sensitivity . . . and an easy reversion to automatism" (Galvan 12), which allowed the medium to contact the dead and act as the passive vehicle through which they would communicate. Thus Alex Owen notes that spiritualism "privileged women" in ways denied to them outside the movement but did this under the restrictive rubric of feminine stereotypes that defined women as passive and self-denying (4). The movement was consequently predicated upon the contradictions of the "separate spheres" ideology that both empowered and imprisoned women in the home, a paradox at the heart of Eleanor's struggles in Jackson's novel and both film adaptations. In the 1999 film, Eleanor's success at reconciling "masculine" assertion with "feminine" receptivity as a psychic medium and investigator is rooted in the spiritualist movement's potential for female empowerment, despite its reinforcement of contemporary feminine stereotypes. Ann Braude points out that spiritualism's valorization of women's spiritual capacities eventually brought it into conjunction with the women's rights movement in America (3), while Alex Owen sees spiritualism as a forerunner of the Womanspirit movement of the late twentieth century that returned to "matriarchal legend and myth" to celebrate femininity as a source of power (240–41), an ideology which seems to inform the depiction of Eleanor in the 1999 film.

De Bont's adaptation further underscores the novel's connections with spiritualism through Eleanor's methods of detection and mediation, which bear striking resemblance to the investigative techniques of the Society for Psychical Research (SPR), an organization established in the late nineteenth century with the aim of providing scientific proof of spiritualist phenomena (Galvan 4). While preparing to write her novel, Jackson purportedly studied a transcript of an SPR investigation of a haunted house (Metcalf 149). Some of the tools Eleanor relies on for her investigation of Hill House in De Bont's film match mechanisms frequently used by the SPR, particularly photography and telecommunication technologies. Jill Nicole Galvan points out that because the rise of spiritualism in the nineteenth century coincided with the development of new communication media, it became common to "associate occult modes of communication and projection with technological ones" (8). The uncanny nature of technologies such as telephones, telegraphs, phonographs, photographs, and X-rays, which offered means of accessing information from invisible worlds, made their connection to occult detection natural. In the 1999 film, Eleanor relies on three of these media for communication with the dead – the telephone, the phonograph, and photography.

When she is evicted from her dead mother's apartment, a phone call from her dead great-great-grandmother invites Eleanor to Hill House. Her explorations of the house bring her to the nursery, which appears to be a replica of her own mother's bedroom, where an antique phonograph plays the musical motif "A Place for Everything," confirming that Eleanor has finally come home. As she investigates the family history and discovers that the house is occupied by her great-great-grandfather's ghost, she uncovers the truth of his crimes through examination of factory ledgers that list the child laborers he murdered and family photographs that reveal the location of their remains. In keeping with the conventions of haunted house films, in which "photographs of previous owners are often early signs that the house is still possessed by other subjectivities and narratives" (Curtis 124), the photographs of her dead grandparents have the most significant impact on Eleanor's investigation. Film historian David Curtis notes the "powerful evidential effect" of still photographs inserted into the moving picture in many haunted house films, an effect of which director De Bont takes uncanny advantage in the scene in which Eleanor locates the Crain family photo album. The album contains nineteenth-century photographs of Hugh and Caroline Crain, first featuring pictures of the couple together, with Crain looming over his wife in a dominant position, followed by a series of portraits of Caroline alone. As a ghostly breeze flips the pages of the album, still photography becomes cinema, animating the dead woman, allowing her to tell her story and reveal her husband's atrocities (Figure 10.8).[5]

Finally, consideration of photography's uncanny revelatory power brings us back to cinema as a medium for visualizing marginalized perspectives and communicating the needs and desires that haunt a culture. While Robert Wise's 1963 adaptation of *The Haunting of Hill House* reveals that audiences at the nascence of second-wave feminism were most haunted by the need to escape the deadly domestic trap, De Bont's 1999 adaptation reveals the postfeminist need to recover domesticity from its depreciation by both patriarchal and feminist ideologies. De Bont's film places Jackson's narrative into the context of a turn-of-the-millennium surge of ghost films that reflected postfeminist gender crises. The transformation of Eleanor into a triumphant heroine owes something to the popularity of television shows that featured powerful female paranormal investigators (e.g., *Buffy the Vampire Slayer*, *The X-Files*, and *Medium*), indicating a cultural need for females to exercise power without sacrificing femininity,[6] while the successful exorcism of

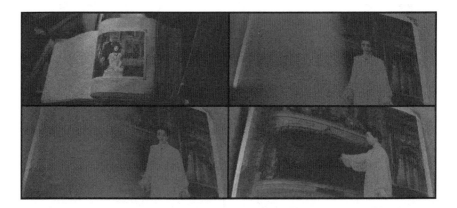

Fig. 10.8 As psychic detective, Eleanor relies on technologies such as photography to communicate with the dead. The flipping pages of a photo album bring still photographs to life, allowing Eleanor's great-great-grandmother to reveal stories of patriarchal abuse. *The Haunting*, 1999, Warner Home Video.

Hugh Crain's ghost relates the Hill House narrative to many millennial ghost movies that featured the laying of male ghosts who represented "distant or absent husbands and fathers" (e.g., *Ghost*, *Always*, *Ghost Dad*, and *The Sixth Sense*) (Fowkes 190).[7] While such productions indicate that the challenges of gendered subjectivity continue to haunt us, the differing film adaptations of Jackson's novel signify that we continue to turn to past texts to address these concerns. In demonstrating the novel's relevance to both feminist and postfeminist discourse, the film adaptations speak to the uncanny prescience of Jackson's text in foreshadowing the complexity of women's concerns as cultural constructs of gender evolve.

Notes

1. For instance, Darryl Hattenhauer claims that Hill House represents Eleanor's mother, citing Jackson's own annotation on a working draft of the novel: "'leaving house = betrayal of mother.'" Noting that "[t]he mother is one of Jackson's most obsessive themes," Hattenhauer points out that the problematics of female subjectivity in Jackson's works are often expressed through the female protagonist's relationships with phallic and feminized mothers that serve as maternal doubles for the protagonist (*American Gothic* 161).
2. Robert Wise's portrayal of Hill House is perhaps indebted to the Gothic trappings of another famous cinematic edifice, the mansion Xanadu in Orson Welles's *Citizen Kane* (1941), which Wise edited. Like Hill House, Xanadu is a manifestation of its patriarch's oppressive ego and the imprisoning ideology on which he founds his identity, a parallel reinforced by the similar camerawork and *mise-en-scène* depicting both dwellings. But while Wise's film focuses on Hill House's history of subsuming female victims, Welles allows Charles Foster Kane's wife to escape her incarceration at Xanadu, leaving Kane to be assimilated by the prison that he himself created.
3. The 1963 film's depiction of this scene as the consummation of Eleanor's marriage to the patriarchy is implied in the change of the character's surname from "Vance" to the more phallically suggestive "Lance."
4. Darryl Hattenhauer's analysis of the variations between David Self's original screenplay for the 1999 adaptation, Michael Tolkin's revised script, and the final film indicates that Self's initial script took a feminist approach to the narrative, depicting the home as an inescapable "domestic trap" for Eleanor ("Spielberg's *The Haunting*" 259). Despite transforming Eleanor into the psychic detective who actively uncovers domestic abuse at Hill House, Self's screenplay concludes with "Crain's ghost, not Eleanor, as the winner in the power struggle." While Eleanor succumbs to "domestic victimhood," Dr. Marrow is "rewarded for reproducing the patriarchy" with an endowed university chair in honor of his unethical experiments in the Crain home ("Spielberg's *The Haunting*" 262). The transformation of Eleanor into the victorious postfeminist matriarch of the finished film apparently occurred during reshoots ordered by executive producer Steven Spielberg ("Spielberg's *The Haunting*" 254). The adaptation's evolution from Self's screenplay to the final film thus reflects the developing postfeminist zeitgeist of 1990s American culture. Hattenhauer concludes by calling for an analysis of the film's narrative (particularly "the impulse to make Nell a savior and detective") using "historicist methods in tandem with feminism" ("Spielberg's *The Haunting*" 264). I attempt such an analysis by examining the film within the historical context of feminist and postfeminist developments in Gothic literature, detective fiction, and horror cinema.
5. The film's use of still photography to reveal the horrors of the patriarchy recalls Jackson's anecdote about accidentally locating a disturbing photo that inspired her depiction

of Hill House. Consulting her mother about the history of the house in the photo, she made the unsettling discovery that her grandfather was the architect, and the townspeople had deliberately burned down the house (Metcalf 151). The scene is also strikingly similar to one of the first pieces of nineteenth-century occult detective fiction, Fitz-James O'Brien's short story "The Pot of Tulips," in which the narrator investigates the haunting of a mansion built by a dead patriarch for his wife. The investigator's encounter with photographs of the unhappy couple prompts a ghostly manifestation revealing the man's crimes against his wife and child. This scene likewise evokes the nineteenth-century phenomenon of "spirit photography" in which the photographer acted as a medium to produce a family portrait featuring living subjects alongside spectral manifestations of dead relatives, often in poses of communication. For more on spirit photography, see Gunning.

6 The casting of Lili Taylor as Eleanor also brings Jackson's narrative into conjunction with Taylor's body of work, particularly another more recent haunted house narrative in which she starred, *The Conjuring* (2013). Set in the 1970s during the period of second-wave feminism, the film, like the 1999 adaptation of *The Haunting*, seems to express postfeminist anxieties about domesticity. The narrative recounts the "true" exploits of husband and wife paranormal investigators Ed and Lorraine Warren as they purge a family home haunted by the ghost of a witch who sacrificed her child in exchange for satanic powers. The ghost has since developed a history of possessing the female inhabitants of the house and forcing them to murder their own children. Whereas Taylor plays the maternal defender of children against demonic forces in *The Haunting*, her character in *The Conjuring* succumbs to demon possession and attempts to kill her five daughters. Mrs. Warren exorcises the ghost by reminding the possessed woman of her maternal joys and duties. The need to restore the family and the threat to motherhood from the vengeful ghost that seeks female victims reflect obvious fears of feminist empowerment.

7 While many millennial ghost narratives (such as the 1999 *The Haunting*) empowered women, recovering them from spectralization in patriarchal culture, Katherine A. Fowkes identifies a converse phenomenon of male spectralization in ghost movies of the period that placed male protagonists in the passive roles of ghosts who before death were "obsessed or distracted by work, distant from their wives and children and unable to express their emotions" (194). This cinematic phenomenon could be read as the result of the feminization of American culture in the wake of the feminist movement, as women and children demanded a level of emotional involvement from males for which they were not socialized under patriarchal structures. Hence they became the ghosts of popular narratives, unable to communicate according to the new cultural expectations.

Works cited

Anderson, Melanie. "'Whatever Walked There, Walked Alone': What Is Haunting Shirley Jackson's Hill House?" *Journal of the Georgia Philological Association* (2009): 198–205. EBSCOhost. Web. 1 Dec. 2013.

Ascari, Maurizio. *A Counter-History of Crime Fiction. Supernatural, Gothic, Sensational.* Basingstoke and New York: Palgrave, 2007. Print.

Birke, Lynda. *Women, Feminism, and Biology: The Feminist Challenge.* New York: Methuen, 1986. Print.

Braude, Ann. *Radical Spirits: Spiritualism and Women's Rights in Nineteenth-Century America.* Bloomington: Indiana UP, 2001. Print.

Brunsdon, Charlotte. *Screen Tastes: Soap Opera to Satellite Dishes.* New York: Routledge, 1997. Print.

The Conjuring. Dir. James Wan. Perf. Lili Taylor, Vera Farmiga, and Patrick Wilson. New Line, 2013. *Amazon Instant Video*. Web. 15 July 2014.

Curtis, Barry. *Dark Places: The Haunted House in Film*. London: Reaktion, 2008. Print.

Dilley, Kimberly. *Busybodies, Meddlers, and Snoops: The Female Hero in Contemporary Women's Mysteries*. Westport, CT: Greenwood P, 1998. Print.

Ellis, Kate Ferguson. *The Contested Castle: Gothic Novels and the Subversion of Domestic Ideology*. Urbana: U of Illinois P, 1989. Print.

Fowkes, Katherine A. "Melodramatic Specters: Cinema and the Sixth Sense." *Spectral America: Phantom and the National Imagination*. Ed. Jeffrey Andrew Weinstock. Madison: U of Wisconsin P, 2004. 185–206. Print.

Galvan, Jill Nicole. *The Sympathetic Medium: Feminine Channeling, the Occult, and Communication Technologies, 1859–1919*. Ithaca: Cornell UP, 2010. Print.

Gunning, Tom. "Phantom Images and Modern Manifestations: Spirit Photography, Magic Theater, Trick Films, and Photography's Uncanny." *Fugitive Images: From Photography to Video*. Ed. Patrice Petro. Bloomington: Indiana UP, 1995. 42–71. Print.

Hattenhauer, Darryl. *Shirley Jackson's American Gothic*. New York: State U of New York P, 2003. Print.

———. "Steven Spielberg's *The Haunting*: A Reconsideration of David Self's Script." *Shirley Jackson: Essays on the Literary Legacy*. Ed. Bernice M. Murphy. Jefferson, NC: McFarland and Company, 2005. 251–66. Print.

The Haunting. Dir. Jan De Bont. Perf. Lili Taylor, Liam Neeson, Catherine Zeta-Jones, and Luke Owen. DreamWorks, 1999. *Netflix*. Web. 15 Feb. 2014.

The Haunting. Dir. Robert Wise. Perf. Julie Harris, Claire Bloom, Russ Tamblyn, and Richard Johnson. 1963. Warner Home Video, 2010. DVD.

Irons, Glenwood, ed. "Introduction: Gender and Genre: The Woman Detective and the Diffusion of Generic Voices." *Feminism in Women's Detective Fiction*. Toronto, Buffalo, and London: U of Toronto P, 1995. ix–xxiv. Print.

Jackson, Shirley. *The Haunting of Hill House*. 1959. New York: Penguin, 2006. Print.

Klein, Kathleen Gregory. *The Woman Detective: Gender and Genre*. Second Edition. Urbana, IL: U of Chicago P, 1988, 1995. Print.

Lareau, Normand. "*The Haunting* by Robert Wise: Review." *Film Quarterly* 17.2 (Winter 1963–1964): 44–47. JSTOR. Web. 1 Dec. 2013.

Lootens, Tricia. "'Whose Hand Was I Holding?' Familial and Sexual Politics in Shirley Jackson's *The Haunting of Hill House*." *Haunting the House of Fiction: Feminist Perspectives on Ghost Stories by American Women*. Eds. Lynette Carpenter and Wendy K. Kolmar. Knoxville: U of Tennessee P, 1991. 166–92. Print.

McGuire, Ann and David Buchbinder. "The Forensic Gothic: Knowledge, the Supernatural, and the Psychic Detective." *Canadian Review of American Studies* 40.3 (2010): 289–307. Electronic.

Metcalf, Linda Trichter. *Shirley Jackson in Her Fiction: A Rhetorical Search for the Implied Author*. Dissertation. New York U. Ann Arbor: U Microfilms International Dissertation Service, 1989. Print.

Nollen, Elizabeth. "Female Detective Figures in British Fiction: Coping with Madness and Imprisonment." *Clue: A Journal of Detection* 15.2 (1994): 39–49. Electronic.

Owen, Alex. *The Darkened Room: Women, Power, and Spiritualism in Late Nineteenth-Century England*. London: Virago, 1989. Print.

Parks, John Gordon. *The Possibility of Evil: The Fiction of Shirley Jackson*. Dissertation. U of New Mexico. Ann Arbor: U Microfilms International Dissertation Service, 1973. Print.

Schneider, Steven Jay. "Thrice-Told Tales: 'The Haunting,' from Novel to Film . . . to Film." *Journal of Popular Film & Television* 30.3 (Fall 2002): 166–76. ProQuest. Web. 1 Dec. 2013.

Tibbetts, John. "Phantom Fighters: 150 Years of Occult Detection." *Armchair Detective: A Quarterly Journal Devoted to the Appreciation of Mystery, Detective, and Suspense Fiction* 29.3 (1996): 340–45. Electronic.

Williams, Anne. *Art of Darkness: A Poetics of Gothic*. Chicago: U of Chicago P, 1995. Print.

11 Girl anachronism
We Have Always Lived in the Castle and the depiction of adolescent psychosis in *Excision* (2012) and *Stoker* (2013)

Bernice M. Murphy

When Korean auteur Park Chan-Wook's English-language debut *Stoker* was released in 2013, critics and viewers alike were quick to note the film's obvious homage to earlier movies. As screenwriter Wentworth Miller noted, "*Stoker* began as a mash-up of Hitchcock's *Shadow of a Doubt*, *The Stepfather* with Terry O'Quinn, and bits and pieces of vampire mythology."[1] Those familiar with the work of Shirley Jackson, however, also will have noted some striking resemblances between *Stoker* and *We Have Always Lived in the Castle* (1962). As we shall see, its eerily self-possessed heroine, India Stoker, has much in common with Mary Katherine ("Merricat") Blackwood, whose narrative voice is so beguilingly frank that readers at first hardly notice that they have been drawn into the mindset of a psychotic mass-murderer. Jackson's sensitive evocation of Merricat's profoundly skewed worldview remains one of the most compelling depictions of the mentally disturbed teenage girl in American popular culture, and yet the novel's obvious influence on later narratives has often been sorely overlooked. I shall attempt to remedy this state of affairs by discussing *We Have Always Lived in the Castle* in relation to two recent films, *Excision* (2012) and *Stoker* (2013). Although neither of the films concerned directly refers to Jackson's work, both of them dramatize themes, tones, and anxieties remarkably similar to those featured in *We Have Always Lived in the Castle*. *Excision* and *Stoker* feature murderous protagonists whose refusal – or inability – to conform to conventional societal norms closely resembles that of Merricat.

Female adolescence has, of course, been depicted frequently in horror cinema as a time during which monstrous deviations from the "norm" take place, but it also has often been the case that teenage girls are permitted to express rage, disobedience, and homicidal impulses only when their actions are related to a supernatural force connected to the perceived "otherness" of the female body. As Barbara Creed notes of *The Exorcist* (1973), in an observation that could apply equally to the many other subsequent on-screen depictions of demonic possession in teenage girls, it "becomes the excuse for legitimizing a display of aberrant feminine behavior which is depicted as depraved, monstrous, abject – and perversely appealing" (31).[2] One of the most well-known examples of this "monstrous feminine" trope identified by Creed can be found in the form of the downtrodden protagonist in *Carrie* (1976), who is able to access devastating telekinetic power after the traumatic onset of her first menstrual period. More recently, feuding teenage witches wreak mayhem in *The Craft* (1996). In *Ginger Snaps* (2000), a disaffected suburban teen is turned into a jock-murdering beast after being bitten by a werewolf. *Jennifer's Body* (2009) features a high-school murder victim who returns from the dead as a sexually rapacious predator. In *Teeth* (2007), radiation leaks from a nuclear power plant transform a previously conventional teenager into a *vagina dentata*–possessing mutant.[3] The supernaturally empowered and deeply threatening teenage girl is also a staple of Japanese horror cinema, most famously epitomized in the form of Sadako Yamamura, the vengeful antagonist of *Ring* (1998).

What interests me here, however, are horror narratives in which the female adolescent is rendered dangerous by the kind of decidedly *non*supernatural "aberrant behavior" manifested by Merricat. The teenage girl who murders for nonsupernatural reasons is, I would argue, a great deal more threatening to the status quo than her more fantastically empowered sisters. Most of them, after all, would never have killed anyone if they had not been granted uncanny abilities by freak happenstance (*The Exorcist*, *Ginger Snaps*, *Teeth*, *Jennifer's Body*) or heredity (*Carrie*, *Ring*, *The Craft*). By way of contrast, like Jackson's protagonist, the heroines of *Stoker* and *Excision* violently dispatch family members because their own unique (and troubling) psychological landscapes, in very different ways, leave them with no other obvious choice in the matter.

Although the murderous female adolescent in popular culture usually is rendered threatening by dint of her aberrant supernatural abilities, there are some notable exceptions to this tendency, and unlike Merricat, not every exception is necessarily mentally ill. While they are both precocious female murderers who first made it to print within a decade of one another, Merricat's pathology differs substantially from that displayed by Rhoda Penmark, the scheming twelve-year-old sociopath depicted in William March's best-selling potboiler *The Bad Seed* (1954). From the very beginning of Jackson's novel, it is clear that Merricat is experiencing psychotic symptoms and finds it extremely difficult to relate to anyone other than Constance and her feline companion, Jonas. Rhoda, by contrast, displays glib assurance in social situations, has a notably "mature" demeanor and ominously tidy appearance, and manifests a total absence of imagination or compassion.[4] March's novel hinges on the scientifically unsound premise that Rhoda, like Jackson's Hill House, was "born bad." She is sane, but by dint of her tainted maternal bloodline, is completely devoid of empathy and morality. Merricat, unlike Rhoda, cannot morally or legally be considered fully responsible for her actions: whatever the specific cause of her inability to fully differentiate between reality and fantasy (a common trait in Jackson heroines), she has obviously been severely warped by her family circumstances.

For instance, Karen J. Hall (1993) suggests that sexual abuse has caused Merricat's break from reality, as well as Constance's tacit approval of her arsenic-dispensing actions. However, as Darryl Hattenhauer (2005) notes, the novel doesn't provide any firm evidence on this score (207). Jackson does imply that

Hangsaman's Natalie Waite and *The Bird's Nest*'s Elizabeth Richmond may have experienced sexual abuse at the hands of older men, so Hall's reading is certainly not out of line with preoccupations found elsewhere in Jackson's oeuvre. Depictions of homicidal prepubescent and teenage girls in American horror cinema have tended to feature either Merricat-style psychotics or, less commonly, Rhoda Penmark–style "Born Bad" sociopaths, although *Stoker*'s protagonist ultimately combines elements drawn from the two main types of nonsupernatural teenage murderer.

The most well-known depiction of the murderous teenage girl in 1960s popular cinema came in *Pretty Poison* (1968), in which Tuesday Weld starred as a scheming psychopath/cheerleader whose all-American looks blind everyone to her true nature. In *Alice, Sweet Alice* (1976), a troubled and neglected twelve-year-old girl is chief suspect in a series of brutal murders (including that of her younger sister). In *The Little Girl Who Lives Down the Lane* (1976), Jodie Foster played a precociously self-sufficient thirteen-year-old determined to keep out meddling outsiders. In an interesting echo of Merricat's penchant for poisoning the sugar bowl, her character's methods include administering cyanide in cups of tea, accompanied by almond cookies to hide the distinctive flavor. (This contamination of the "sugar" associated with little girls represents an obvious subversion of the "sugar and spice" cliché. Many of the most prolific female murderers in the Victorian era in particular were associated with poison, with the victims often being family members.) More recently, *Hard Candy* (2005) featured a sociopathic fourteen-year-old vigilante whose behavior soon becomes even more disturbing than that of the predatory pedophile she torments.[5]

A more obviously Merricat-like character can be found in the home-invasion movie *The Bleeding House* (2011), which features an extremely disturbed teenage girl named Gloria (Alexandra Chando), who later is revealed to be a murderous arsonist. Like Merricat, Gloria prefers the name she has given herself – "Blackbird." Her obvious mental disturbance is underlined by her penchant for pinning live insects to the walls of her bedroom. She also is, ominously, forbidden from going near the knife drawer. As in *Stoker*, much of the tension in the film revolves around a controlling older man encouraging a teenage girl to fully embrace her inherently violent "true" nature.

Jackson had a long-standing interest in depicting the inner lives of disturbed young women and returned to this trope throughout her career. This trend would reach its apotheosis in *Castle*, which one critic has memorably described as "not so much a depiction of madness as a poetic participation in it" (Sullivan 227). Unstable young women feature prominently in *The Bird's Nest* (1956) – a fictionalized psychiatric case study – and in *The Haunting of Hill House* (1959), but Jackson's most obvious precursor to Merricat is Natalie Waite, the protagonist of *Hangsaman* (1951). Natalie's rapid descent into a dangerously dissociative state (which may be caused by undiagnosed schizophrenia) is hastened by her departure for college and her unwilling induction into a world in which the officially sanctioned fate of educated middle-class girls like her is marriage, home, and children. It is a prospect that fills her with genuine horror. Natalie is preoccupied by violent fantasies, many of them centered on the murder of her overbearing father. Though she never acts upon these fantasies – and, if anything, turns her potential for violence inwards – the implicit threat that she represents to the patriarchal order is one that will later be violently realized by Merricat.

It has often been argued by critics, including me, that Jackson's recurrent portrayal of female madness is a reflection of the limited range of choices and the powerful pressures facing American women during the 1950s. Joan Wylie Hall has suggested that "imperiled females embody a post war sensibility of dislocation and loss. Their sex, Jackson implies, is no badge of protection; rather it almost ensures their defeat" (xiv). As Sylvia Hewitt observes, in 1945, American women, who had played such a vital role in keeping the war machine on the right track, were more powerful than they had ever been before (151). Yet the years that followed were characterized by a succession of major losses in the battle for women's rights and the firm reinstatement of "traditional" gender stereotypes (Hewitt 152).

It seems obvious that the women most affected by the decade's reversion to "traditional" female models of behavior would be those experiencing adolescence and early adulthood. After all, they would be expected to conform most enthusiastically to these radically redefined expectations of female behavior. It is surely significant then that while middle-aged housewives frequently feature in Jackson's short stories, her novels tend to focus upon younger, unattached women.[6] Even in her panoramic first novel, *The Road Through the Wall* (1948), Jackson finds time to focus upon adolescent misfit Harriet Merriam. Natalie Waite is seventeen years old, whereas *The Bird's Nest*'s Elizabeth Richmond is twenty-three. Merricat is eighteen; Constance is twenty-eight. They were twelve and twenty-two, respectively, when the rest of the Blackwood clan was poisoned. Eleanor Vance, at thirty-two, is rather older, but, typically, she is emotionally and sexually immature.

We Have Always Lived in the Castle also represents a novel-length "fleshing-out" of an intriguing spot of local color dramatized in *The Sundial* (1956). The village that the squabbling Halloran family's founding father chose as the site for his mansion had, we are told, "been, shortly before his time, very much the subject of sensational publicity" (*Sundial* 78). The reason was that fifteen-year-old local girl Harriet Stuart was believed to have arisen early one fateful morning in order to bludgeon her parents and two younger brothers to death with a hammer (*Sundial* 78). The obvious comparisons with Lizzie Borden are emphasized by the wry observation that "Fall River, Massachusetts, was nothing to the villagers near Mr. Halloran's proposed big house; Harriet Stuart was their enshrined murderess" (*Sundial* 78).

The story the locals eagerly relate to tourists drawn to the scene of the infamous crime runs as follows:

> They couldn't prove it on her see, because no one knew *why* she did it, and being fifteen years old and all, she got off. They said at the time it was a crazy idea she was even put on trial, because no jury in their right minds could see

her sitting there, quiet and sad and looking like any young kid, and really *believe* she did it.

(*Sundial* 78–79)

This observation is obviously intended to bring to mind the famous defense offered by Borden's attorney: "To find her guilty, you must believe her a fiend. Does she look it?" (Lincoln 284). The Borden allusions take on extra significance when we note that the novel begins and ends with the scenes of probable interfamilial homicide and that the most likely suspect in the second death is a little girl – ten-year-old Fancy Halloran.

Borden is the most famous suspected parricide in American legal history, the so-called Lady with the Axe who has passed into popular legend (Lincoln 19).[7] Jackson's clear interest in the case probably lay in the fact that it allowed her to implicitly critique the era's stifling domestic ideology by splitting the "American Clytemnestra" (Lincoln 19) into two halves: the "ladylike" accused murderer, Constance, who, after all, "told the police that those people deserved to die," and the culprit, Merricat, whose crimes Constance has actively concealed. Therefore *Castle* can be considered Jackson's broad fictionalization of the long and curious aftermath of the Borden trial, during which Lizzie and her older sister Emma returned home to Fall River. One suspects from the evidence provided in *Castle* that despite the seemingly overwhelming evidence of her guilt, Constance likely was acquitted because the jury could not bring themselves to believe that a well-bred young lady from a "respectable" home could have committed such a terrible crime. The wider social and domestic implications of such an act would seem too disruptive to be countenanced. Tellingly, it simply does not occur to anyone that the then twelve-year-old Merricat could have spiked the sugar bowl. Constance is the only one who knows just how far her little sister's resentment of the rest of the family went, and the reason why she did it. (Sibling relationships are also of key importance in *Excision* and *Stoker*.)

Although Lizzie Borden was thirty-two when her father and stepmother were murdered, Jackson's Borden surrogates in *Sundial* and *Castle* are, as noted, teenagers. As suggested earlier, this may well have much to do with the postwar reimposition of highly conservative expectations for young American women. This inability – or outright refusal – to "grow up" and engage with the socially expected models of female behavior is also apparent in Natalie Waite, Elizabeth Richmond, and Eleanor Vance, but it is particularly acute in Merricat. It is also a characteristic found in *Excision*'s deeply disturbed protagonist, Pauline, who consistently rejects both the stifling notions of "lady-like" behavior foisted upon her by her nagging mother and the hypersexualized social conformity of her bullying peers. As will become clear later on, *Stoker*, by contrast, much more actively engages with the idea of embracing adulthood, even though the heroine is still in a state of decidedly Merricat-like arrested development at the beginning of the movie.

Although *We Have Always Lived in the Castle* takes place six years after the murders, Merricat has willingly clung to childhood ever since that fateful family dinner. Constance, by comparison, is achingly conscious of the passing years. Although Merricat briefly mentions attending school in the village before the murders (in a jarring moment for the reader, in that it is difficult for us to imagine Merricat ever leading a "normal" childhood), there is no reference to her doing so afterwards. Until the disruptive arrival of the charmless usurper, Cousin Charles, she spends her days doing pretty much what she pleases, playing in the fields around the Blackwood house and erecting protective totems. The only apparent interruption comes in the form of her torturous trips to the village for supplies. For Merricat, the only rules are those which Constance has imposed (she is banned from handling or preparing food) or self-imposed taboos, such as her intriguing refusal to enter their mother's bedroom or to eat in the presence of others.

Although the film's debt to Jackson is by no means as obvious as that seen in *Stoker*, the protagonist of *Excision*, one of the most interesting on-screen depictions of the psychotic teenage girl in recent years, has much in common with Merricat. *Excision* began life as an award-winning 2008 short film, but was later expanded into a full-length feature by writer/director Richard Bates, Jr. The film's ultimately devastating conclusion is telegraphed by the disturbing opening sequence. In it, the protagonist, eighteen-year-old high-school student Pauline (AnnaLynne McCord) luxuriates in a blood-soaked, hyper-real, and highly sexualized fantasy of death and dismemberment. The sequence establishes that, like her literary predecessor, Pauline's inner life is dominated by vivid fantasies of violent transgression. Just as Merricat's fervent desire, which is expressed in the first chapter, to enact poisonous retribution upon the villagers that she perceives as hateful and "dirty" takes on horrific significance once we realize that her murderous impulses have not previously been confined to the realms of imagination, so too does the opening of *Excision* provide vital clues as to the true nature of the narrative to come.

For instance, Pauline's status as a high-school misfit is confirmed by her earnest classroom inquiry as to whether it is possible to "contract an STD from having sex with a dead person." Although the query arouses laughter, Pauline's pathology goes far beyond morbid curiosity. Just as *Castle*'s community at large, and even regular visitors such as Helen Clarke, see Merricat as odd but essentially harmless, in *Excision*, even those closest to Pauline perceive her consistently off-kilter behavior as eccentricity or defiance, when it actually is symptomatic of something immeasurably more serious. Indeed, another key similarity between *Excision* and *Castle* is that in both narratives the only person who truly understands the protagonist is her sister, and in each instance that sister is the center of the main character's world. The depths of Pauline's psychological distress go largely unnoticed until it is too late.

This is a trope seen in films dealing with female madness as far back as Roman Polanski's *Repulsion* (1965). The beauty and seemingly passive demeanor of beautician Carol (Catherine Deneuve) are perceived by the men around her as evidence of her docility when in actuality, like Pauline, she is tormented by violent psychosexual impulses. Even Merricat's psychological problems exist in plain sight, but, as noted earlier, because the community simply cannot conceive of a child – and a female one at that – committing such a horrific and apparently motiveless act, the possibility of her guilt has never occurred to anyone except for Constance. Merricat's invisibility to the wider world is confirmed by Uncle Julian's chilling insistence that she died in the orphanage six years before, "of neglect" (93).[8]

Pauline's indifference toward conventional social expectations is accentuated, as is usually the case in these kinds of narratives, by her unkempt physical appearance. This is another characteristic shared with Merricat, who is happy to run about the fields in her mother's old shoes, and positively relishes the prospect of having to dress up in a tablecloth at the end of *Castle*. Pauline has long, lank hair (characteristics she shares with Gloria from *The Bleeding House*, and India Stoker), acne, and cold sores. She also has slumping shoulders and a vaguely masculine stride. Her unfashionable attire is a stark visual contrast to the preppy, colorful dress of her jeering classmates. Even when forced into a dress so that she can take part in the Southern social ritual of "cotillion," she is ungainly. It is obvious from the outset that Pauline is a constant source of concern and embarrassment to her elegant, religious, and socially conservative mother Phyllis (Traci Lords).[9] Her relationship with her long-suffering father Bob (Roger Bart), though obviously loving, is of much less importance to the narrative.

A tense relationship between mother and daughter also features in *Stoker*, and is frequently a significant feature of supernatural and psychotic/psychopathic teen-girl films, such as *Ginger Snaps*, *Heavenly Creatures* (1994), and *Carrie*. As has frequently been noted, the troubled mother-daughter relationship is a recurrent trope in Jackson's novels.[10] While *Castle* tends to focus mainly upon the figure of the domineering father, what information we do glean about Merricat and Constance's mother suggests that she was as unpleasant as her spouse. It was she who insisted that the Blackwood house be fenced off from the surrounding community. The isolation and snobbery of the sisters clearly started with their mother's aversion toward the outside world. Though they show reverence for her elegant drawing room, there is no suggestion of there ever having been warmth or love in the relationship Mrs. Blackwood had with her daughters: Constance was obviously a much more loving (and enabling) mother figure to Merricat.

The first exchange between mother and daughter in *Excision* involves Phyllis asking Pauline not to eat with her mouth open, because "I raised you better than that." While Phyllis abhors discussion of bodily functions and is appalled by her firstborn's obvious disregard for grooming and personal hygiene, Pauline is absolutely fascinated by the abject – a tendency which allows Bates to include some genuinely challenging (and extremely bloody) sequences. Visually, as well as thematically, the film straddles an uneasy line between gross-out comedy and genuine horror.

As is the case in *We Have Always Lived in Castle*, the eighteen-year-old protagonist is also coded as an outsider as a result of her unconventional attitudes (or apparent indifference) toward the opposite sex. Merricat is so obviously unable to tolerate anyone besides her beloved Constance that even as the latter wistfully remarks, "You should have boyfriends," Merricat tells us that "she began to laugh, because she sounded funny even to herself" (*Castle* 82). Sex is seldom explicitly referenced in Jackson – and even romantic attachments are few and far between (and seldom convincing) in her work – but *Stoker* and *Excision* feature scenes in which the protagonist's sexual "coming of age" is graphically depicted. Pauline sets about losing her virginity – more, she declares, as an anthropological exercise than anything else – by propositioning a boy in her class. Although this sexual encounter may in part indicate an attempt to "fit in" with her peers, it may more likely be a subconscious attempt to explore her unsettling compulsions in a socially acceptable manner. Indeed, the psychosexual underpinnings of Pauline's mental illness are evident from the very beginning of the film; therefore, much of *Excision* focuses upon Pauline's crude and progressively more disturbing attempts to satisfy these impulses. In contrast, psychosexual compulsions do not appear to be a motivating factor in Merricat's behavior in *Castle*. Merricat appears to have, consciously or otherwise, completely repressed this aspect of herself, as though her own psychological and sexual development has been frozen at the age of twelve. She is, however, subject to compulsive behaviors of a different kind, usually revolving around her belief in various protective "rituals" and her frequent display of obsessive thought patterns related to her fear of losing Constance, her desire to be "kinder" to Uncle Julian, and her mistrust of outsiders.

Still it should be noted as well that Pauline's fascination with the workings of the human body has another increasingly important cause. Though her low grades and erratic behavior clearly make medical school an impossibility, she wants to become a surgeon so that she can save her beloved little sister, Grace (Ariel Levy), who has cystic fibrosis and will soon need a lung transplant. Just as much of what motivates Merricat's more desperate actions in *Castle* can be traced back to her deeply possessive love for Constance (her climatic act of arson is, after all, an attempt to expel the outsider who threatens what she sees as their mutual idyll), so too are Pauline's ultimately terrible actions at least partially motivated by her misguided but earnest longing to "save" her sister.

One of the most interesting things about *Excision* is that despite the more obviously lurid aspects of the film, Pauline's relationship with her family is often depicted with touching nuance. Even as Phyllis berates Pauline, she worries that she's being too hard on her daughter and is privately appalled by the possibility that she might be turning into her own mother. Furthermore, Bates provides a reason as to why the severity of Pauline's psychological distress appears to have bypassed her parents. The family has for many years been under a great deal of emotional and financial strain as a result of Grace's condition, and it seems obvious that as well as contributing to Pauline's psychiatric problems, the understandable familial focus upon Grace's illness has left Phyllis and Bob unaware of just how disturbed their eldest daughter has become.

As we have seen, for Pauline, as for Merricat, the relationship with her sister is the most important one in her life. Just as Merricat believes that she can always rely upon Constance (at least until Cousin Charles turns up on the doorstep), Pauline's one comfortable and wholly accepting relationship is with Grace, her sole confidant and defender. As the film progresses and Pauline further alienates herself from her mother and the outside world, she becomes ever more fixated upon the idea that she alone can save Grace. Unlike Merricat, Pauline does display a degree of self-awareness. She recognizes that she is in urgent need of outside intervention, at one point even asking to see a clinical psychologist, and she self-diagnoses "borderline personality disorder" (a condition characterized by erratic and impulsive behavior, a profound fear of abandonment, paranoia, inappropriate behavior, and severe dissociative symptoms).[11] Typically, her teachers and parents interpret her statement as a self-dramatizing attempt to get out of trouble.

There is a telling line later in the film when Pauline's father, Bob, in a weary attempt to bridge the widening gap between mother and daughter, says, "Everything she does, she does out of love. Someday you'll understand." The tragedy here is that Pauline and Phyllis are in this respect far more alike than he realizes. For all of their obvious differences, there is an unmistakable kinship between mother and daughter that is underscored by the alliterative quality of their names and by the similar colors of their clothing. Moreover, they both adore Grace and would give anything for her to be healthy. Pauline's horrific actions in the last ten minutes of the film are certainly influenced by her transgressive fantasies of sex and death, but they are also, crucially, motivated by a genuine desire to help her favorite person in the world. This means that when Pauline performs her own horrifically misguided attempt at a lung transplant in the family garage, she does so in the heartfelt belief that she is ultimately bringing about the "miracle" that the family has been praying for. The "black sheep" of the family will finally make her parents proud. In words that echo sentiments expressed by her mother throughout the film, just before she chloroforms Grace in preparation for the ghastly "procedure," Pauline says to her sister, "You're not going to understand what I'm about to do, but someday you'll thank me." It's a statement that brings to mind the final pages of *Castle*, wherein Merricat finally succeeds in "saving" Constance from the outside world.

Castle and *Excision* do ultimately differ substantially in relation to where they leave their respective protagonists once the main characters' most treasured fantasy has been transformed into reality. Tellingly, Merricat's final assertion is a declaration of absolute contentment: "'Oh, Constance,' I said, 'We are so happy'" (214). By way of contrast, the closing moments of *Excision* explicitly emphasize the horrific consequences of the protagonist's irrational actions. The true scope of the family tragedy we have watched unfold becomes chillingly evident in the film's final scene, when Phyllis returns home and discovers what her eldest daughter has done. We see a shot of Pauline with her head shaved, dressed in a blood-spattered medical gown, standing above the two crudely mutilated dead girls, scalpel in hand. She is clearly completely detached from reality: "I know it's a mess. It's just my first surgery; I haven't perfected my technique yet." Though Phyllis initially cries, "What have you done!" she then embraces her daughter, uttering a single, agonizing scream of horror, grief, and rage. Lords memorably conveys Phyllis's effort to grasp what has happened to Grace, as well as her sudden realization of the true depths of Pauline's psychosis. Enclosed in her mother's arms for the first time in the film, Pauline suddenly seems to take in what has happened. Whereas Merricat's violence has resulted in the creation of the insular, Constance-centric world that she had always desired, Pauline has just killed the one person in her life who unconditionally loved her. It is a hideous irony accentuated by the film's conclusion with Pauline's anguished screams of sudden, gut-wrenching self-awareness.

Though it shares some intriguing (and even stronger) similarities to *We Have Always Lived in the Castle*, *Stoker* differs from *Excision* in many key respects, not the least of which is that while Bates's film was a low-budget cult endeavor with limited distribution, *Stoker* is a studio production with recognizable actors and a well-known director. As in *Shadow of a Doubt*, the focus is on the troubling relationship between a teenage girl and her mysterious uncle. *Stoker*, however, fully develops Hitchcock's subtle suggestion that the pair are in some sense doubles of one another with an unresolved incestuous attraction to boot. The film's premise and character development also strongly evoke Jackson's final completed novel.[12]

Just as Merricat informs us in the second sentence of *Castle* that she is eighteen years old, India Stoker's (Mia Wasikowska) age is emphasized from the outset. The main plot even begins on her eighteenth birthday, an early indication that the film is essentially an unconventional female *bildungsroman*. Park economically conveys (through the sound of an off-screen car crash) the news that India's father Richard (Dermot Mulroney) has been killed on the day that she officially passes into adulthood. We later find out that this milestone is the reason why Uncle Charlie (Matthew Goode) has come back into the Stoker family sphere. He sees India as a kindred spirit possessed of the same murderous urges and psychological tics that he has experienced since childhood, and, against his older brother's wishes, has "come home" in order to act as malevolent mentor, substitute father figure, and, possibly, lover to his niece.

The film opens with an elliptical but deeply evocative scene that we later realize is taken from the end of the narrative. Like *We Have Always Lived in the Castle*, this is a tale told in retrospect. Just as Merricat's striking opening lines lay the groundwork for the revelation that she was the one behind the Blackwood family massacre, India's opening (and sole) voice-over establishes her clear sense of difference from the rest of the world. As she strides confidently across a rural highway, her progress intermittently interrupted by jarring freeze-frames, the voice-over runs as follows:

> My ears hear what others cannot hear. Small, faraway things people cannot normally see are visible to me. These senses are the fruits of a lifetime of longing. Longing to be rescued – to – be completed. Just as the skirt needs the wind to billow. I am not formed by things that are of myself alone. I wear my father's belt tied around my mother's blouse, and shoes which are from my uncle. This is me. Just as a flower does not choose its color, we are not responsible for what we have come to be. Only once you realize this do you become free, and to become adult is to become free.

The rest of the film details the events that have led up to this blood-spattered roadside interlude.

Like Blackwood farm, the Stoker house is a large and elegantly furnished mansion separated from the community by gates and a fence. Prior to the death of her father, India, like Merricat, appears to spend much of her time wandering around the large family estate. As the opening credits unfurl, we see her aimlessly upending tennis balls, running through the grass of a meadow, and lurking in the garden next to the stone ornaments, which will later take on distinctly sinister significance. In these scenes, Wasikowska is clad in a virginal white dress that resembles the kind of billowy nightgown worn by the classic Gothic heroine-in-peril.[13] It is an impression wholly undermined by the end of the film, when it has become clear that it is those who cross India who are in danger, and not the other way around. The effect is only marred by her clunky and childlike shoes, which she has, suggestively, clearly outgrown. Like Pauline in *Excision*, India is also styled in a manner that accentuates her apparent indifference toward conventional social norms. Wasikowska's preexisting pallor is highlighted by the character's dark brown hair and eyes (rather different from the actor's usually lighter coloring), and she here looks like an older version of Wednesday Addams. This a similarity highlighted by India's penchant for old-fashioned, high-necked dresses and blouses that emphasize the character's intense self-containment and sense of restraint. (They may also remind the viewer that Wasikowska had just starred in screen adaptations of two key texts about Victorian girlhood: *Jane Eyre* [2011] and *Alice in Wonderland* [2010].)

We soon learn that on every birthday prior to her eighteenth, Uncle Charlie has gifted India with a new pair of shoes made to the same childish design every time. There is an evocative shot in which we see India lying on her bed, surrounded by a horseshoe shaped barricade of shoeboxes – one for every year. It's a detail which highlights the obsessive nature of both uncle and niece: he sends her the same present every year, and India, who believes them to be a present from her father, appears to have worn the shoes that he has gifted her every single day of her life so far. The shoebox she receives on this birthday is a notable exception, however. In lieu of footwear, this time it contains an old-fashioned key, which India will later deploy in order to discover the secrets of Uncle Charlie's murky past, as well as of her own true nature.

As in *We Have Always Lived in the Castle*, therefore, clothing, shoes, and accessories are of considerable symbolic import in *Stoker*. One of the first things that Cousin Charles does after his arrival is to establish himself in the room of Merricat's late and unlamented father, John Blackwood, and start wearing his fine clothing and jewelry. Similarly, *Uncle* Charlie in *Stoker* has soon appropriated both his brother Richard's room and his tennis whites (which are too big for him – a subtle detail which foreshadows the final-act revelation that Charlie is a deranged fantasist desperate for his brother's approval and his place in the family). India's discovery of Richard's distinctive sunglasses while snooping around in Charlie's room (another very Merricat-like activity) sparks the realization that he staged the car crash that supposedly killed her father. In an echo of Cousin

Charles's calculating bid for Constance's affections, Uncle Charlie also seems to have his eye on India's mother, Evelyn (Nicole Kidman): "I would like to know my brother's wife," he says, during one of their many innuendo-laden conversations. The ownership of Richard's leather belt is particularly important. Charlie uses it to murder his interfering Aunt Gwendolyn (Jacki Weaver) and a teenage boy who tries to rape India, and he eventually almost kills Evelyn with it. Yet when we see the belt for the last time, it is tied around India's waist as a powerful symbol of her triumph over Charlie as well as her newfound acceptance of her own inherently dangerous nature.

Indeed, in contrast to *We Have Always Lived in the Castle* and *Excision*, which feature obviously psychotic teenage girls who appear at times to have little or no conscious control of their actions (Merricat, like Pauline, is what she is, through no obvious fault of her own), in an echo of issues raised by *The Bad Seed* almost sixty years previously, one of the main questions asked by *Stoker* is whether it is *desirable* – or even possible – to resist a genetic predisposition toward violence. But unlike Rhoda Penmark, who does display an ability to "fit in" when necessary – at least well enough to fool adults – and is resolutely, and chillingly "sane," India is shown to be "different" in some powerful but indefinable way. Her behavior at times seems to suggest high-functioning autism or Asperger's syndrome. She has an aversion to being touched – even by her despairing mother – and appears to have a considerable degree of visual and audio hyperacuity (which Park frequently highlights through his use of extreme close-up and exaggerated sound). Additionally, India has an Usher-esque tendency to focus on minute details and patterns to the exclusion of the larger picture, a trait that is highlighted during a high-school art class: everyone else draws what is in front of them, but she creates an obsessively detailed picture of the barely glimpsed pattern on the inside of the vase instead. She is extremely articulate, musical, and well read, but has a very flat emotional affect, and for much of the film appears unable to engage with others on a deeper emotional level – with the exception of Charlie, her manipulative kindred spirit.

It is eventually revealed that Evelyn always felt excluded from the close relationship between India and Richard, who spent much of their time on hunting trips. Charlie's arrival presents Evelyn with what she sees as an opportunity to gain back something of what she had lost even before her husband was killed. India even observes, "You look like my father" in one of several key scenes that take place between the two of them on the central staircase of the house (their shifting positions provide a visual clue as to who has the upper hand). Similarly, the striking resemblance between Cousin Charles and deposed patriarch John Blackwood in *Castle* helps explain why Constance passively allows him to establish a firm foothold within the Blackwood home, and cannot bring herself to interfere when he begins to lay down the law to Merricat and Uncle Julian. In yet another echo of Jackson in *Stoker*, within days of Richard's funeral, Evelyn has virtually installed Charlie as the new head of the household. Uncle Charlie also resembles Cousin Charles in that he repeatedly declares his intention to be "friends" with India. "We don't need to be friends. We're family," she retorts. There is a vitally important difference here, though. Whereas Cousin Charles's "friendly" overtures in *Castle* are obviously bogus – it is soon clear that if he had his way, he would pack Merricat off to an institution as soon as possible – Uncle Charlie is absolutely sincere when he says that he wants to be friends with India. His obsession with her drives the entire plot. Although she initially resists his overtures, it becomes obvious that as noted previously, the two have much in common.

Like India, Charlie has an oddly timeless quality about him that makes him hard to situate in the modern world (the same could also be said of Merricat). In another echo of *Castle*, it comes as something of a shock when we realize that India attends a resolutely normal-looking high school. Though she appears to have no willing interaction with her peers, she is subject to sexually aggressive bullying from boys in her class. One of the early turning points in the film comes when she coolly reacts to the ringleader's threats by efficiently stabbing him in the hand with a pencil. India later gazes at the gory shavings with obvious fascination. Her growing fixation upon blood and violence allies her with Pauline in *Excision*, although here, crucially, we have the sense that India is *becoming* something rather than being *overcome* by something. The ends of each film further confirm this reading. Whereas the final moments of *Stoker* reveal a newly confident India setting out to create her own life, as has already been established, Pauline finishes *Excision* in a state of abject devastation and complete psychological breakdown.

The sense of growing mutual attraction (and recognition) between uncle and niece is emphasized by the strikingly shot scene in which the two of them play Philip Glass's "Duet" on the piano. Previously, India has always played alone, but once Charlie sits next to her on the stool and joins in, her almost swooning response to his presence emphasizes the undertow of erotic tension that has existed between them from their very first encounter. India's burgeoning sexual maturation is linked to her growing infatuation with her uncle and her escalating willingness to use violence against others. This is highlighted in the scene that follows. In a jealous (and aroused) reaction to having just watched her mother and Charlie kiss, India leaves the house in search of Whip, a boy from school who had earlier defended her from the bullies.

The encounter between the teenagers initially has an eerily romantic quality to it. The two of them talk in a moonlit playground, as India, clad in another flowing white dress, slowly whirls round and round the merry-go-round. While doing so, she says,

> Have you ever seen a photograph of yourself – taken when you didn't know you were being photographed? From an angle you don't get to see when you look in the mirror? And you think that's *me*. That's *also* me. Do you know what I'm talking about?

Charlie has obviously sparked in India the ability to look at herself in a new way, although the ramifications of this do not become apparent until the rest of the scene plays out. Asked by Whip if "You're not afraid of being touched anymore," she answers, "Please don't spoil it," and runs into the woods, clearly wanting him to follow. She kisses him first, and he eagerly responds, but when she bites his lip (another vaguely vampiric action), he quickly becomes hostile and tries to rape her. At this instant, Uncle Charlie comes to the rescue, choking Whip to unconsciousness. There follows an impressionistic scene in which India relives memories of the incident while showering later that night. Charlie broke the boy's neck while she watched, and with her help, he buried Whip on the Stoker lawn (alongside Aunt Gwen). Though it initially seems as if India is traumatized, the scene develops into a fairly graphic masturbation sequence. India's "coming of age" has not come about as the result of a sexual encounter with a boy her own age, but rather as a result of her unmistakably aroused response to Charlie's brutal actions and her de facto collusion in his homicidal behavior (flashbacks suggest that she has already repressed her awareness that he murdered the family housekeeper).

India's new sense of self-awareness, as a sexual being and as a potential killer, is highlighted in the following scene, when she enters her mother's lush bedroom while wearing one of the decidedly grown-up looking silk nightdresses she had previously refused to put on (in fact, mother and daughter are for the first time in the film dressed alike). In the only moment of physical closeness we see between them, India slowly brushes her mother's hair, and a remarkably close-up shot of Kidman's red locks leads into a revealing flashback (here, as in his previous films, Park is a talented visual stylist). We learn – and India herself soon realizes – that Richard taught her to hunt because he decided early on that she was indeed just like his brother – a born killer. He decided to channel her latent violent impulses into hunting because "sometimes you need to do something bad to stop you from doing something much worse." In the film's most melodramatic development, it transpires that far from being a debonair man of the world, Charlie has only just been released from a high-class mental institution funded by the Stoker family. He was placed there as a child because he murdered his younger brother, Jonathan (who was buried alive on the lawn); as a result, he has no experience whatsoever of the outside world. It is implied that he was jealous because the little boy was Richard's favorite.

Once India discovers the truth, it becomes obvious to her that her uncle is essentially an overgrown child with deeply unrealistic expectations about their relationship. Devastated by Richard's insistence that he never return home or contact India, Charlie bludgeoned his brother to death and decided to take his place in the family, because he believes that he and India "share the same blood." Though India demands that he leave immediately, Charlie's ability to smoothly intervene when the local sheriff (investigating Whip's disappearance) turns up on the doorstep appears to redeem him. The boy's murder seems to have cemented their relationship. Charlie's desire to shepherd India through his own twisted version of the "coming of age" story is underlined by his final birthday present: a pair of elegant high heels, a revealing contrast to the childish brogues he had given her in previous years.

In the scenes that follow, it seems as if India has decided to team up with Charlie for good and embark for a new life in New York with him. Evelyn finally realizes that they are involved with one another, and in retaliation she burns the contents of Richard's study before tearfully denouncing her daughter. "India – who are you? You were supposed to love me. Weren't you?" she asks. India, characteristically, says nothing. Although she seems indifferent to her mother's emotional distress, she does, however, decisively intervene when Charlie tries to murder Evelyn, shooting him in the head with her trusty rifle. Typically, India's motives here, like her facial expression, remain tantalizingly opaque. Did she shoot Charlie because a part of her does care for Evelyn, or at least feels that she owes her this mercy? Was he killed in revenge for her father's murder? Or did India realize that in order to achieve true independence, she needs to rid herself of her childish, manipulative, and obsessive "mentor"? It is impossible to know which possibility is the likeliest, although some combination of all three may well be closest to the truth.

After burying Charlie next to his victims on the lawn, India pragmatically appropriates the car, money, and accommodation that Richard had set aside for his brother and leaves Evelyn and the family estate behind with barely a backwards glance. As the voice-over with which the film began indicated, she is literally and metaphorically stepping into Charlie's shoes. Significantly, she is completing a transition that Charlie (who, like Merricat, will always be defined by his childhood act of murder) was unable to make. India, therefore, differs substantially from Pauline and Merricat in that by the end of the narrative she has, in her own estimation at least, become a fully individuated adult.

The final seconds of the story make it clear, however, that this final "step" involves becoming a cold-blooded murderer. Whatever her motives, India's shooting of Charlie saved Evelyn's life and could therefore be characterized as a purely defensive act. The same cannot be said of her murder of the local sheriff on the way out of town, which is motivated entirely by the need to clean up loose ends. The final shot of the film is a very revealing one: a close-up of India as she aims her rifle at her cowering victim. The sheriff is already bleeding out from the gaping neck wound that she inflicted with the secateurs previously wielded by Uncle Charlie. India has a genuine smile on her face for the first time in the film. She is, by her own reckoning at least, finally "free" (this is even the final word in the film, thanks to the song that is playing on the soundtrack as we fade to black), but that freedom is inextricably bound to her newfound willingness to embrace her homicidal impulses.

The final moments of *Stoker* highlight an interesting contrast to Jackson's dramatization of a rather similar plot just over fifty years earlier. Merricat's actions ultimately mean that she never has to conform to the stifling expectations of the cruel and judgmental world around her, which can see only one officially sanctioned path for young women through marriage and motherhood, or in her case, probable institutionalization.[14] The end result, as we have seen, is a situation that she has always desired – finally, she and Constance can "live on the moon." Still, depending on how we read the conclusion, it may not seem like such a desirable outcome. Merricat's arson, the villagers' violence, Cousin Charles's inevitable betrayal, and Uncle Julian's sadly anticlimactic death have meant that Constance has, now, understandably, internalized Merricat's paranoid worldview. They will live out the rest of their days as isolated, feared outcasts – modern-day witches, as Jackson makes clear – willingly hiding in the ruins of their once fine house. This may well be a much more loving and mutually supportive way of life than that which they would have had in the outside world, but it is telling that empowerment here means concealment and the gleeful embrace of Gothic stereotypes about "aberrant" female behavior. At the conclusion of *Stoker*, however, India leaves the family home behind and drives off into the big city to live an independent life on her own terms. In this, India differs not only from Merricat and Pauline but also from many of the other homicidal young women featured in American horror cinema, who are often rendered completely insane, institutionalized, or dead – usually by their own hands – by the end of the story. The way in which India's trajectory differs from Merricat's may therefore provide some indication of the greater sense of opportunity being offered to teenage girls five decades after Jackson's death. Merricat will happily live out her days as a "witch" in the ruins of her once fine "castle." India Stoker leaves home and family behind in order to pursue her own destiny, free of outside interference and controlling male relatives, although the nature of the troubling connection this seems to create between female empowerment and homicidal violence is one that the film, perhaps wisely, leaves unresolved. Despite the notable deviations from Jackson seen in both *Excision* and *Stoker*, it seems clear that, like her creator, Merricat Blackwood continues to cast a long, if often overlooked, shadow over narratives of this type.

Notes

1 Setoodeh, Ramin. "Whatever Happened to 'Prison Break' Hunk Wentworth Miller?" *The Daily Beast*. The Newsweek Daily Beast Company Mag., 6 March 2013. Web. 29 July 2014.
2 See also: *The Exorcism of Emily Rose* (2005); *The Last Exorcism* (2010); *The Quiet Ones* (2014).
3 In *Misfit Sisters: Screen Horror as Female Rights of Passage* (New York: Palgrave Macmillan, 2007), Sue Short notes that in these later films, the female outsider locates a latent power within herself as she attempts to cope with puberty (2).
4 From *The Turn of the Screw* onwards, suspiciously well-turned out children are always a cause for alarm in horror film and fiction. *Orphan* (2009) provides one of the most memorable recent dramatizations of this trope.
5 There also have been some notable films featuring twenty-something young women driven to murder by psychotic urges: the protagonist of *May* (2002) is a socially awkward loner whose intense desire for companionship is complicated by her fascination with topics such as murder and cannibalism; *Black Swan*'s (2010) lead character is a repressed ballerina with Eleanor Vance–style mother issues whose lurid visions of Gothic transformation soon take over her life; and an initially more self-assured young woman also goes spectacularly off the rails in *Alyce Kills* (2011).
6 The most intriguing "what-if" of Jackson's sadly abbreviated career is how her unfinished novel *Come Along with Me* would have developed. The protagonist was a middle-aged widow whose generous girth and warmly sarcastic narrative voice seemed to suggest a figure much more at ease with herself than Jackson's previous protagonists.

7 Hattenhauer persuasively characterizes Constance as a "passive-aggressive enabler who unconsciously uses her cloying sweetness to get the dark Merricat to do the dirty work" (177).
8 Julian's remarks here may also be a subconscious admission that he sees her as the rest of the family did. As the "wicked" second daughter in a family that already had the ever-capable Constance and a "greedy" male heir, Merricat always was surplus to requirements. Though she is always resolving to be "kinder" to him – the closest she can ever come to admit feeling guilty for poisoning him – Merricat and Julian seldom interact.
9 *Excision*'s critique of the conservative middle-class milieu is slyly reflected in the casting: though she has been working in mainstream cinema for years, Lords first came to national prominence as a porn star. Similarly, the pastor who ineffectively counsels Pauline is played by cult cinema icon John Waters.
10 For further reading on troubled mother-daughter relationships in Jackson, see: Oppenheimer (1988); Newman (1990); Rubenstein (1996); and Hattenhauer (2003).
11 DSM – IV "Diagnostic Criteria for 301.83 Borderline Personality Disorder." http://behavenet.com/node/21651. Accessed 1 August 2014.
12 As a quick Internet search establishes, many other viewers have noted the striking similarities between *Stoker* and *Castle*, but as of the time of writing, Jackson's influence has not been acknowledged by either Park or Miller.
13 Interestingly, some of the prerelease publicity material for Guillermo del Toro's baroque haunted house movie *Crimson Peak* (2015) also depicts Wasikowska as a nightgown-clad, candle-carrying classic Gothic heroine.
14 For more on *Castle* as a feminist text, see Lynette Carpenter (1993) and Karen J. Hall (1993). Hall sees the behavior of the Blackwood sisters as "feminist interventions against the patriarchy which violates and oppresses them" (111).

Works cited

Alice, Sweet Alice. Dir. Alfred Sole. Harristown Funding, 1976. DVD.
Alyce Kills. Dir. Jay Lee. Social Construct, 2011. DVD.
The Bleeding House. Dir. Philip Gelatt. Reno Productions, 2011. DVD.
Carpenter, Lynette. "The Establishment and Preservation of Female Safety in *We Have Always Lived in the Castle*." *Frontiers* 8.1 (1984): 32–8. Print.
Carrie. Dir. Brian De Palma. United Artists, 1976. DVD.
The Craft. Dir. Andrew Fleming. Columbia Pictures, 1996. DVD.
Creed, Barbara. *The Monstrous Feminine: Film, Feminism and Psychoanalysis*. London: Routledge, 1993. Print.
Excision. Dir. Richard Bates, Jr. Perf. AnnaLynne McCord, Traci Lords, Roger Bart, and Ariel Winter. New Normal Films, 2012. DVD.
The Exorcist. Dir. William Friedkin. Warner Bros, 1973. DVD.
Ginger Snaps. Dir. John Fawcett. Copperheart Entertainment, 2000. DVD.
Hall, Joan Wylie. *Shirley Jackson: A Study in the Short Fiction*. New York: Twayne, 1993. Print.
Hall, Karen J. "Sisters in Collusion: Safety and Revolt in Shirley Jackson's *We Have Always Lived in the Castle*." *The Significance of Sibling Relationships in Literature*. Eds. Joanna Stephens Mink and Janet Douber Ward. Bowling Green: Bowling Green UP, 1993. 110–19. Print.
Hattenhauer, Darryl. *Shirley Jackson's American Gothic*. New York: SUNY P, 2005. Print.
Hewitt, Sylvia Anne. *A Lesser Life: The Myth of Women's Liberation*. London: Michael Joseph, 1987. Print.
Jackson, Shirley. *The Sundial*. New York: Farrar, Straus and Cudahy, 1958. Print.

———. *We Have Always Lived in the Castle*. New York: Penguin, 1962; 2006. Print.
Jennifer's Body. Dir. Karyn Kusama. Fox Atomic, 2009. DVD.
Lincoln, Victoria. *A Private Disgrace: Lizzie Borden by Daylight*. London: Souvenir P, 1967; 1989. Print.
The Little Girl Who Lives Down the Lane. Dir. Nicolas Gessner. Braun Entertainment, 1976. DVD.
Newman, Judie. "Shirley Jackson and the Reproduction of Mothering: *The Haunting of Hill House*." *American Horror Fiction: From Brockden Brown to Stephen King*. New York: Palgrave MacMillan, 1990. 120–34. Print.
Oppenheimer, Judy. *Private Demons: The Life of Shirley Jackson*. New York: Ballantine Books, 1988. Print.
Pretty Poison. Dir. Noel Black. Twentieth Century Fox, 1968. DVD.
Ring. Dir. Hideo Nakata. Omega Project, 1998. DVD.
Stoker. Dir. Park Chan Wook. Perf. Mia Wasikowska, Nicole Kidman, and Matthew Goode. Fox Searchlight, 2013. DVD.
Sullivan, Jack. *The Penguin Encyclopaedia of Horror and the Supernatural*. New York: Viking, 1986. Print.
Teeth. Dir. Mitchell Lichtenstein. Pierpoline Films, 2007. DVD.

Index

abduction 4, 14
adolescence 5, 47, 49, 79, 89, 183–4, 186
agency 18, 35, 42, 44, 48, 50, 72, 93, 95, 112, 161, 165, 167–8, 172–3
Alice, Sweet Alice (1976 film) 185
alienation 42, 57, 65, 144
The Alleged Haunting of B— House 38
alter ego 58, 63, 158n1
Alyce Kills (2011 film) 198n5
American Society of Psychical Research 38–9, 42, 52n8
anxiety 10, 22, 35, 44, 72, 90, 106, 148
apocalypse 20, 34–5, 118
Arents Pioneer Medal 3
aristocracy 84, 60
Askew, Alice and Claude 42, 52n9; Aylmer Vance stories 42, 52n9

Baden-Powell, Robert 41; *Scouting for Boys* 41
Ballechin House 37–8, 46, 50–1
barbarism 55
Bascom, William 57, 72n5
Bates, Richard Jr. 188; *Excision* 5, 183–4, 187–95, 198, 199n9
Bechdel, Alison i, 5, 142–5, 151–7, 158n1, 158n5; *Dykes to Watch Out For* 152; *The Essential Dykes to Watch Out For* 152; *Fun Home* (graphic novel) 142–2, 151, 153–7, 158n1, 158n5
Bergson, Henri 99
Bible 18–19, 80, 94, 155, 164; Old Testament Book of *Habakkuk* 94
Bierce, Ambrose 4, 25–6; *In the Midst of Life: Tales of Soldiers and Civilians* 26; "The Man and the Snake" 26; "An Occurrence at Owl Creek Bridge" 26; *A Sole Survivor: Bits of Autobiography* 25; "A Tough Tussle" 26; "A Watcher by the Dead" 26
"Biography of a Story" *see* Jackson
Bird's Nest, The see Jackson
bisexual 166, 171
Blackwood, Algernon 39, 41–2, 176; "Ancient Sorceries" 42; "The Camp of the Dog" 42; "A Psychical Invasion" 39, 42; "Secret Worship" 39
Bleeding House, The (2011 film) 185, 189
Borden, Lizzie 186–7
Borley Rectory 37, 45, 51n4
British Society for Psychical Research 38–9, 42, 52n8
Burke, Kenneth 2, 126

carnivalesque 67
Chan-Wook, Park 183; *Stoker* 5, 183–98, 199n12
Chaucer, Geoffrey 20, 32; *The Knight's Tale* 20
Cheever, John 4, 76
civilization 2, 55
Cixous, Hélenè 98, 101, 105; "The Laugh of the Medusa" 98
Cleaver, June (TV character) 43
Cold War 97–9, 108, 112–13, 116–18
Come Along With Me see Jackson
Commedia dell'arte 81
Common Lives, Lesbian Lives (magazine) 152
community 57, 64–5, 67–9, 71–2, 77–83, 86–7, 90–4, 98, 100, 102–8, 116–17, 136, 139, 144, 150, 174, 188–9, 193; academic 125, 130; and Jackson 28, 129–30; LGBTQ 152–3, 156
Conan Doyle, Sir Arthur 41; *see also* Holmes, Sherlock
Cowley, Malcolm 2

Index

Cozzens, James Gould 4
Craft, The (1996 film) 184

Danielewski, Mark Z. 3
De Bont, Jan 160, 168–9, 171, 173–4, *175*, 176–8; *The Haunting* 169–73, *175*, 176, 178, *178*, 180n6, 180n7
del Toro, Guillermo 198n13
detective 35–6, 59–60, 133–4, 169, 173–4, 178; detective fiction i, 4, 40–2, 45–7, 50, 51n7, 52n8, 52n11, 179n4, 180n5; female detective 174, 176; *see also* psychic detective
Dewitt, Sarah Hyman 1, 23n1
Diana (goddess) 64
Diana's Mirror (myth) 64
domesticity i, 2, 4–5, 7–8, 43, 51n2, 51n3, 69, 82, 84–5, 87, 89, 91, 97–101, 103, 105–8, 108n1, 108n6, 112–14, 116–17, 121n3, 121n9, 129–30, 134, 143–51, 153–57, 158n2, 161, 164–5, 168–74, 176, 178, 179n4, 180n6, 187
double 14–16, 22, 40, 60, 91, 135–6, 158n1, 158n4, 160, 179n1, 192
Duke Parapsychology Laboratory 38–9, 51n6

Edenic 66, 80; *see also* Garden of Eden
Edgar Allan Poe Award 3
Ellis, Bret Easton: 131; *The Rules of Attraction* 132
Ellison, Ralph 2, 131
estate 8, 13, 38, 77–8, 82, 84–6, 92–4, 100–1, 115, 146, 161, 193, 197
Excision (2012 film) *see* Bates, Richard Jr.
exile 69–70
Exorcist, The (1973 film) 183–4
"Experience and Fiction" *see* Jackson
extrasensory perception (ESP) 38–9, 40, 43–4, 51n6

fairytale 1–2, 4, 46, 48, 51n7, 54, 57, 61–2, 65, 68–72, 72n2, 73n9, 115, 120
family 7–8, 10–11, 14, 16, 21–2, 27, 29–31, 35–6, 43, 47–8, 51n2, 51n3, 51n5, 59–62, 65–6, 68–9, 83–5, 87, 95n1, 99–102, 104, 112–14, 116–17, 119, 121n1, 121n6, 126–30, 134–5, 138, 143, 145–6, 149–57, 160–2, 165, 167–70, 172–8, 180n5, 180n6, 184–7, 190–4, 196–8, 199n8; and Jackson's personal life 36, 107–8, 129–30, 145
fantasy 5, 30, 60, 66, 69, 80–1, 88, 108, 115, 133–4, 147–8, 150, 174, 184, 188, 191

fate 12, 14, 33, 59, 77, 93–4, 162, 165, 176, 185–7
Faulkner, William 3
feminism 4–5, 42, 51, 102, 108, 112, 116, 123, 156, 158n2, 160, 168–72, 174, 176, 178–9, 179n4, 180n6, 180n7, 199n14
fertility 47, 55, 58, 131
feudal 77
Fitzgerald, F. Scott 154; *The Great Gatsby* 156; *This Side of Paradise* 124, 126, 156
folklore 1, 54–8, 60, 64–9, 71–2, 72n1, 72n2, 72n3, 72n5, 73n7
forest 59, 63, 118
Franklin, Ruth 1
Frazer, James 64–5, 73n8; *The Golden Bough* 61, 63–4, 73n8
Freud, Sigmund 55, 72n2, 99, 103
Friedan, Betty 97–8, 103; *The Feminine Mystique* 97, 103, 115
Friedman, Lenemaja 7, 15, 106, 136–7

garden 8–9, 30, 59, 64, 79–81, 83, 85, 91, 114, 134, 161, 193
Garden of Eden 29, 62, 80
gender 4, 41, 43, 52n11, 89, 99, 104, 113, 154, 160, 167–9, 178–9, 186
ghost 3, 29, 35–46, 51n4, 51n7, 52n10, 69, 144, 146–9, 152, 160–1, 163, 164–75, 177–9, 179n4, 180n5, 180n6, 180n7
ghost hunter(s) 39, 42, 167
Ghost Hunters (TV show) 43
Ginger Snaps (2000 film) 184, 189
Good Housekeeping (magazine) 2, 106, 111–12, 119
Gothic 3–4, 7, 19–20, 28, 35, 40, 45, 76, 97–100, 105–8, 108n8, 113, 125, 131, 143–7, 151, 157, 158n4, 161, 172–4, 176, 179n2, 193, 198, 198n5, 199n13
"Green Grow the Rushes, O" (folk ballad) 60, 62
gynocracy 100

Hall, Joan Wylie xi, 80, 101, 186
Hall, Radclyffe 155
Hangsaman see Jackson
Hattenhauer, Darryl 3, 7, 40, 44, 51n2, 51n7, 54, 56, 58–9, 62, 65, 76, 103, 106, 112–13, 117, 121n1, 138, 161, 179n1, 179n4, 184, 199n7, 199n10
Haunting, The (1963 film) *see* Wise, Robert
Haunting, The (1999 film) *see* de Bont, Jan
Haunting of Hill House, The see Jackson

Heavenly Creatures (1994 film) 189
Hell House see Matheson, Richard
Herrington, H. W. 54
Hodgson, William Hope (W. H.) 41, 176; *The Casebook for Carnacki the Ghost Finder* 41–2, 176
Holmes, Sherlock 41–2
horror 3, 26, 35–6, 40, 42, 59, 63, 90, 97, 106–7, 112, 121n9, 143, 151, 173, 189, 191; in cinema i, 5, 183, 179n4, 179n5, 183–5, 198, 198n3, 198n4
housewife 4, 36, 51n3, 97, 107–8, 111, 120, 129–30
humanity 4, 28, 30, 34, 56, 119
humor 4, 29, 36–7, 61, 97–105, 107–8, 108n5, 129, 145
Hyman, Laurence Jackson 1, 23n1
Hyman, Stanley Edgar 2, 36–7, 54–8, 61, 63–5, 67–8, 73n8, 97, 106–7, 112, 126–7, 129–31

identity 7–9, 11, 13–16, 18, 20, 22–3, 38, 42, 44, 49, 56–9, 61, 65, 72, 78, 97, 108n1, 112, 116, 143, 154, 156–7, 162, 170, 174, 179n2
initiation/initiation story 57–8, 60, 135, 138
innocence 33, 80, 87, 155
isolation 15, 28, 77, 82, 85, 112, 189

Jackson, Shirley: "Biography of a Story" 1; *The Bird's Nest* 9, 12, 17–18, 22, 28, 35, 44, 51n1, 185–6; "Colloquy" 44; *Come Along With Me* 35, 37–8, 40, 46, 50, 198n6; "Epilogue: Fame" 108n1; "Experience and Fiction" 37, 158n2, 158n3; "Family Treasure" 138; *Hangsaman* 1, 4, 14, 16, 20, 35, 51n1, 54, 57–8, 60, 63–5, 68, 71, 72n7, 123–4, 126, 128, 133–4, 138–40, 140n1, 185; *The Haunting of Hill House* i, 1, 3–5, 7, 10–11, 16, 19, 28, 35–40, 42–4, 47, 51, 51n1, 51n6, 51n7, 76, 128, 142–7, 149–51, 153, 157, 158n3, 160, 178, 185; "Janice" 127–8; *Just An Ordinary Day* 27, 127–8; *Let Me Tell You* 1, 23n1, 51n4; *Life Among the Savages* 106–8, 108n1, 129, 145 "The Lottery" i, 1–3, 5, 26, 35–6, 51n1, 54, 76–7, 80, 90–2, 111, 126; "Louisa, Please Come Home" 3; "The Man in the Woods" 1, 128; "The Missing Girl" 127–8; "Mrs. Anderson" 108n6; "The Night We All Had Grippe" 39–40; "Of Course" 129; "On Being a Faculty Wife" 129; "One Ordinary Day, With Peanuts" 26; "The Possibility of Evil" 3; *Raising Demons* 106–8, 145; *The Road Through the Wall* 4, 16, 20, 36, 51, 76–7, 80, 91–3, 95n2, 126, 186; "Still Life with Teapot and Students" 140n3; "The Story We Used to Tell" 108n6; *The Sundial* 4, 8–9, 13, 20, 25–35, 51n1, 56, 76, 145, 186–7; "The Third Baby is the Easiest" 108n1; "The Very Hot Sun in Bermuda" 128; *We Have Always Lived in the Castle* 1, 4–5, 27–8, 35, 51n1, 54, 56, 65, 67–8, 70–1, 76, 97–100, 106, 108, 111–13, 116–18, 121n4, 131, 145, 183, 185–95, 199n12, 199n14; "What a Thought" 108n6
James, Henry: *The Turn of the Screw* 33
Jennifer's Body (2009 Film) 184
Johnson, Owen: *Stover at Yale* 124
Joshi, S. T. 25, 41, 51n2
jouissance 63
Journal of American Folklore 60
Just an Ordinary Day see Jackson

King, Stephen 3, 51

Lacanian mirror stage 9
Lang, Andrew 55
laughter 97–108; and gallows humor 97, 103; and Hélène Cixous 101–2; and Henri Bergson 99
Leave it to Beaver 108
LeFanu, Sheridan 176
legend 4, 54–55, 57, 59, 65, 71–2, 73n10
lesbian 63, 143, 146–7, 152–6, 158n4, 166; apparitionality of 147
L'Estrange, Sir Roger: *Fables of Aesop and Other Eminent Mythologists* 19
Let Me Tell You see Jackson
Lethem, Jonathan 111, 131
library 29–31, 43, 49, 69, 114, 121n5, 148, 152, 154–56, 160–61
Life Among the Savages see Jackson
literacy 154–55; visual 40
Little Girl Who Lives Down the Lane, The 185
Lootens, Tricia 51n5, 149, 161
"Lottery, The" *see* Jackson
Lyons, John O. 58, 62–3, 139; *The College Novel in America* 123–25

McCall's 98
McCarthy, Mary: *The Groves of Academe* 123

McCarthyism 116
Mademoiselle 106, 129
madness 4–5, 10, 21, 41, 106, 145, 148, 171, 174, 185–6, 188
magic 2, 26, 36–7, 51n2, 55, 61–3, 65, 68–70, 72, 73n8, 98, 116–18, 145, 158n2
"Maid Freed From the Gallows" (folk ballad) 59
maps 156–7
March, William: *The Bad Seed* 184
Marchalonis, Shirley 125–6
marginalization 98, 105, 125, 160
maternal 13, 46, 107, 160–2, 164–5, 168–70, 173–4, 179n1, 180n6, 184
Matheson, Richard: *Hell House* 3
matriarchy 100
Medusa 98, 101, 108n7
memory 9, 19, 21, 77, 81, 126
Mencken, H. L. 26
Metcalf, Linda 161, 176–7, 180n5
Miller, Wentworth 183, 189; *see also* Park Chan-wook
Millet, Kate 156
misanthropy 4, 25–8, 32–3
misogyny 25
Modernity 77, 79, 82, 84, 93
Murphy, Bernice M. 35, 63, 91, 99, 105, 106, 121n1, 148
myth 2, 4, 19, 41, 54–8, 61–2, 63–5, 68–9, 71–2, 72n2–3, 72n5, 73n8, 77, 80, 118–19, 154, 177, 183

National Book Award 3
Nemerov, Howard 131
neodomestic 5, 144
neurosis 171
Newman, John Henry: *The Idea of a University* 123
Newman, Judie 37, 161
New Yorker, The 1–2, 111, 126, 128
New York Times Book Review 3
nihilism 103
North Bennington (Vermont) 27–8, 126, 130–1

occult 4, 36–8, 40–2, 45–7, 50–1, 52n9, 76, 111, 121n9, 171, 173, 176–7, 180n5
occult detective fiction 4, 40–2, 45–7, 50, 52n9, 176, 180n5
Oedipal 61
O'Hara, John 4, 76
Oliver, Mary 131

"One Ordinary Day with Peanuts" *see* Jackson
Oppenheimer, Judy 2, 7, 23n3, 26–8, 36–7, 44, 54, 56, 68, 71, 95n2, 106, 108, 111, 121n1, 121n3, 140n2
Owen, Alex 176–7
Ozzie and Harriet 108

Park Chan-wook: *Stoker* 5, 183–85, 187–98, 199n12
paternal 36, 43, 78, 162, 165, 169, 173
patriarchy 43, 99–100, 108n5, 119, 121n2, 164, 166, 168, 170–1, 174, 179n3–5, 199n14
phallic 43, 68, 160–5, 167–8, 174–5, 179n1, 179n3; mother 162
Porter, Katherine Anne 3
Pretty Poison 185
psychic detective 173, 176, 179n4
psychical residue 38
psychosis 58, 191
pulp fiction 60

queer 143–8, 151–2, 154–5, 157–8

race 113
Raising Demons see Jackson
rape 4, 11, 14, 16, 21, 60, 63, 132, 194, 196
Reader's Digest 95n1, 119
Real, the (Lacanian) 63
repression 13, 51n5, 55, 60, 69, 112, 135, 149, 161
Repulsion 188
Rhine, J. B. 39
Rhine, Louisa E. 39
Richardson, Samuel 4, 7–10, 12–23; *Clarissa* 10–12, 16–17, 19, 21; *Pamela* 7–8, 13–14, 16–20, 22–3; *Sir Charles Grandison* 7–8, 14, 18, 23
Ring, The (*Ringu*) (1998 film) 184
ritual 1–2, 4, 10, 19, 21, 26, 54–62, 64–73, 79–80, 89, 91–2, 134–5, 189–90
Road Through the Wall, The see Jackson

sacred 57, 64, 71, 73n10, 83, 85
Salinger, J. D. 2
San Francisco, California 77, 82
Sarton, May: *The Small Room* 124, 126
Saturday Evening Post, The 3, 95n1
savage 55, 67
Savoy, Eric 151
schizophrenia 185
seduction 4, 11, 58, 63, 71, 165

"Seven Types of Ambiguity" *see* Jackson
Shakespeare, William 19; *Hamlet* 16; *The Rape of Lucrece* 16; *Twelfth Night* 19
Shilts, Randy: *And the Band Played On* 152
Showalter, Elaine 125
Siddons, Anne Rivers: *The House Next Door* 3
Societies for Psychical Research 38–40, 42, 52n8, 177
spectralization 161, 172, 180n7
Spiritualism 176–7; role of women in 176–7; and Kate and Margaret Fox 176
Spock, Benjamin 107
Stoker see Park Chan-Wook
Stonewall Riots 152
Straub, Peter: *Ghost Story* 3
suburbia 93–4, 148
subversion 18, 58, 65, 90, 101–2, 116, 185
Sundial, The see Jackson
supernatural 3–4, 28, 31–2, 35–52, 55, 128, 142, 145–6, 171–6, 183–5, 189
superstition 56–7, 68–9
Swift, Jonathan 4, 26
Syfy (TV network) 43
Symbolic, the (Lacanian) 63
Syracuse University 3, 54, 127

Tartt, Donna 4, 131–2, 140
Teeth (2007 film) 184
Telepathy 38–9, 47
Thackeray, William Makepeace: *Vanity Fair* 20
Tin-tin (game) 19, 80
trauma 8, 13, 17, 21–2, 50, 54, 57, 60, 63–5, 133, 135–6, 155, 184, 196
Turn of the Screw, The see James, Henry
Tylor, E. B. 55

uncanny 2, 8, 35, 40, 68, 76, 98, 160–1, 173, 177–9, 184
University of Mississippi 131
unreliable narrator 70, 112

vampire 42, 62, 178, 183
Van Gennep, Arnold 57
victimization 42, 77, 91
Victorian 40–1, 87; homes 142–3, 164; literature 40–1, 193; domesticity 164; female murderers 185
Vidal, Gore 26; *Kalki* 28
violation 14, 17, 21
voodoo 36

Waldman, Anne 131
Walpole, Horace: *The Castle of Otranto* 28
Waugh, Evelyn 26
We Have Always Lived in the Castle see Jackson
Welden, Paula Jean: influence on Jackson 127–8; influence on Tartt 131
West, Nathanael 26
Whyte, William H.: *The Organization Man* 79, 93
Wise, Robert: *The Haunting* (1963) 160, 162–5, 168, 173, 178, 179n2–3
witchcraft 22, 36, 51n2, 65, 111; witched-like sounds 7
Wolfe, Tom: *I Am Charlotte Simmons* 124
Woman's Day 95n1
Woman's Home Companion 2, 106
Womanspirit movement 177
World War II 43, 82, 97

Yates, Richard 76